Georg Ebers, Eleanor Grove

An Egyptian Princess

Vol. II

Georg Ebers, Eleanor Grove

An Egyptian Princess
Vol. II

ISBN/EAN: 9783337172916

Printed in Europe, USA, Canada, Australia, Japan

Cover: Foto ©ninafisch / pixelio.de

More available books at **www.hansebooks.com**

AN
EGYPTIAN PRINCESS

BY

GEORG EBERS
Author of "Uarda," etc.

FROM THE GERMAN BY ELEANOR GROVE.

IN TWO VOLUMES.—VOL. II.

AUTHORIZED EDITION.

REVISED, CORRECTED AND ENLARGED FROM THE
LATEST GERMAN EDITION.

NEW YORK
WILLIAM S. GOTTSBERGER, PUBLISHER
11 MURRAY STREET
1884

Copyright, 1880, by WILLIAM S. GOTTSBERGER.

Published by authority of the

AUTHOR AND OF BARON TAUCHNITZ.

PRESS OF
WILLIAM S. GOTTSBERGER
NEW YORK

AN EGYPTIAN PRINCESS.

CHAPTER I.

THE principal steward of the banquet went forward to meet the guests as they entered, and, assisted by other noble staff-bearers (chamberlains and masters of the ceremonies), led them to their appointed places.

When they were all seated, a flourish of trumpets announced that the king was near. As he entered the hall every one rose, and the multitude received him with a thundering shout of "Victory to the king!" again and again repeated.

The way to his seat was marked by a purple Sardian carpet, only to be trodden by himself and Kassandane. His blind mother, led by Crœsus, went first and took her seat at the head of the table, on a throne somewhat higher than the golden chair for Cambyses[1], which stood by it. The king's lawful wives sat on his left hand; Nitetis next to him, then Atossa, and by her side the pale, plainly-dressed Phædime; next to this last wife of Cambyses sat Boges, the eunuch. Then came the high-priest Oropastes, some of the principal Magi, the satraps of various provinces (among them the Jew Belteshazzar), and a number of Persians, Medes and eunuchs, all holding high offices under the crown.

Bartja sat at the king's right hand, and after him

1. Plutarch, *Artaxerxes* 5.

Crœsus, Hystaspes, Gobryas, Araspes, and others of the Achæmenidæ, according to their rank and age. Of the concubines, the greater number sat at the foot of the table; some stood opposite to Cambyses, and enlivened the banquet by songs and music. A number of eunuchs stood behind them, whose duty it was to see that they did not raise their eyes towards the men.[2]

Cambyses' first glance was bestowed on Nitetis; she sat by him in all the splendor and dignity of a queen, but looking very, very pale in her new purple robes.

Their eyes met, and Cambyses felt that such a look could only come from one who loved him very dearly. But his own love told him that something had troubled her. There was a sad seriousness about her mouth, and a slight cloud, which only he could see, seemed to veil the usually calm, clear and cheerful expression of her eyes. "I will ask her afterwards what has happened," thought he, "but it will not do to let my subjects see how much I love this girl."

He kissed his mother, sister, brother and his nearest relations on the forehead—said a short prayer thanking the gods for their mercies and entreating a happy new year for himself and the Persians—named the immense sum he intended to present to his countrymen on this day, and then called on the staff-bearers to bring the petitioners before his face, who hoped to obtain some reasonable request from the king on this day of grace.

As every petitioner had been obliged to lay his request before the principal staff-bearer the day before, in order to ascertain whether it was admissible, they all

---

2. Herod. IX. 110. 111. Book of Esther I. 10. 11. Brisson. *Regn. Persarum princip.* I. c. 103.

received satisfactory answers. The petitions of the women had been enquired into by the eunuchs in the same manner, and they too were now conducted before their lord and master by Boges, Kassandane alone remaining seated.

The long procession was opened by Nitetis and Atossa, and the two princesses were immediately followed by Phædime and another beauty. The latter was magnificently dressed and had been paired with Phædime by Boges, in order to make the almost poverty-stricken simplicity of the fallen favorite more apparent.

Intaphernes and Otanes looked as annoyed as Boges had expected, on seeing their grandchild and daughter so pale, and in such miserable array, in the midst of all this splendor and magnificence.

Cambyses had had experience of Phædime's former extravagance in matters of dress, and, when he saw her standing before him so plainly dressed and so pale, looked both angry and astonished. His brow darkened, and as she bent low before him, he asked her in an angry and tyrannical tone: "What is the meaning of this beggarly dress at my table, on the day set apart in my honor? Have you forgotten, that in our country it is the custom never to appear unadorned before the king? Verily, if it were not my birthday, and if I did not owe you some consideration as the daughter of our dearest kinsman, I should order the eunuchs to take you back to the harem, that you might have time to think over your conduct in solitude."

These words rendered the mortified woman's task much easier. She began to weep loud and bitterly, raising her hands and eyes to her angry lord in such a beseeching manner that his anger was changed into compassion, and he raised her from the ground with the question: "Have you a petition to ask of me?"

"What can I find to wish for, now that the sun of my life has withdrawn his light?" was her faltering answer, hindered by sobs.

Cambyses shrugged his shoulders, and asked again: "Is there nothing then that you wish for? I used to be able to dry your tears with presents; ask me for some golden comfort to-day."

"Phædime has nothing left to wish for now. For whom can she put on jewels when her king, her husband, withdraws the light of his countenance?"

"Then I can do nothing for you," exclaimed Cambyses, turning away angrily from the kneeling woman.

Boges had been quite right in advising Phædime to paint herself with white, for underneath the pale color her cheeks were burning with shame and anger. But, in spite of all, she controlled her passionate feelings, made the same deep obeisance to Nitetis as to the queen-mother, and allowed her tears to flow fast and freely in sight of all the Achæmenidæ.

Otanes and Intaphernes could scarcely suppress their indignation at seeing their daughter and grandchild thus humbled, and many an Achæmenide looked on, feeling deep sympathy with the unhappy Phædime and a hidden grudge against the favored, beautiful stranger.

The formalities were at last at an end and the feast began. Just before the king, in a golden basket, and gracefully bordered round with other fruits, lay a gigantic pomegranate, as large as a child's head.[3]

---

[3]. The Pishkesh or gift, which the Persians of the present day are in the habit of presenting to their guests, usually consists of sweets or baskets of fruit arranged in the most graceful manner. Brugsch, in

Cambyses noticed it now for the first time, examined its enormous size and rare beauty with the eye of a connoisseur, and said: "Who grew this wonderful pomegranate?"

"Thy servant Oropastes," answered the chief of the Magi, with a low obeisance. "For many years I have studied the art of gardening, and have ventured to lay this, the most beautiful fruit of my labors, at the feet of my king."[4]

"I owe you thanks," cried the king: "My friends, this pomegranate will assist me in the choice of a governor at home when we go out to war, for, by Mithras, the man who can cherish and foster a little tree so carefully will do greater things than these. What a splendid fruit! Surely it's like was never seen before. I thank you again, Oropastes, and as the thanks of a king must never consist of empty words alone, I name you at once vicegerent of my entire kingdom, in case of war. For we shall not dream away our time much longer in this idle rest, my friends. A Persian gets low-spirited without the joys of war."

A murmur of applause ran through the ranks of the Achæmenidæ and fresh shouts of "Victory to the king" resounded through the hall. Their anger on account of the humiliation of a woman was quickly forgotten; thoughts of coming battles, undying renown and conqueror's laurels to be won by deeds of arms, and recollections of their former mighty deeds raised the spirits of the revellers.

The king himself was more moderate than usual

his *Reise nach Persien* praises very highly the good taste, with which these baskets are arranged.
    4. The story which follows in the text is told by Ælian. (*V. H.* I. 23.) of Artaxerxes and a certain Omises.

to-day, but he encouraged his guests to drink, enjoying their noisy merriment and overflowing mirth;—taking, however, far more pleasure still in the fascinating beauty of the Egyptian Princess, who sat at his side, paler than usual, and thoroughly exhausted by the exertions of the morning and the unaccustomed weight of the high tiara. He had never felt so happy as on this day. What indeed could he wish for more than he already possessed? Had not the gods given him every thing that a man could desire? and, over and above all this, had not they flung into his lap the precious gift of love? His usual inflexibility seemed to have changed into benevolence, and his stern severity into good-nature, as he turned to his brother Bartja with the words: "Come brother, have you forgotten my promise? Don't you know that to-day you are sure of gaining the dearest wish of your heart from me? That's right, drain the goblet, and take courage! but do not ask anything small, for I am in the mood to give largely to-day. Ah, it is a secret! come nearer then. I am really curious to know what the most fortunate youth in my entire kingdom can long for so much, that he blushes like a girl when his wish is spoken of."

Bartja, whose cheeks were really glowing from agitation, bent his head close to his brother's ear, and whispered shortly the story of his love. Sappho's father had helped to defend his native town Phocæa* against the hosts of Cyrus, and this fact the boy cleverly brought forward, speaking of the girl he loved as the daughter of a Greek warrior of noble birth. In so saying he spoke the truth, but at the same time he suppressed the

* See vol. I. note 22.

fact,[5] that this very father had acquired great riches by mercantile undertakings. He then told his brother how charming, cultivated and loving his Sappho was, and was just going to call on Crœsus for a confirmation of his words, when Cambyses interrupted him by kissing his forehead and saying: "You need say no more, brother; do what your heart bids you. I know the power of love too, and I will help you to gain our mother's consent."

Bartja threw himself at his brother's feet, overcome with gratitude and joy, but Cambyses raised him kindly and, looking especially at Nitetis and Kassandane, exclaimed: "Listen, my dear ones, the stem of Cyrus is going to blossom afresh, for our brother Bartja has resolved to put an end to his single life, so displeasing to the gods.[6] In a few days the young lover will leave us for your country, Nitetis, and will bring back another jewel from the shores of the Nile to our mountain home."

"What is the matter, sister?" cried Atossa, before her brother had finished speaking. Nitetis had fainted, and Atossa was sprinkling her forehead with wine as she lay in her arms.

"What was it?" asked the blind Kassandane, when Nitetis had awakened to consciousness a few moments later.

"The joy—the happiness—Tachot," faltered Nitetis.

Cambyses, as well as his sister, had sprung to the fainting girl's help. When she had recovered conscious-

5. The Persians were forbidden by law to contract debts, because debtors were necessarily led to say much that was untrue. Herod. I. 138. For this reason they held all money transactions in contempt, such occupations being also very uncongenial to their military tastes. They despised commerce and abandoned it to the conquered nations.

6. The Persians were commanded by their religion to marry, and the unmarried were held up to ridicule. *Vendid.* IV. Fargard. 130. The highest duty of man was to create and promote life, and to have many children was therefore considered praiseworthy. Herod. I. 136.

ness, he asked her to take some wine to revive her completely, gave her the cup with his own hand, and then went on at the point at which he had left off in his account: "Bartja is going to your own country, my wife—to Naukratis on the Nile—to fetch thence the granddaughter of a certain Rhodopis, and daughter of a noble warrior, a native of the brave town of Phocæa, as his wife."

"What was that?" cried the blind queen-mother.

"What is the matter with you?" exclaimed Atossa again, in an anxious, almost reproachful tone.

"Nitetis!" cried Crœsus admonishingly. But the warning came too late; the cup which her royal lover had given her slipped from her hands and fell ringing on the floor. All eyes were fixed on the king's features in anxious suspense. He had sprung from his seat pale as death; his lips trembled and his fist was clenched.

Nitetis looked up at her lover imploringly, but he was afraid of meeting those wonderful, fascinating eyes, and turned his head away, saying in a hoarse voice: "Take the women back to their apartments, Boges. I have seen enough of them—let us begin our drinking-bout—good-night, my mother; take care how you nourish vipers with your heart's blood. Sleep well, Egyptian, and pray to the gods to give you a more equal power of dissembling your feelings. To-morrow, my friends, we will go out hunting. Here, cup-bearer, give me some wine! fill the large goblet, but taste it well—yes, well—for to-day I am afraid of poison; to-day for the first time. Do you hear, Egyptian? I am afraid of poison! and every child knows—ah—ha—that all the poison, as well as the medicine[7] comes from Egypt."

7. The reputation of Egypt for medicines was known even to Homer. The number of different drugs mentioned in the inscriptions on the walls of the temple-laboratories, especially at Dendera and

Nitetis left the hall,—she hardly knew how,—more staggering than walking. Boges accompanied her, telling the bearers to make haste.

When they reached the hanging-gardens he gave her up to the care of the eunuch in attendance, and took his leave, not respectfully as usual, but chuckling, rubbing his hands, and speaking in an intimate and confidential tone: "Dream about the handsome Bartja and his Egyptian lady-love, my white Nile-kitten! Haven't you any message for the beautiful boy, whose love-story frightened you so terribly? Think a little. Poor Boges will very gladly play the go-between; the poor despised Boges wishes you so well—the humble Boges will be so sorry when he sees the proud palm-tree from Sais cut down. Boges is a prophet; he foretells you a speedy return home to Egypt, or a quiet bed in the black earth in Babylon, and the kind Boges wishes you a peaceful sleep. Farewell, my broken flower, my gay, bright viper, wounded by its own sting, my pretty fir-cone, fallen from the tall pine-tree!"

"How dare you speak in this impudent manner?" said the indignant princess.

"Thank you," answered the wretch, smiling.

"I shall complain of your conduct," threatened Nitetis.

"You are very amiable," answered Boges.

"Go out of my sight," she cried.

Edfoo, (published by Dümichen), and in the medical papyri, is surprising. *Odyssey* IV. 299. Pliny, XXV. 2. mentions the great number of useful herbs which flourished on the shores of the Nile. Neither were the Egyptian poisons less celebrated, especially the Strychnus. Plin. XXI. 15. The Halicacabon, called by Homer, (*Odyss.* 304), μῶλυ, was a very strong Egyptian poison. The number and variety of drugs mentioned in the Papyrus Ebers proves the great wealth of the Egyptian *materia medica*.

"I will obey your kind and gentle hints;" he answered softly, as if whispering words of love into her ear.

She started back in disgust and fear at these scornful words; she saw how full of terror they were for her, turned her back on him and went quickly into the house, but his voice rang after her: "Don't forget me, my lovely queen, think of me now and then; for everything that happens in the next few days will be a keepsake from the poor despised Boges."

As soon as she had disappeared he changed his tone, and commanded the sentries in the severest and most tyrannical manner, to keep a strict watch over the hanging-gardens. "Certain death," said he, "to whichever of you allows any one but myself to enter these gardens. No one, remember—no one—and least of all messengers from the queen-mother, Atossa or any of the great people, may venture to set foot on these steps. If Crœsus or Oropastes should wish to speak to the Egyptian Princess, refuse them decidedly. Do you understand? I repeat it, whoever is begged or bribed into disobedience will not see the light of to-morrow's sun. Nobody may enter these gardens without express permission from my own mouth. I think you know me. Here, take these gold staters, your work will be heavier now; but remember, I swear by Mithras not to spare one of you who is careless or disobedient."

The men made a due obeisance and determined to obey; they knew that Boges' threats were never meant in joke, and fancied something great must be coming to pass, as the stingy eunuch never spent his staters without good reason.

Boges was carried back to the banqueting-hall in the same litter, which had brought Nitetis away.

The king's wives had left, but the concubines were still standing in their appointed place, singing their monotonous songs, though quite unheard by the uproarious men.

The drinkers had already long forgotten the fainting woman. The uproar and confusion rose with every fresh wine-cup. They forgot the dignity of the place where they were assembled, and the presence of their mighty ruler.

They shouted in their drunken joy; warriors embraced one another with a tenderness only excited by wine, here and there a novice was carried away in the arms of a pair of sturdy attendants, while an old hand at the work would seize a wine-jug instead of a goblet, and drain it at a draught amid the cheers of the lookers-on.

The king sat on at the head of the table, pale as death, staring into the wine-cup as if unconscious of what was going on around him. But at the sight of his brother his fist clenched.

He would neither speak to him, nor answer his questions. The longer he sat there gazing into vacancy, the firmer became his conviction that Nitetis had deceived him,—that she had pretended to love him while her heart really belonged to Bartja. How shamefully they had made sport of him! How deeply rooted must have been the faithlessness of this clever hypocrite, if the mere news that his brother loved some one else could not only destroy all her powers of dissimulation, but actually deprive her of consciousness!

When Nitetis left the hall, Otanes, the father of Phædime had called out: "The Egyptian women seem to take great interest in the love-affairs of their brothers-in-law. The Persian women are not so generous with their feelings; they keep them for their husbands."

Cambyses was too proud to let it be seen that he had heard these words; like the ostrich, he feigned deafness and blindness in order not to seem aware of the looks and murmurs of his guests, which all went to prove that he had been deceived.

Bartja could have had no share in her perfidy; she had loved this handsome youth, and perhaps all the more because she had not been able to hope for a return of her love. If he had had the slightest suspicion of his brother, he would have killed him on the spot. Bartja was certainly innocent of any share in the deception and in his brother's misery, but still he was the cause of all; so the old grudge, which had only just been allowed to slumber, woke again; and, as a relapse is always more dangerous than the original illness, the newly-roused anger was more violent than what he had formerly felt.

He thought and thought, but he could not devise a fitting punishment for this false woman. Her death would not content his vengeance, she must suffer something worse than mere death!

Should he send her back to Egypt, disgraced and shamed? Oh, no! she loved her country, and she would be received by her parents with open arms. Should he, after she had confessed her guilt, (for he was determined to force a confession from her) shut her up in a solitary dungeon? or should he deliver her over to Boges, to be the servant of his concubines? Yes! now he had hit upon the right punishment. Thus the faithless creature should be disciplined, and the hypocrite, who had dared to make sport of him—the All-powerful—forced to atone for her crimes.

Then he said to himself: "Bartja must not stay here; fire and water have more in common than we two—he always fortunate and happy, and I so miserable. Some day or other his descendants will divide my treasures, and wear my crown; but as yet I am king, and I will show that I am."

The thought of his proud, powerful position flashed through him like lightning. He woke from his dreams into new life, flung his golden goblet far into the hall, so that the wine flew round like rain, and cried: "We have had enough of this idle talk and useless noise. Let us hold a council of war, drunken as we are,[8] and consider what answer we ought to give the Massagetæ. Hystaspes, you are the eldest, give us your opinion first."

Hystaspes, the father of Darius, was an old man. He answered: "It seems to me, that the messengers of this wandering tribe have left us no choice. We cannot go to war against desert wastes; but as our host is already under arms and our swords have lain long in their scabbards, war we must have. We only want a few good enemies, and I know no easier work than to make them."

At these words the Persians broke into loud shouts of delight; but Crœsus only waited till the noise had ceased to say: "Hystaspes, you and I are both old men; but you are a thorough Persian and fancy you can only be happy in battle and bloodshed. You are now obliged to lean for support on the staff, which used to be the badge of your rank as commander, and yet you speak like a hot-blooded boy. I agree with you that enemies are easy enough to find, but only fools go out to look for them. The man who tries to make enemies is like

---

8. Herod. I. 134. The Persians deliberated and resolved when they were intoxicated, and when they were sober reconsidered their determinations. Tacitus tells the same of the old Germans. *Germ.* c. 22.

a wretch who mutilates his own body. If the enemies are there, let us go out to meet them like wise men who wish to look misfortune boldly in the face; but let us never try to begin an unjust war, hateful to the gods. We will wait until wrong has been done us, and then go to victory or death, conscious that we have right on our side."

The old man was interrupted by a low murmur of applause, drowned however quickly by cries of "Hystaspes is right! let us look for an enemy!"

It was now the turn of the envoy Prexaspes to speak, and he answered laughing: "Let us follow the advice of both these noble old men. We will do as Crœsus bids us and not go out to seek an enemy, but at the same time we will follow Hystaspes' advice by raising our claims and pronouncing every one our enemy, who does not cheerfully consent to become a member of the kingdom founded by our great father Cyrus. For instance, we will ask the Indians if they would feel proud to obey your sceptre, Cambyses. If they answer no, it is a sign that they do not love us, and whoever does not love us, must be our enemy."

"That won't do," cried Zopyrus. "We must have war at any price."

"I vote for Crœsus," said Gobryas.

"And I too," said the noble Artabazus.

"We are for Hystaspes," shouted the warrior Araspes, the old Intaphernes, and some more of Cyrus's old companions-in-arms.

"War we must have at any price," roared the general Megabyzus, the father of Zopyrus, striking the table so sharply with his heavy fist, that the golden vessels rang again, and some goblets even fell; "but not with the Massagetæ—not with a flying foe."

"There must be no war with the Massagetæ," said the high-priest Oropastes. "The gods themselves have avenged Cyrus's death upon them."

Cambyses sat for some moments, quietly and coldly watching the unrestrained enthusiasm of his warriors, and then, rising from his seat, thundered out the words: "Silence, and listen to your king!"

The words worked like magic on this multitude of drunken men. Even those who were most under the influence of wine, listened to their king in a kind of unconscious obedience. He lowered his voice and went on: "I did not ask whether you wished for peace or war—I know that every Persian prefers the labor of war to an inglorious idleness—but I wished to know what answer you would give the Massagetan warriors. Do you consider that the soul of my father—of the man to whom you owe all your greatness—has been sufficiently avenged?"

A dull murmur in the affirmative, interrupted by some violent voices in the negative, was the answer. The king then asked a second question: "Shall we accept the conditions proposed by their envoys, and grant peace to this nation, already so scourged and desolated by the gods?" To this they all agreed eagerly.

"That is what I wished to know," continued Cambyses. "To-morrow, when we are sober, we will follow the old custom and reconsider what has been resolved on during our intoxication. Drink on, all of you, as long as the night lasts. To-morrow, at the last crow of the sacred bird Parodar,[9] I shall expect you to meet me for the chase, at the gate of the temple of Bel."

9. The cock was held sacred by the Persians, because it scared the dark Divs of night back into their dens. Jasht, *Avân*, 21. It was

So saying, the king left the hall, followed by a thundering "Victory to the king!" Boges had slipped out quietly before him. In the forecourt he found one of the gardener's boys from the hanging-gardens.

"What do you want here?" asked Boges.

"I have something for the prince Bartja."

"For Bartja? Has he asked your master to send him some seeds or slips?"

The boy shook his sunburnt head and smiled roguishly.

"Some one else sent you then?" said Boges becoming more attentive.

"Yes, some one else."

"Ah! the Egyptian has sent a message to her brother-in-law?"

"Who told you that?"

"Nitesis spoke to me about it. Here, give me what you have; I will give it to Bartja at once."

"I was not to give it to any one but the prince himself."

"Give it to me; it will be safer in my hands than in yours."

"I dare not."

"Obey me at once, or—"

At this moment the king came up. Boges thought a moment, and then called in a loud voice to the whip-bearers on duty at the palace-gate, to take the astonished boy up.

"What is the matter here?" asked Cambyses.

"This fellow," answered the eunuch, "has had the

---

called Parôdar (Parôdarsh) and also Kahrkatâç (he who raises and lowers his comb?). Vendid. XVIII. 34.

audacity to make his way into the palace with a message from your consort Nitetis to Bartja."

At sight of the king, the boy had fallen on his knees, touching the ground with his forehead.

Cambyses looked at him and turned deadly pale. Then, turning to the eunuch, he asked: "What does the Egyptian Princess wish from my brother?"

"The boy declares that he has orders to give up what has been entrusted to him to no one but Bartja."

On hearing this the boy looked imploringly up at the king, and held out a little papyrus roll.

Cambyses snatched it out of his hand, but the next moment stamped furiously on the ground at seeing that the letter was written in Greek, which he could not read.

He collected himself, however, and, with an awful look, asked the boy who had given him the letter.

"The Egyptian lady's waiting-woman Mandane," he answered; "the Magian's daughter."

"For my brother Bartja?"

"She said I was to give the letter to the handsome prince, before the banquet, with a greeting from her mistress Nitetis, and I was to tell him . . ."

Here the king stamped so furiously, that the boy was frightened and could only stammer: "Before the banquet the prince was walking with you, so I could not speak to him, and now I am waiting for him here, for Mandane promised to give me a piece of gold if I did what she told me cleverly."

"And that you have not done," thundered the king, fancying himself shamefully deceived. "No, indeed you have not. Here, guards, seize this fellow!"

The boy begged and prayed, but all in vain; the

whip-bearers seized him quick as thought, and Cambyses, who went off at once to his own apartments, was soon out of reach of his whining entreaties for mercy.

Boges followed his master, rubbing his fat hands, and laughing quietly to himself.

The king's attendants began their work of disrobing him, but he told them angrily to leave him at once.

As soon as they were gone, he called Boges and said in a low voice: "From this time forward the hanging-gardens and the Egyptian are under your control. Watch her carefully! If a single human being or a message reaches her without my knowledge, your life will be the forfeit."

"But if Kassandane or Atossa should send to her?"

"Turn the messengers away, and send word that every attempt to see or communicate with Nitetis will be regarded by me as a personal offence."

"May I ask a favor for myself, O King?"

"The time is not well chosen for asking favors."

"I feel ill. Permit some one else to take charge of the hanging-gardens for to-morrow only."

"No!—now leave me."

"I am in a burning fever and have lost consciousness three times during the day—if when I am in that state any one should . . ."

"But who could take your place?"

"The Lydian captain of the eunuchs, Kandaules. He is true as gold, and inflexibly severe. One day of rest would restore me to health. Have mercy, O King!"

"No one is so badly served as the king himself. Kandaules may take your place to-morrow, but give him the strictest orders, and say that the slightest neglect will put his life in danger.—Now depart."

"Yet one word, my King: to-morrow night the rare blue lily in the hanging-gardens will open. Hystaspes, Intaphernes, Gobyras, Crœsus and Oropastes, the greatest horticulturists at your court, would very much like to see it. May they be allowed to visit the gardens for a few minutes? Kandaules shall see that they enter into no communication with the Egyptian."

"Kandaules must keep his eyes open, if he cares for his own life.—Go!"

Boges made a deep obeisance and left the king's apartment. He threw a few gold pieces to the slaves who bore the torches before him. He was so very happy. Every thing had succeeded beyond his expectations:—the fate of Nitetis was as good as decided, and he held the life of Kandaules, his hated colleague, in his own hands.

Cambyses spent the night in pacing up and down his apartment. By cock-crow he had decided that Nitetis should be forced to confess her guilt, and then be sent into the great harem to wait on the concubines. Bartja, the destroyer of his happiness, should set off at once for Egypt, and on his return become the satrap of some distant provinces. He did not wish to incur the guilt of a brother's murder, but he knew his own temper too well not to fear that in a moment of sudden anger, he might kill one he hated so much, and therefore wished to remove him out of the reach of his passion.

Two hours after the sun had risen, Cambyses was riding on his fiery steed, far in front of a countless train of followers armed with shields, swords, lances, bows and lassos, in pursuit of the game which was to be found in the immense preserves near Babylon, and was to be started from its lair by more than a thousand dogs.[10]

CHAPTER II.

THE hunt was over. Waggons full of game, amongst which were several enormous wild boars killed by the king's own hand, were driven home behind the sportsmen. At the palace-gates the latter dispersed to their several abodes, in order to exchange the simple Persian leather hunting-costume for the splendid Median court-dress.

In the course of the day's sport Cambyses had (with difficulty restraining his agitation) given his brother the seemingly kind order to start the next day for Egypt

[10]. The same immense trains of followers of course accompanied the kings on their hunting expeditions, as on their journeys. As the Persian nobility were very fond of hunting, their boys were taught this sport at an early age. According to Strabo, kings themselves boasted of having been mighty hunters in the inscriptions on their tombs. A relief has been found in the ruins of Persepolis, on which the king is strangling a lion with his right arm, but this is supposed to have a historical, not a symbolical meaning. Similar representations occur on Assyrian monuments. Izdubar strangling a lion and fighting with a lion (relief at Khorsabad) is admirably copied in Delitzsch's edition of G. Smith's Chaldean Genesis. Texier, *Description de l'Arménie* pl. 98. Layard discovered some representations of hunting-scenes during his excavations; as, for instance, stags and wild boars among the reeds; and the Greeks often mention the immense troops of followers on horse and foot who attended the kings of Persia when they went hunting. According to Xenophon, *Cyrop*. I. 2. II. 4. every hunter was obliged to be armed with a bow and arrows, two lances, sword and shield. In Firdusi's Book of Kings we read that the lasso was also a favorite weapon. Hawking was well known to the Persians more than 900 years ago. Book of Kabus XVIII. p. 495. The boomerang was used in catching birds as well by the Persians as by the ancient Egyptians and the present savage tribes of New Holland. Brugsch tells us that the present Sh..h of Persia, Nasr-ed-din, is a bold sportsman and passionately fond of hunting.

in order to fetch Sappho and accompany her to Persia. At the same time he assigned him the revenues of Bactra, Rhagæ and Sinope for the maintenance of his new household, and to his young wife, all the duties levied from her native town Phocæa, as pin-money.

Bartja thanked his generous brother with undisguised warmth, but Cambyses remained cold as ice, uttered a few farewell words, and then, riding off in pursuit of a wild ass, turned his back upon him.

On the way home from the chase the prince invited his bosom-friends* Crœsus, Darius, Zopyrus and Gyges to drink a parting-cup with him.

Crœsus promised to join them later, as he had promised to visit the blue lily at the rising of the Tistar-star.

He had been to the hanging-gardens that morning early to visit Nitetis, but had been refused entrance by the guards, and the blue lily seemed now to offer him another chance of seeing and speaking to his beloved pupil. He wished for this very much, as he could not thoroughly understand her behavior the day before, and was uneasy at the strict watch set over her.

The young Achæmenidæ sat cheerfully talking together in the twilight in a shady bower in the royal gardens, cool fountains plashing round them. Araspes, a Persian of high rank, who had been one of Cyrus's friends, had joined them, and did full justice to the prince's excellent wine.

"Fortunate Bartja!" cried the old bachelor, "going out to a golden country to fetch the woman you love; while I, miserable old fellow, am blamed by every-

---

* See vol. I. note 193.

body,* and totter to my grave without wife or children to weep for me and pray the gods to be merciful to my poor soul."

"Why think of such things?" cried Zopyrus, flourishing the wine-cup. "There's no woman so perfect that her husband does not, at least once a day, repent that he ever took a wife. Be merry, old friend, and remember that it's all your own fault. If you thought a wife would make you happy, why did not you do as I have done? I am only twenty-two years old and have five stately wives and a troop of the most beautiful slaves in my house."

Araspes smiled bitterly.

"And what hinders you from marrying now?" said Gyges. "You are a match for many a younger man in appearance, strength, courage and perseverance. You are one of the king's nearest relations too—I tell you, Araspes, you might have twenty young and beautiful wives."

"Look after your own affairs," answered Araspes. "In your place, I certainly should not have waited to marry till I was thirty."

"An oracle has forbidden my marrying."

"Folly? how can a sensible man care for what an oracle says? It is only by dreams, that the gods announce the future to men. I should have thought that your own father was example enough of the shameful way in which those lying priests deceive their best friends."

"That is a matter which you do not understand, Araspes."

"And never wish to, boy, for you only believe in

* See note 6

oracles because you don't understand them, and in your short-sightedness call everything that is beyond your comprehension a miracle. And you place more confidence in anything that seems to you miraculous, than in the plain simple truth that lies before your face. An oracle deceived your father and plunged him into ruin, but the oracle is miraculous, and so you too, in perfect confidence, allow it to rob you of happiness!"

"That is blasphemy, Araspes. Are the gods to be blamed because we misunderstand their words?"

"Certainly: for if they wished to benefit us they would give us, with the words, the necessary penetration for discovering their meaning. What good does a beautiful speech do me, if it is in a foreign language that I do not understand?"

"Leave off this useless discussion," said Darius, "and tell us instead, Araspes, how it is that, though you congratulate every man on becoming a bridegroom, you yourself have so long submitted to be blamed by the priests, slighted at all entertainments and festivals, and abused by the women, only because you choose to live and die a bachelor?"

Araspes looked down thoughtfully, then shook himself, took a long draught from the wine-cup, and said, "I have my reasons, friends, but I cannot tell them now."

"Tell them, tell them," was the answer.

"No, children, I cannot, indeed I cannot. This cup I drain to the health of the charming Sappho, and this second to your good fortune, my favorite, Darius."

"Thanks, Araspes!" exclaimed Bartja, joyfully raising his goblet to his lips.

"You mean well, I know," muttered Darius, looking down gloomily.

"What's this, you son of Hystaspes?" cried the old man, looking more narrowly at the serious face of the youth. "Dark looks like these don't sit well on a betrothed lover, who is to drink to the health of his dearest one. Is not Gobryas' little daughter the noblest of all the young Persian girls after Atossa? and isn't she beautiful?"

"Artystone has every talent and quality that a daughter of the Achæmenidæ ought to possess," was Darius's answer, but his brow did not clear as he said the words.

"Well, if you want more than that, you must be very hard to please."

Darius raised his goblet and looked down into the wine.

"The boy is in love, as sure as my name is Araspes!" exclaimed the elder man.

"What a set of foolish fellows you are," broke in Zopyrus at this exclamation. "One of you has remained a bachelor in defiance of all Persian customs; another has been frightened out of marrying by an oracle; Bartja has determined to be content with only one wife; and Darius looks like a Destur chanting the funeral-service, because his father has told him to make himself happy with the most beautiful and aristocratic girl in all Persia!"

"Zopyrus is right," cried Araspes. "Darius is ungrateful to fortune."

Bartja meanwhile kept his eyes fixed on the friend, who was thus blamed by the others. He saw that their jests annoyed him, and feeling his own great happiness doubly in that moment, pressed Darius's hand, saying: "I am so sorry that I cannot be present at your wedding. By the time I come back, I hope you will be reconciled to your father's choice."

"Perhaps," said Darius, "I may be able to show a second and even a third wife by that time."

"Anahita* grant it!" exclaimed Zopyrus. "The Achæmenidæ would soon become extinct, if every one were to follow such examples as Gyges and Araspes have set us. And your one wife, Bartja, is really not worth talking about. It is your duty to marry three wives at once, in order to keep up your father's family—the race of Cyrus."

"I hate our custom of marrying many wives," answered Bartja. "Through doing this, we make ourselves inferior to the women, for we expect them to remain faithful to us all our lives, and we, who are bound to respect truth and faithfulness above every thing else, swear inviolable love to one woman to-day, and to another to-morrow."

"Nonsense!" cried Zopyrus. "I'd rather lose my tongue than tell a lie to a man, but our wives are so awfully deceitful, that one has no choice but to pay them back in their own coin."

"The Greek women are different," said Bartja, "because they are differently treated. Sappho told me of one, I think her name was Penelope, who waited twenty years faithfully and lovingly for her husband, though every one believed he was dead, and she had fifty lovers a day at her house."

"My wives would not wait so long for me," said Zopyrus laughing. "To tell the truth, I don't think I

* See vol. 1. note 253.

should be sorry to find an empty house, if I came back after twenty years. For then I could take some new wives into my harem, young and beautiful, instead of the unfaithful ones, who, besides, would have grown old. But alas! every woman does not find some one to run away with her, and our women would rather have an absent husband than none at all."

"If your wives could hear what you are saying!" said Araspes.

"They would declare war with me at once, or, what is still worse, conclude a peace with one another."

"How would that be worse?"

"How? it is easy to see, that you have had no experience."

"Then let us into the secrets of your married life."

"With pleasure. You can easily fancy, that five wives in one house do not live quite so peacefully as five doves in a cage; mine at least carry on an uninterrupted, mortal warfare. But I have accustomed myself to that, and their sprightliness even amuses me. A year ago, however, they came to terms with one another, and this day of peace was the most miserable in my life."

"You are jesting."

"No, indeed, I am quite in earnest. The wretched eunuch who had to keep watch over the five, allowed them to see an old jewel-merchant from Tyre. Each of them chose a separate and expensive set of jewels. When I came home Sudabe came up and begged for money to pay for these ornaments. The things were too dear, and I refused. Every one of the five then came and begged me separately for the money; I refused each of them point blank and went off to court. When I came back, there were all my wives weeping side by side, embracing one another and calling each other fellow-sufferers. These former enemies rose up against me with the most touching unanimity, and so overwhelmed me with revilings and threats that I left the room. They closed their doors against me. The next morning the lamentations of the evening before were continued. I fled once more and went hunting with the king, and when I came back, tired, hungry and half-frozen—for it was in spring, we were already at Ecbatana, and the snow was lying an ell deep on the Orontes—there was no fire on the hearth and nothing to eat. These noble creatures had entered into an alliance in order to punish me, had put out the fire, forbidden the cooks to do their duty and, which was worse than all—had kept the jewels! No sooner had I ordered the slaves to make a fire and prepare food, than the impudent jewel-dealer appeared and demanded his money. I refused again, passed another solitary night, and in the morning sacrificed ten talents for the sake of peace. Since that time harmony and peace among my beloved wives seems to me as much to be feared as the evil Divs themselves, and I see their little quarrels with the greatest pleasure."

"Poor Zopyrus!" cried Bartja.

"Why poor?" asked this five-fold husband. "I tell you I am much happier than you are. My wives are young and charming, and when they grow old, what is to hinder me from taking others, still handsomer, and who, by the side of the faded beauties, will be doubly charming. Ho! slave—bring some lamps. The sun has gone down, and the wine loses all its flavor when the table is not brightly lighted."

At this moment the voice of Darius, who had left the

arbor and gone out into the garden, was heard calling: "Come and hear how beautifully the nightingale is singing."

"By Mithras, you son of Hystaspes, you must be in love," interrupted Araspes. "The flowery darts of love" *must* have entered the heart of him, who leaves his wine to listen to the nightingale."

"You are right there, father," cried Bartja. "Philomel, as the Greeks call our Gulgul, is the lovers' bird among all nations, for love has given her her beautiful song. What beauty were you dreaming of, Darius, when you went out to listen to the nightingale?"

"I was not dreaming of any," answered he. "You know how fond I am of watching the stars, and the Tistar-star rose so splendidly to-night, that I left the wine to watch it. The nightingales were singing so loudly to one another, that if I had not wished to hear them I must have stopped my ears."

"You kept them wide open, however," said Araspes laughing. "Your enraptured exclamation proved that."

"Enough of this," cried Darius, to whom these jokes were getting wearisome. "I really must beg you to leave off making allusions to matters, which I do not care to hear spoken of."

"Imprudent fellow!" whispered the older man; "now you really have betrayed yourself. If you were not in love, you would have laughed instead of getting angry.

---

11. We have borrowed this idea from the Indians, the arrows of whose love-god Kama were made of sharpened flower-blossoms. The nightingale "gulgul" plays a great part in the Persian love-songs. Her song is spoken of as the perfection of sweet sound, and she herself as the lovers' bird. See J. von Hammer's *Geschichte der schönen Redekünste Persiens*.

Still I won't go on provoking you—tell me what you have just been reading in the stars."

At these words Darius looked up again into the starry sky and fixed his eyes on a bright constellation hanging over the horizon. Zopyrus watched him and called out to his friends, "Something important must be happening up there. Darius, tell us what's going on in the heavens just now."

"Nothing good," answered the other. "Bartja, I have something to say to you alone."

"Why to me alone? Araspes always keeps his own counsel, and from the rest of you I never have any secrets."

"Still—"

"Speak out."

"No, I wish you would come into the garden with me."

Bartja nodded to the others, who were still sitting over their wine, laid his hand on Darius' shoulder and went out with him into the bright moonlight. As soon as they were alone, Darius seized both his friend's hands, and said: "To-day is the third time that things have happened in the heavens, which bode no good for you. Your evil star has approached your favorable constellation so nearly, that a mere novice in astrology could see some serious danger was at hand. Be on your guard, Bartja, and start for Egypt to-day; the stars tell me that the danger is here on the Euphrates, not abroad."

"Do you believe implicitly in the stars?"

"Implicitly. They never lie."

"Then it would be folly to try and avoid what they have foretold."

"Yes, no man can run away from his destiny; but

that very destiny is like a fencing-master—his favorite pupils are those who have the courage and skill to parry his own blows. Start for Egypt to-day, Bartja."

"I cannot—I haven't taken leave of my mother and Atossa."

"Send them a farewell message, and tell Crœsus to explain the reason of your starting so quickly."

"They would call me a coward."

"It is cowardly to yield to any mortal, but to go out of the way of one's fate is wisdom."

"You contradict yourself, Darius. What would the fencing-master say to a runaway-pupil?"

"He would rejoice in the stratagem, by which an isolated individual tried to escape a superior force."

"But the superior force must conquer at last.—What would be the use of my trying to put off a danger which, you say yourself, cannot be averted? If my tooth aches, I have it drawn at once, instead of tormenting and making myself miserable for weeks by putting off the painful operation as a coward or a woman would, till the last moment. I can await this coming danger bravely, and the sooner it comes the better, for then I shall have it behind me."

"You do not know how serious it is."

"Are you afraid for my life?"

"No."

"Then tell me, what you are afraid of."

"That Egyptian priest with whom I used to study the stars, once cast your horoscope with me. He knew more about the heavens, than any man I ever saw. I learnt a great deal from him, and I will not hide from you that even then he drew my attention to dangers that threaten you now."

"And you did not tell me?"

"Why should I have made you uneasy beforehand? Now that your destiny is drawing near, I warn you."

"Thank you,—I will be careful. In former times I should not have listened to such a warning, but now that I love Sappho, I feel as if my life were not so much my own to do what I like with, as it used to be."

"I understand this feeling . . ."

"You understand it? Then Araspes was right? You don't deny?"

"A mere dream without any hope of fulfilment."

"But what woman could refuse you?"

"Refuse!"

"I don't understand you. Do you mean to say that you—the boldest sportsman, the strongest wrestler—the wisest of all the young Persians—that you, Darius, are afraid of a woman?"

"Bartja, may I tell you more, than I would tell even to my own father?"

"Yes."

"I love the daughter of Cyrus, your sister and the king's,—Atossa."

"Have I understood you rightly? you love Atossa? Be praised for this, O ye pure Amescha çpenta!* Now I shall never believe in your stars again, for instead of the danger with which they threatened me, here comes an unexpected happiness. Embrace me, my brother, and tell me the whole story, that I may see whether I can help you to turn this hopeless dream, as you call it, into a reality."

"You will remember that before our journey to Egypt, we went with the entire court from Ecbatana to Susa. I

* See note 17.

was in command of the division of the "Immortals" appointed to escort the carriages containing the king's mother and sister, and his wives. In going through the narrow pass which leads over the Orontes, the horses of your mother's carriage slipped. The yoke to which the horses were harnessed[12] broke from the pole, and the heavy, four-wheeled carriage fell over the precipice without obstruction. On seeing it disappear, we were horrified and spurred our horses to the place as quickly as possible. We expected of course to see only fragments of the carriages and the dead bodies of its inmates, but the gods had taken them into their almighty protection, and there lay the carriage, with broken wheels, in the arms of two gigantic cypresses which had taken firm root in the fissures of the slate rocks, and whose dark tops reached up to the edge of the carriage-road.

"As quick as thought I sprang from my horse and scrambled down one of the cypresses. Your mother and sister stretched their arms to me, crying for help. The danger was frightful, for the sides of the carriage had been so shattered by the fall, that they threatened every moment to give way, in which case those inside it must inevitably have fallen into the black, unfathomable abyss which looked like an abode for the gloomy Divs, and stretched his jaws wide to crush its beautiful victims.

"I stood before the shattered carriage as it hung over the precipice ready to fall to pieces every moment, and then for the first time I met your sister's imploring

---

12. There was a yoke at the end of the shaft of a Persian carriage, which was fastened on to the backs of the horses and took the place of our horse-collar and pole-chain. See illustration in Gosse's *Assyria*, *p*. 224. Layard, p. 151 and 447-451. The Egyptian horses were harnessed in the same manner. See Vol. I. note 30. The horses represented on the Persian and Assyrian monuments are without question a different race from those on the Egyptian.

look. From that moment I loved her, but at the time I was much too intent on saving them, to think of anything else, and had no idea what had taken place within me. I dragged the trembling women out of the carriage, and one minute later it rolled down the abyss crashing into a thousand pieces. I am a strong man, but I confess that all my strength was required to keep myself and the two women from falling over the precipice until ropes were thrown to us from above. Atossa hung round my neck, and Kassandane lay on my breast, supported by my left arm; with the right I fastened the rope round my waist, we were drawn up, and I found myself a few minutes later on the high-road—your mother and sister were saved.

"As soon as one of the Magi had bound up the wounds cut by the rope in my side, the king sent for me, gave me the chain I am now wearing and the revenues of an entire satrapy, and then took me to his mother and sister. They expressed their gratitude very warmly; Kassandane allowed me to kiss her forehead, and gave me all the jewels she had worn at the time of the accident, as a present for my future wife. Atossa took a ring from her finger, put it on mine and kissed my hand in the warmth of her emotion—you know how eager and excitable she is. Since that happy day—the happiest in my life—I have never seen your sister, till yesterday evening, when we sat opposite to each other at the banquet. Our eyes met. I saw nothing but Atossa, and I think she has not forgotten the man who saved her. Kassandane . . ."

"Oh, my mother would be delighted to have you for a son-in-law; I will answer for that. As to the king, your father must apply to him; he is our uncle and has a right to ask the hand of Cyrus's daughter for his son."

"But have you forgotten your father's dream? You know that Cambyses has always looked on me with suspicion since that time."

"Oh, that has been long forgotten. My father dreamt before his death that you had wings,[13] and was misled by the soothsayers into the fancy that you, though you were only eighteen then, would try to gain the crown. Cambyses thought of this dream too; but, when you saved my mother and sister, Crœsus explained to him that this must have been its fulfilment, as no one but Darius or a winged eagle could possibly have possessed strength and dexterity enough to hang suspended over such an abyss."

"Yes, and I remember too that these words did not please your brother. He chooses to be the only eagle in Persia; but Crœsus does not spare his vanity—"

"Where can Crœsus be all this time?"

"In the hanging-gardens. My father and Gobryas have very likely detained him."

Just at that moment the voice of Zopyrus was heard exclaiming, "Well, I call that polite! Bartja invites us to a wine-party and leaves us sitting here without a host, while he talks secrets yonder."

"We are coming, we are coming," answered Bartja. Then taking the hand of Darius heartily, he said: "I am very glad that you love Atossa. I shall stay here till the day after to-morrow, let the stars threaten me with all the dangers in the world. To-morrow I will find out what Atossa feels, and when every thing is in

---

13. Herod. I. 209.

the right track I shall go away, and leave my winged Darius to his own powers."

So saying Bartja went back into the arbor, and his friend began to watch the stars again. The longer he looked the sadder and more serious became his face, and when the Tistar-star set, he murmured, "Poor Bartja!" His friends called him, and he was on the point of returning to them, when he caught sight of a new star, and began to examine its position carefully. His serious looks gave way to a triumphant smile, his tall figure seemed to grow taller still, he pressed his hand on his heart and whispered: "Use your pinions, winged Darius; your star will be on your side," and then returned to his friends.

A few minutes after, Crœsus came up to the arbor. The youths sprang from their seats to welcome the old man, but when he saw Bartja's face by the bright moonlight, he stood as if transfixed by a flash of lightning.

"What has happened, father?" asked Gyges, seizing his hand anxiously.

"Nothing, nothing," he stammered almost inaudibly, and pushing his son on one side, whispered in Bartja's ear: "Unhappy boy, you are still here? don't delay any longer,—fly at once! the whip-bearers are close at my heels, and I assure you that if you don't use the greatest speed, you will have to forfeit your double imprudence with your life."

"But Crœsus, I have . . ."

"You have set at nought the law of the land and of the court, and, in appearance at least, have done great offence to your brother's honor . . ."

"You are speaking . . ."

"Fly, I tell you—fly at once; for if your visit to the hanging-gardens was ever so innocently meant, you are still in the greatest danger. You know Cambyses' violent temper so well; how could you so wickedly disobey his express command?"

"I don't understand."

"No excuses,—fly! don't you know that, Cambyses has long been jealous of you, and that your visit to the Egyptian to-night . . ."

"I have never once set foot in the hanging-gardens, since Nitetis has been here."

"Don't add a lie to your offence, I . . ."

"But I swear to you . . ."

"Do you wish to turn a thoughtless act into a crime by adding the guilt of perjury? The whip-bearers are coming, fly!"

"I shall remain here, and abide by my oath."

"You are infatuated! It is not an hour ago since I myself, Hystaspes, and others of the Achæmenidæ, saw you in the hanging-gardens . . ."

In his astonishment Bartja had, half involuntarily, allowed himself to be led away, but when he heard this he stood still, called his friends and said "Crœsus says he met me an hour ago in the hanging-gardens, you know that since the sun set I have not been away from you. Give your testimony, that in this case an evil Div must have made sport of our friend and his companions."

"I swear to you, father," cried Gyges, "that Bartja has not left this garden for some hours."

"And we confirm the same," added Araspes, Zopyrus and Darius with one voice.

"You want to deceive me?" said Crœsus getting

very angry, and looking at each of them reproachfully. "Do you fancy that I am blind or mad? Do you think that your witness will outweigh the words of such men as Hystaspes, Gobryas, Artaphernes and the high-priest, Oropastes? In spite of all your false testimony, which no amount of friendship can justify, Bartja will have to die unless he flies at once."

"May Angramainjus destroy me," said Araspes interrupting the old man, "if Bartja was in the hanging-gardens two hours ago!" and Gyges added:

"Dont call me your son any longer, if we have given false testimony."

Darius was beginning to appeal to the eternal stars, but Bartja put an end to this confusion of voices by saying in a decided tone: "A division of the body-guard is coming into the garden. I am to be arrested; I cannot escape because I am innocent, and to fly would lay me open to suspicion. By the soul of my father, the blind eyes of my mother, and the pure light of the sun, Crœsus, I swear that I am not lying."

"Am I to believe you, in spite of my own eyes which have never yet deceived me? But I will, boy, for I love you. I do not and I will not know whether you are innocent or guilty, but this I do know, you must fly, and fly at once. You know Cambyses. My carriage is waiting at the gate. Don't spare the horses, save yourself even if you drive them to death. The soldiers seem to know what they have been sent to do; there can be no question that they delay so long only in order to give their favorite time to escape. Fly, fly, or it is all over with you."

Darius, too, pushed his friend forward, exclaiming:

"Fly, Bartja, and remember the warning that the heavens themselves wrote in the stars for you."

Bartja, however, stood silent, shook his handsome head, waved his friends back, and answered: "I never ran away yet, and I mean to hold my ground to-day. Cowardice is worse than death in my opinion, and I would rather suffer wrong at the hands of others than disgrace myself. There are the soldiers! Well met, Bischen. You've come to arrest me, haven't you? Wait one moment, till I have said good-bye to my friends."

Bischen, the officer he spoke to, was one of Cyrus's old captains; he had given Bartja his first lessons in shooting and throwing the spear, had fought by his side in the war with the Tapuri, and loved him as if he were his own son. He interrupted him, saying: "There is no need to take leave of your friends, for the king, who is raging like a madman, ordered me not only to arrest you, but every one else who might be with you."

And then he added in a low voice: "The king is beside himself with rage and threatens to have your life. You must fly. My men will do what I tell them blindfold; they will not pursue you; and I am so old that it would be little loss to Persia, if my head were the price of my disobedience."

"Thanks, thanks, my friend," said Bartja, giving him his hand; "but I cannot accept your offer, because I am innocent, and I know that though Cambyses is hasty, he is not unjust. Come friends, I think the king will give us a hearing to-day, late as it is."

CHAPTER III.

Two hours later Bartja and his friends were standing before the king. The gigantic man was seated on his golden throne; he was pale and his eyes looked sunken; two physicians stood waiting behind him with all kinds of instruments and vessels in their hands. Cambyses had, only a few minutes before, recovered consciousness, after lying for more than an hour in one of those awful fits, so destructive both to mind and body, which we call epileptic.

Since Nitetis' arrival he had been free from this illness; but it had seized him to-day with fearful violence, owing to the overpowering mental excitement he had gone through."

If he had met Bartja a few hours before, he would have killed him with his own hand; but though the epileptic fit had not subdued his anger it had at least so far quieted it, that he was in a condition to hear what was to be said on both sides.

At the right hand of the throne stood Hystaspes, Darius's grey-haired father, Gobryas, his future father-in-law, the aged Intaphernes, the grandfather of that Phædime whose place in the king's favor had been given to Nitetis, Oropastes the high-priest, Crœsus, and behind them Boges, the chief of the eunuchs. At its left Bartja, whose hands were heavily fettered, Araspes, Darius,

---

14. The dangerous disease to which Herodotus says Cambyses had been subject from his birth, and which was called "sacred" by some, can scarcely be other than epilepsy. See Herod. III. 33.

Zopyrus and Gyges. In the background stood some hundred officials and grandees.

After a long silence Cambyses raised his eyes, fixed a withering look on his fettered brother, and said in a dull hollow voice: "High-priest, tell us what awaits the man who deceives his brother, dishonors and offends his king, and darkens his own heart by black lies."

Oropastes came forward and answered: "As soon as such a one is proved guilty, a death full of torment awaits him in this world, and an awful sentence on the bridge Chinvat;[15] for he has transgressed the highest commands, and, by committing three crimes, has forfeited the mercy of our law, which commands that his life shall be granted to the man who has sinned but once, even though he be only a slave."[16]

"Then Bartja has deserved death. Lead him away, guards, and strangle him! Take him away! Be silent, wretch! never will I listen to that smooth, hypocritical tongue again, or look at those treacherous eyes. They come from the Divs and delude every one with their wanton glances. Off with him, guards!"

Bischen, the captain, came up to obey the order, but in the same moment Crœsus threw himself at the king's feet, touched the floor with his forehead, raised

---

15. On the third day after death, at the rising of the bright sun, the souls are conducted by the Divs to the bridge Chinvât, where they are questioned as to their past lives and conduct. *Vendid.* Fargard. XIX. 93. On that spot the two supernatural powers fight for the soul. *Vendid* Farg. VII. 132. In this struggle the soul of the good, the odor of which is feared by the Divs as wolves by sheep, is helped by the *Yazatas* or pure spirits and enters heaven victorious, while the soul of the impure finds no help and is dragged down, bound, into hell by the Div Vizareshô. Different, and according to Rogge, more beautiful (?) conceptions of this idea are to be found in Tiele's *d. gedsd. v. Zarathustra p.* 251. This subject is admirably treated by Spiegel, *Ausland* 1872.

16. Herod. I. 137.

his hands and cried: "May thy days and years bring nought but happiness and prosperity; may Auramazda pour down all the blessings of this life upon thee, and the Amescha çpenta[17] be the guardians of thy throne! Do not close thine ear to the words of the aged, but remember that thy father Cyrus appointed me to be thy counsellor. Thou art about to slay thy brother; but I say unto thee, do not indulge anger; strive to control it. It is the duty of kings and of the wise, not to act without due enquiry. Beware of shedding a brother's blood; the smoke thereof will rise to heaven and become a cloud that must darken the days of the murderer, and at last cast down the lightnings of vengeance on his head. But I know that thou desirest justice, not murder. Act then as those who have to pronounce a sentence, and hear both sides before deciding. When this has been done, if the criminal is proved guilty and confesses his crime, the smoke of his blood will rise to heaven as a friendly shadow, instead of a darkening cloud, and thou wilt have earned the fame of a just judge instead of deserving the divine judgments."

Cambyses listened in silence, made a sign to Bischen to retire, and commanded Boges to repeat his accusation.

The eunuch made an obeisance, and began: "I was ill and obliged to leave the Egyptian and the hanging-gardens in the care of my colleague Kandaules, who has paid for his negligence with his life. Finding myself better towards evening, I went up to the hanging-gardens to see if everything was in order there, and also to look

[17]. The *Amescha çpenta*, "holy immortal ones," may be compared to the archangels of the Hebrews. They surround the throne of Auramazda and symbolize the highest virtues. Later we find their number fixed at six.

at the rare flower which was to blossom in the night. The king, (Auramazda grant him victory!) had commanded that the Egyptian should be more strictly watched than usual, because she had dared to send the noble Bartja . . ."

"Be silent," interrupted the king "and keep to the matter in hand."

"Just as the Tistar-star was rising, I came into the garden, and staid some time there with these noble Achæmenidæ, the high-priest and the king Crœsus, looking at the blue lily, which was marvellously beautiful. I then called my colleague Kandaules and asked him, in the presence of these noble witnesses, if everything was in order. He affirmed that this was the case and added, that he had just come from Nitetis, that she had wept the whole day, and neither tasted food nor drink. Feeling anxious lest my noble mistress should become worse, I commissioned Kandaules to fetch a physican, and was just on the point of leaving the noble Achæmenidæ, in order in person to ascertain my mistress's state of health, when I saw in the moonlight the figure of a man. I was so ill and weak, that I could hardly stand and had no one near to help me, except the gardener.

"My men were on guard at the different entrances, some distance from us.

"I clapped my hands to call some of them, but, as they did not come, I went nearer to the house myself, under the protection of these noblemen. The man was standing by the window of the Egyptian Princess's apartment, and uttered a low whistle when he heard us coming up. Another figure appeared directly—clearly recognizable in the bright moonlight—sprang out of the sleeping-room window and came towards us with her companion.

"I could hardly believe my eyes on discovering that the intruder was no other than the noble Bartja. A fig-tree concealed *us* from the fugitives, but we could distinctly see *them*, as they passed us at a distance of not more than four steps. While I was thinking whether I should be justified in arresting a son of Cyrus, Crœsus called to Bartja, and the two figures suddenly disappeared behind a cypress. No one but your brother himself can possibly explain the strange way in which he disappeared. I went at once to search the house, and found the Egyptian lying unconscious on the couch in her sleeping-room."

Every one listened to this story in the greatest suspense. Cambyses ground his teeth and asked in a voice of great emotion: "Can you testify to the words of the eunuch, Hystaspes?"

"Yes."

"Why did you not lay hands on the offender?"

"We are soldiers, not policemen."

"Or rather you care for every knave more than for your king."

"We honor our king, and abhor the criminal just as we formerly loved the innocent son of Cyrus."

"Did you recognize Bartja distinctly?"

"Yes."

"And you, Crœsus,—can you too give no other answer?"

"No! I fancied I saw your brother in the moonlight then, as clearly as I see him now; but I believe we must have been deceived by some remarkable likeness."

Boges grew pale at these words; Cambyses, however, shook his head as if the idea did not please him, and said: "Whom am I to believe then, if the eyes of my best warriors fail them? and who would wish to be a judge, if testimony such as yours is not to be considered valid?"

"Evidence quite as weighty as ours, will prove that we must have been in error."

"Will any one dare to give evidence in favor of such an outrageous criminal?" asked Cambyses, springing up and stamping his foot.

"We will," "I," "we," shouted Araspes, Darius, Gyges and Zopyrus with one voice.

"Traitors, knaves!" cried the king. But as he caught sight of Crœsus' warning eye fixed upon him, he lowered his voice, and said: "What have you to bring forward in favor of this fellow? Take care what you say, and consider well what punishment awaits perjurers."

"We know that well enough," said Araspes, "and yet we are ready to swear by Mithras, that we have not left Bartja or his garden one moment since we came back from hunting."

"As for me," said Darius, "I, the son of Hystaspes, have especially convincing evidence to give in favor of your brother's innocence; I watched the rising of the Tistar-star with him; and this, according to Boges, was the very star that shone on his flight."

Hystaspes gazed on his son in astonishment and doubt at hearing these words, and Cambyses turned a scrutinizing eye first on the one and then on the other party of these strange witnesses, who wished so much, and yet found it so impossible, to believe one another, himself unable to come to a decision.

Bartja, who till now had remained perfectly silent, looking down sadly at his chained hands, took advantage of the silence to say, making at the same time a deep obeisance: "May I be allowed to speak a few words, my King?"

"Speak!"

"From our father we learnt to strive after that which was pure and good only; so up to this time my life has been unstained. If you have ever known me take part in an evil deed, you have a right not to believe me, but if you find no fault in me then trust to what I say, and remember that a son of Cyrus would rather die than tell a lie. I confess that no judge was ever placed in such a perplexing position. The best men in your kingdom testify against one another, friend against friend, father against son. But I tell you that were the entire Persian nation to rise up against you, and swear that Cambyses had committed this or that evil deed, and you were to say, 'I did not commit it,' I, Bartja, would give all Persia the lie and exclaim, 'Ye are all false witnesses; sooner could the sea cast up fire than a son of Cyrus allow his mouth to deal in lies.' No, Cambyses, you and I are so high-born that no one but yourself can bear evidence against me; and you can only be judged out of your own mouth."

Cambyses' looks grew a little milder on hearing these words, and his brother went on: "So I swear to you by Mithras, and by all pure spirits, that I am innocent. May my life become extinct and my race perish from off the earth, if I tell you a lie, when I say that I have not once set foot in the hanging-gardens since my return!"

Bartja's voice was so firm and his tone so full of

assurance, as he uttered this oath that Cambyses ordered his chains to be loosened, and, after a few moments' thought, said: "I should like to believe you, for I cannot bear to imagine you the worst and most abandoned of men. To-morrow we will summon the astrologers, soothsayers and priests. Perhaps they may be able to discover the truth. Can you see any light in this darkness, Oropastes?"

"Thy servant supposes, that a Div has taken upon him the form of Bartja, in order to ruin the king's brother and stain thine own royal soul with the blood of thy father's son."

Cambyses and every one present nodded their assent to this proposition, and the king was just going to offer his hand to Bartja, when a staff-bearer came in and gave the king a dagger. A eunuch had found it under the windows of Nitetis' sleeping-apartment.

Cambyses examined the weapon carefully. Its costly hilt was thickly set with rubies and turquoises. As he looked he turned pale, and dashed the dagger on the ground before Bartja with such violence, that the stones fell out of their setting.

"This is your dagger, you wretch!" he shrieked, seized by the same violent passion as before. "This very morning you used it to give the last thrust to the wild boar, that I had mortally wounded. Crœsus, you ought to know it too, for my father brought it from your treasure-house at Sardis. At last you are really convicted, you liar!—you impostor! The Divs require no weapons, and such a dagger as this is not to be picked up everywhere. Ah, ha! you are feeling in your girdle! You may well turn pale; your dagger is gone!"

"Yes, it is gone. I must have lost it, and some enemy . . ."

"Seize him, Bischen, put on his fetters! Take him to prison—the traitor, the perjurer! He shall be strangled to-morrow. Death is the penalty of perjury. Your heads for theirs, you guards, if they escape. Not one word more will I hear; away with you, you perjured villains! Boges, go at once to the hanging-gardens and bring the Egyptian to me. Yet no, I won't see that serpent again. It is very near dawn now, and at noon she shall be flogged through the streets. Then I'll . . ."

But here he was stopped by another fit of epilepsy, and sank down on to the marble floor in convulsions.

At this fearful moment Kassandane was led into the hall by the old general Megabyzus. The news of what had happened had found its way to her solitary apartments, and, notwithstanding the hour, she had risen in order to try and discover the truth and warn her son against pronouncing a too hasty decision. She believed firmly that Bartja and Nitetis were innocent, though she could not explain to herself what had happened. Several times she had tried to put herself in communication with Nitetis, but without avail. At last she had been herself to the hanging-gardens, but the guards had actually had the hardihood to refuse her admission.

Crœsus went at once to meet her, told her what had happened, suppressing as many painful details as possible, confirmed her in her belief of the innocence of the accused, and then took her to the bedside of the king.

The convulsions had not lasted long this time. He lay on his golden bed under purple silk coverlets, pale and exhausted. His blind mother seated herself at his side, Crœsus and Oropastes took their station at the foot of the bed, and in another part of the room, four physicians [18] discussed the patient's condition in low whispers.

Kassandane was very gentle with her son; she begged him not to yield to passionate anger, and to remember what a sad effect every such outburst had on his health.

"Yes, mother, you are right," answered the king, smiling bitterly; "I see that I must get rid of everything that rouses my anger. The Egyptian must die, and my perfidious brother shall follow his mistress."

Kassandane used all her eloquence to convince him of the innocence of the accused, and to pacify his anger, but neither prayers, tears, nor her motherly exhortations, could in the least alter his resolution to rid himself of these murderers of his happiness and peace.

At last he interrupted her lamentations by saying: "I feel fearfully exhausted; I cannot bear these sobs and lamentations any longer. Nitetis has been proved guilty. A man was seen to leave her sleeping-apartment

18. It was natural, that medicine should be carefully studied among a people who set such a high value upon life as did the Persians. Pliny indeed, (XXX. 1.) maintains, that the whole of Zoroaster's religion was founded on the science of medicine, and it is true that there are a great many medical directions to be found in the Avesta. In the *Vendidad*, Farg. VII. there is a detailed list of medical fees. "The physician shall treat a priest for a pious blessing or spell, the master of a house for a small draught animal, etc., the lord of a district for a team of four oxen. If the physician cures the mistress of the house, a female ass shall be his fee, etc., etc." We read in the same Fargard, that the physician had to pass a kind of examination. If he had operated thrice successfully on bad men, on whose bodies he had been permitted to try his skill, he was pronounced "capable for ever." If, on the other hand, three evil Dàevayaçna (worshippers of the Divs) died under his hands, he was pronounced "incapable of healing for evermore." Pliny enumerates a multitude of strange Magian prescriptions. The Vendidad mentions the art of healing as the highest attribute of Thrita, a celebrated mythical hero, not unknown to the inhabitants of India. XX. Fargard. 11.

in the night, and that man was not a thief, but the handsomest man in Persia, and one to whom she had dared to send a letter yesterday evening."

"Do you know the contents of that letter?" asked Crœsus, coming up to the bed.

"No; it was written in Greek. The faithless creature made use of characters, which no one at this court can read."

"Will you permit me to translate the letter?"

Cambyses pointed to a small ivory box in which the ominous piece of writing lay, saying: "There it is; read it; but do not hide or alter a single word, for to-morrow I shall have it read over again by one of the merchants from Sinope."

Crœsus' hopes revived; he seemed to breathe again as he took the paper. But when he had read it over, his eyes filled with tears and he murmured: "The fable of Pandora is only too true; I dare not be angry any longer with those poets who have written severely against women.* Alas, they are all false and faithless! O Kassandane, how the Gods deceive us! they grant us the gift of old age, only to strip us bare like trees in winter, and show us that all our fancied gold was dross and all our pleasant and refreshing drinks poison!"

Kassandane wept aloud and tore her costly robes; but Cambyses clenched his fist while Crœsus was reading the following words:

"Nitetis, daughter of Amasis of Egypt, to Bartja, son of the great Cyrus:

"I have something important to tell you; I can tell it to no one but yourself. To-morrow I hope I shall meet you in your mother's apartments. It lies in your

* See vol. 1. note 155.

power to comfort a sad and loving heart, and to give it one happy moment before death. I have a great deal to tell you, and some very sad news; I repeat that I must see you soon."

The desperate laughter, which burst from her son cut his mother to the heart. She stooped down and was going to kiss him, but Cambyses resisted her caresses, saying: "It is rather a doubtful honor, mother, to be one of your favorites. Bartja did not wait to be sent for twice by that treacherous woman, and has disgraced himself by swearing falsely. His friends, the flower of our young men, have covered themselves with indelible infamy for his sake; and through him, your best beloved daughter . . . but no! Bartja had no share in the corruption of that fiend in Peri's form. Her life was made up of hypocrisy and deceit, and her death shall prove that I know how to punish. Now leave me, for I must be alone."

They had scarcely left the room, when he sprang up and paced backwards and forwards like a madman, till the first crow of the sacred bird Parôdar.* When the sun had risen, he threw himself on his bed again, and fell into a sleep that was like a swoon.

Meanwhile Bartja had written Sappho a farewell letter, and was sitting over the wine with his fellow-prisoners and their elder friend Araspes. "Let us be merry," said Zopyrus, "for I believe it will soon be up with all our merriment. I would lay my life, that we are all of us dead by to-morrow. Pity that men haven't got more than one neck; if we 'd two, I would not mind

* See note 9.

wagering a gold piece or two on the chance of our remaining alive."

"Zopyrus is quite right," said Araspes; "we will make merry and keep our eyes open; who knows how soon they may be closed for ever?"

"No one need be sad who goes to his death as innocently as we do," said Gyges. "Here, cup-bearer, fill my goblet!"

"Ah! Bartja and Darius!" cried Zopyrus, seeing the two speaking in a low voice together, "there you are at your secrets again. Come to us and pass the wine-cup. By Mithras, I can truly say I never wished for death, but now I quite look forward to the black Azis,[19] because he is going to take us all together. Zopyrus would rather die with his friends, than live without them."

"But the great point is to try and explain what has really happened," said Darius.

"It's all the same to me," said Zopyrus, whether I die with or without an explanation, so long as I know I am innocent and have not deserved the punishment of perjury. Try and get us some golden goblets, Bischen; the wine has no flavor out of these miserable brass mugs. Cambyses surely would not wish us to suffer from poverty in our last hours, though he does forbid our fathers and friends to visit us."

"It's not the metal that the cup is made of," said Bartja, "but the wormwood of death, that gives the wine its bitter taste."

"No, really, you're quite out there," exclaimed Zopyrus. "Why I had nearly forgotten that strangling

19. An evil spirit who brings death to men. *Vendid.* XVIII. 45. "Azis, who was created by the Daevas may come to me. He appears in order to snatch me from the world."

generally causes death." As he said this, he touched Gyges and whispered: "Be as cheerful as you can! don't you see that it's very hard for Bartja to take leave of this world? What were you saying, Darius?"

"That I thought Oropastes' idea the only admissible one,—that a Div had taken the likeness of Bartja and visited the Egyptian in order to ruin us."

"Folly! I don't believe in such things."

"But don't you remember the legend of the Div, who took the beautiful form of a minstrel and appeared before king Kawus?"

"Of course," cried Araspes. "Cyrus had this legend so often recited at the banquets, that I know it by heart. Would you like to hear it?"

"Yes, yes, let us hear it!" cried the young men. Araspes thought a moment, and then began, half singing, half reciting:

> When Kawus sat upon his father's throne,
> The whole world subject unto him alone,
> And countless treasures heaped around him saw,
> While vassals trembled at his glance for awe,
> Beheld the chains of gold, the jewels bright,
> The steeds of Thasir, matchless in their might,
> The strings of pearls, the crown of gems so rare,
> It seemed no mortal could with him compare.
> One day, in golden arbor, 'neath a vine
> Of roses sweet, he quaffed the ruby wine.
>
> A Div, concealed beneath the beauteous guise
> Of wand'ring minstrel, to a courtier hies.
> With Kawus speech he sought. Thus he began:
> "I am a singer from Masenderan;[20]
> If it doth please the gracious Shah to hear
> My voice, let me unto his throne draw near."

---

20. Mazenderan, (probably more correct than the Masenderan of Schack), a district in the northern borders of Iran, is, on the one hand, praised in the legends of the heroes for its fertility, but on the other,

Quoth Kawus: "Entrance to the singer give
And 'mid my band of minstrels him receive!"
The Div then struck his lyre, and began
To chant the praises of Masenderan. *

"Do you want to hear the song of Masenderan?" asked Araspes.

"Yes, yes; go on."

"My lovely land Masenderan, all hail!
How laughs with plenty each fair mead and vale,
Fresh roses in thy gardens ever bloom,
Anemones and tulips bright, find room
Upon thy hills, their beauty to display.
Within thy borders reigns eternal May,
A spring alike unmarred by frost or heat.
Thy breezes all are pure, thy fields aye greet
The eye with changeless green. Thy woods resound
With songs of nightingales; deer gaily bound
Thy dales and hill-sides o'er; thy streams all flow
With fragrant waters; perfumed breezes blow;
Colors of every hue delight the eye.
Through Bahman, Ader, Ferwerdin and Di **
The tulips bloom; throughout the circling year,
The hunter finds the falcon ever near.
Far as the confines of thy land extend,
The gleam of silks, the flash of jewels blend;
Thy priests are decked with diadems of gold,
And golden girdles wear thy nobles bold;
Whoe'er within thy blest domain doth live
Hath found the highest joy this earth can give."[21] ***

is spoken of as the abode of evil spirits. To this day the district is blessed with an almost tropical vegetation, and its nobles are proud of calling themselves "Divs." See Ritter, *Erdkunde*, VIII. 426.

21. These words are taken from a beautiful song in Firdusi's Book of Kings, which has been very well translated into German by v. Schack. Firdusi was born about 940 A. D. Ancient Persian history is the subject of his immortal epic poems. The Kai Kawus, who was lured to Mazenderan by the Divs, belonged to the family of the Kajanidæ which must not, as some scholars suppose, be placed on a level with the Achæmenidæ, but must be regarded either as purely mythical,

** May, March, July and April.
* *** Translated by Miss M. J. Safford.

"And Kai Kawus hearkened to the words of the disguised Div and went to Masenderan, and was beaten there by the Divs and deprived of his eyesight."

"But," broke in Darius, "Rustem, the great hero, came and conquered Erscheng and the other bad spirits, freed the captives and restored sight to the blind, by dropping the blood of the slaughtered Divs into their eyes. And so it will be with us, my friends! We shall be set free, and the eyes of Cambyses and of our blind and infatuated fathers will be opened to see our innocence. Listen, Bischen; if we really should be executed, go to the Magi, the Chaldæans, and Nebenchari the Egyptian, and tell them they had better not study the stars any longer, for that those very stars had proved themselves liars and deceivers to Darius."

"Yes," interrupted Araspes, "I always said that dreams were the only real prophecies. Before Abradatas fell in the battle of Sardis, the peerless Panthea dreamt that she saw him pierced by a Lydian arrow."

"You cruel fellow!" exclaimed Zopyrus. "Why do you remind us, that it is much more glorious to die in battle than to have our necks wrung off."

"Quite right," answered the elder man; "I confess that I have seen many a death, which I should prefer to our own,—indeed to life itself. Ah, boys, there was a time when things went better than they do now."

"Tell us something about those times."

---

or at least as having reigned earlier than the Achæmenidæ. We have ventured to introduce the words of a poet who lived so long after the date of our story, because his poems are strictly founded on the ancient Persian traditions and are thoroughly Persian. Besides, we think the quotation possesses sufficient poetical beauty, to reconcile our readers to the anachronism.

"And tell us why you never married. It won't matter to you in the next world, if we do let out your secret."

"There's no secret; any of your own fathers could tell you what you want to hear from me. Listen then. When I was young," I used to amuse myself with women, but I laughed at the idea of love. It occurred, however, that Panthea, the most beautiful of all women, fell into our hands, and Cyrus gave her into my charge, because I had always boasted that my heart was invulnerable. I saw her every day, and learnt, my friends, that love is stronger than a man's will. However, she refused all my offers, induced Cyrus to remove me from my office near her, and to accept her husband Abradatas as an ally. When her handsome husband went out to the war, this high-minded, faithful woman decked him out with all her own jewels and told him that the noble conduct of Cyrus, in treating her like a sister, when she was his captive, could only be repaid by the most devoted friendship and heroic courage. Abradatas agreed with her, fought for Cyrus like a lion, and fell. Panthea killed herself by his dead body. Her servants, on hearing of this, put an end to their own lives too at the grave of this best of mistresses. Cyrus shed tears over this noble pair, and had a stone set up to their memory, which you can see near Sardis. On it are the simple words: 'To Panthea, Abradatas, and the most faithful of servants.' You see, children, the man who had loved such a woman could never care for another."

22. The story of Panthea, Abradatas, and Araspes, is given by Xenophon in his Cyropaedia with a strong Greek coloring. He probably invented this romance in honor of his hero, Cyrus. Xenoph. *Cyrop.* V.

The young men listened in silence, and remained some time after Araspes had finished, without uttering a word. At last Bartja raised his hands to heaven and cried: "O thou great Auramazda! why dost thou not grant us a glorious end like Abradatas? Why must we die a shameful death like murderers?"

As he said this Crœsus came in, fettered and led by whip-bearers. The friends rushed to him with a storm of questions, and Bartja too went up to embrace the man who had been so long his tutor and guide. But the old man's cheerful face was severe and serious, and his eyes, generally so mild, had a gloomy, almost threatening, expression. He waved the prince coldly back, saying, in a voice which trembled with pain and reproach: "Let my hand go, you infatuated boy! you are not worth all the love I have hitherto felt for you. You have deceived your brother in a fourfold manner, duped your friends, betrayed that poor child who is waiting for you in Naukratis, and poisoned the heart of Amasis' unhappy daughter."

Bartja listened calmly till he heard the word "deceived"; then his hand clenched, and stamping his foot, he cried: "But for your age and infirmities, and the gratitude I owe you, old man, these slanderous words would be your last."

Crœsus heard this outbreak of just indignation unmoved, and answered: "This foolish rage proves that you and Cambyses have the same blood in your veins. It would become you much better to repent of your crimes, and beg your old friend's forgiveness, instead of adding ingratitude to the unheard-of baseness of your other deeds."

At these words Bartja's anger gave way. His

clenched hands sank down powerless at his side, and
his cheeks became pale as death.

These signs of sorrow softened the old man's indignation. His love was strong enough to embrace the
guilty as well as the innocent Bartja, and taking the
young man's right hand in both his own, he looked at
him as a father would who finds his son, wounded on the
battle-field, and said: "Tell me, my poor, infatuated
boy, how was it that your pure heart fell away so quickly
to the evil powers?"

Bartja shuddered. The blood came back to his
face, but these words cut him to the heart. For the
first time in his life his belief in the justice of the gods
forsook him.

He called himself the victim of a cruel, inexorable
fate, and felt like a hunted animal driven to its last gasp
and hearing the dogs and sportsmen fast coming nearer.
He had a sensitive, childlike nature, which did not yet
know how to meet the hard strokes of fate. His body
and his physical courage had been hardened against
bodily and physical enemies; but his teachers had never
told him how to meet a hard lot in life; for Cambyses
and Bartja seemed destined only to drink out of the cup
of happiness and joy.

Zopyrus could not bear to see his friend in tears.
He reproached the old man angrily with being unjust
and severe. Gyges' looks were full of entreaty, and
Araspes stationed himself between the old man and the
youth, as if to ward off the blame of the elder from cutting deeper into the sad and grieved heart of the younger
man. Darius, however, after having watched them for
some time, came up with quiet deliberation to Crœsus,
and said: "You continue to distress and offend one

another, and yet the accused does not seem to know with what offence he is charged, nor will the accuser hearken to his defence. Tell us, Crœsus, by the friendship which has subsisted between us up to this day, what has induced you to judge Bartja so harshly, when only a short time ago you believed in his innocence?"

The old man told at once what Darius desired to know—that he had seen a letter, written in Nitetis' own hand, in which she made a direct confession of her love to Bartja and asked him to meet her alone. The testimony of his own eyes and of the first men in the realm, nay, even the dagger found under Nitetis' windows, had not been able to convince him that his favorite was guilty; but this letter had gone like a burning flash into his heart and destroyed the last remnant of his belief in the virtue and purity of woman.

"I left the king," he concluded, "perfectly convinced that a sinful intimacy must subsist between your friend and the Egyptian Princess, whose heart I had believed to be a mirror for goodness and beauty alone. Can you find fault with me for blaming him who so shamefully stained this clear mirror, and with it his own not less spotless soul?"

"But how can I prove my innocence?" cried Bartja, wringing his hands. "If you loved me you would believe me; if you really cared for me . . ."

"My boy! in trying to save your life only a few minutes ago, I forfeited my own. When I heard that Cambyses had really resolved on your death, I hastened to him with a storm of entreaties; but these were of no avail, and then I was presumptuous enough to reproach him bitterly in his irritated state of mind. The weak thread of his patience broke, and in a fearful passion he commanded the guards to behead me at once. I was seized directly by Giv, one of the whip-bearers; but as the man is under obligations to me, he granted me my life until this morning, and promised to conceal the postponement of the execution. I am glad, my sons, that I shall not outlive you, and shall die an innocent man by the side of the guilty."

These last words roused another storm of contradiction.

Again Darius remained calm and quiet in the midst of the tumult. He repeated once more the story of the whole evening exactly, to prove that it was impossible Bartja could have committed the crime laid to his charge. He then called on the accused himself to answer the charge of disloyalty and perfidy. Bartja rejected the idea of an understanding with Nitetis in such short, decided, and convincing words, and confirmed his assertion with such a fearful oath, that Crœsus' persuasion of his guilt first wavered, then vanished, and when Bartja had ended, he drew a deep breath, like a man delivered from a heavy burden, and clasped him in his arms.

But with all their efforts they could come to no explanation of what had really happened. In one thing, however, they were all agreed: that Nitetis loved Bartja and had written the letter with a wrong intention.

"No one who saw her," cried Darius, "when Cambyses announced that Bartja had chosen a wife, could doubt for a moment that she was in love with him. When she let the goblet fall, I heard Phædime's father say that the Egyptian women seemed to take a great interest in the affairs of their brothers-in-law."

While they were talking, the sun rose and shone pleasantly into the prisoners' room.

Bartja murmured: "Mithras means to make our parting difficult."

"No," answered Crœsus, "he only means to light us kindly on our way into eternity."

CHAPTER IV.

THE innocent originator of all this complicated misery had passed many a wretched hour since the birthday banquet. Since those harsh words with which Cambyses had sent her from the hall, not the smallest fragment of news had reached her concerning either her angry lover, or his mother and sister. Not a day had passed since her arrival in Babylon, that had not been spent with Kassandane and Atossa; but now, on her desiring to be carried to them, that she might explain her strange conduct, her new guard, Kandaules, forbade her abruptly to leave the house. She had thought that a free and full account of the contents of her letter from home, would clear up all these misunderstandings. She fancied she saw Cambyses holding out his hand as if to ask forgiveness for his hastiness and foolish jealousy. And then a joyful feeling stole into her mind as she remembered a sentence she had once heard Ibykus say: "As fever attacks a strong man more violently than one of weaker constitution; so a heart that loves strongly and deeply can be far more awfully tormented by jealousy, than one which has been only superficially seized by passion."

If this great connoisseur in love were right, Cambyses must love her passionately, or his jealousy could not have caught fire so quickly and fearfully. Sad thoughts about her home, however, and dark forebodings of the future would mix with this confidence in Cambyses' love, and she could not shut them out. Mid-day came, the sun stood high and burning in the sky, but no news came from those she loved so well; and a feverish restlessness seized her which increased as night came on. In the twilight Boges came to her, and told her, with bitter scorn, that her letter to Bartja had come into the king's hands, and that the gardener's boy who brought it had been executed. The tortured nerves of the princess could not resist this fresh blow, and before Boges left, he carried the poor girl senseless into her sleeping-room, the door of which he barred carefully.

A few minutes later, two men, one old, the other young, came up through the trap-door which Boges had examined so carefully two days before. The old man remained outside, crouching against the palace-wall; a hand was seen to beckon from the window: the youth obeyed the signal, swung himself over the ledge and into the room at a bound. Then words of love were exchanged, the names Gaumata and Mandane whispered softly, kisses and vows given and received. At last the old man clapped his hands. The youth obeyed, kissed and embraced Nitetis' waiting-maid once more, jumped out of the window into the garden, hurried past the admirers of the blue lily who were just coming up, slipped with his companion into the trap-door which had been kept open, closed it carefully, and vanished.

Mandane hurried to the room in which her mistress generally spent the evening. She was well acquainted with her habits and knew that every evening, when the stars had risen, Nitetis was accustomed to go to the window looking towards the Euphrates, and spend hours gazing into the river and over the plain; and that at that time she never needed her attendance. So she felt quite safe from fear of discovery in this quarter, and knowing she was under the protection of the chief of the eunuchs himself, could wait for her lover calmly.

But scarcely had she discovered that her mistress had fainted, when she heard the garden filling with people, a confused sound of men's and eunuchs' voices, and the notes of the trumpet used to summon the sentries. At first she was frightened and fancied her lover had been discovered, but Boges appearing and whispering: "He has escaped safely," she at once ordered the other attendants, whom she had banished to the women's apartments during her rendezvous, and who now came flocking back, to carry their mistress into her sleeping-room, and then began using all the remedies she knew of, to restore her to consciousness. Nitetis had scarcely opened her eyes when Boges came in, followed by two eunuchs, whom he ordered to load her delicate arms with fetters.

Nitetis submitted; she could not utter one word, not even when Boges called out as he was leaving the room: "Make yourself happy in your cage, my little imprisoned bird. They've just been telling your lord that a royal marten has been making merry in your dove-cote. Farewell, and think of the poor tormented Boges in this tremendous heat, when you feel the cool damp earth. Yes, my little bird, death teaches us to know our real friends, and so I won't have you buried in a coarse linen sack, but in a soft silk shawl. Farewell, my darling!"

The poor, heavily-afflicted girl trembled at these words, and when the eunuch was gone, begged Mandane to tell her what it all meant. The girl, instructed by Boges, said that Bartja had stolen secretly into the hanging-gardens, and had been seen by several of the Achæmenidæ as he was on the point of getting in at one of the windows. The king had been told of his brother's treachery, and people were afraid his jealousy might have fearful consequences. The frivolous girl shed abundant tears of penitence while she was telling the story, and Nitetis, fancying this a proof of sincere love and sympathy, felt cheered.

When it was over, however, she looked down at her fetters in despair, and it was long before she could think of her dreadful position quietly. Then she read her letter from home again, wrote the words, "I am innocent," and told the sobbing girl to give the little note containing them to the king's mother after her own death, together with her letter from home. After doing this she passed a wakeful night which seemed as if it would never end. She remembered that in her box of ointments there was a specific for improving the complexion, which, if swallowed in a sufficiently large quantity, would cause death. She had this poison brought to her, and resolved calmly and deliberately, to take her own life directly the executioner should draw near. From that moment she took pleasure in thinking of her last hour, and said to herself: "It is true he causes my death; but he does it out of love." Then she thought she would write to him, and confess all her love. He should not receive the letter until she was dead, that he might not think she had written it to save her life. The hope that this strong, inflexible man might perhaps shed tears over her last words of love filled her with intense pleasure.

In spite of her heavy fetters, she managed to write the following words: "Cambyses will not receive this letter until I am dead. It is to tell him that I love him more than the gods, the world,—yes, more than my own young life. Kassandane and Atossa must think of me kindly. They will see from my mother's letter that I am innocent, and that it was only for my poor sister's sake that I asked to see Bartja. Boges has told me that my death has been resolved upon. When the executioner approaches, I shall kill myself. I commit this crime against myself, Cambyses, to save you from doing a disgraceful deed."

This note and her mother's she gave to the weeping Mandane, and begged her to give both to Cambyses when she was gone. She then fell on her knees and prayed to the gods of her fathers to forgive her for her apostasy from them.

Mandane begged her to remember her weakness and take some rest, but she answered: "I do not need any sleep, because, you know, I have such little waking-time still left me."

As she went on praying and singing her old Egyptian hymns, her heart returned more and more to the gods of her fathers, whom she had denied after such a short struggle. In almost all the prayers with which she was acquainted, there was a reference to the life after death. In the nether world, the kingdom of Osiris, where the forty-two judges of the dead pronounce sentence on the worth of the soul after it has been weighed by the goddess of truth and Thoth, who holds the office of writer in heaven, she could hope to meet her dear ones again, but only in case her unjustified soul were not obliged to enter on the career of transmigration through the bodies of different animals, and her body, to whom the soul had been entrusted, remained in a state of preservation.[23] This, "if" filled her with a feverish restlessness. The doctrine that the well-being of the soul depended on the preservation of the earthly part of every human being left behind at death, had been impressed on her from childhood. She believed in this error, which had built pyramids and excavated rocks, and trembled at the thought that, according to the Persian custom, her body would be

23. See Vol. I. note 121. on the Egyptian dogma, which made the welfare of the soul dependent on the preservation of the body, and on their views of the life to come. We will only mention here, that as the dead were to obtain the use of their limbs, mouths, hearts, feet and hands again in the nether world, it was necessary that these should be preserved. Whatever was deficient in the body, would be deficient also in its phantom or shadow. They certainly seem to have exhausted the thought of immortality in every direction. As the sun at night is not dead but only gone to enlighten the lower world, so the Egyptian only seems to die; the real life of his eternal soul only begins after he has taken leave of the earth. The soul descends into the lower world, either to be pronounced just, and in the pure light of the East, a partaker of salvation, to sow the well-watered fields in the plains of Anulu, or Alu, and reap without trouble that which it has sown, until it has become ripe to be merged in Osiris as a part of the world-soul; or, after suffering fearful torments in the purgatory of hell, to be scourged out of the lower world and begin its wanderings through the bodies of animals. In one of the papyri of the dead, the condemned soul is being scourged out of Hades in the form of a sow. After these wanderings, if purified and pardoned, it is at last permitted to unite itself with Osiris, but if not, must again begin the round of purification. Pythagoras borrowed his doctrine of the transmigration of souls from the Egyptians. Plato divested it of its bodily garment in the delicate manner which only he was capable of doing, and transferred the idea into the spiritual kingdom. The Egyptian idea of the transmigration of souls was very different from the belief prevalent in India. On the duration of the soul's wanderings and the phœnix-period, see Lepsius, *Chronologie p.* 181.

thrown to the dogs and birds of prey, and so given up to the powers of destruction, that her soul must be deprived of every hope of eternal life. Then the thought came to her, should she prove unfaithful to the gods of her fathers again, and once more fall down before these new spirits of light, who gave the dead body over to the elements and only judged the soul? And so she raised her hands to the great and glorious sun, who with his golden sword-like rays was just dispersing the mists that hung over the Euphrates, and opened her lips to sing her newly-learnt hymns in praise of Mithras; but her voice failed her,—instead of Mithras she could only see her own great Ra, the god she had so often worshipped in Egypt, and instead of a Magian hymn could only sing the one with which the Egyptian priests are accustomed to greet the rising sun.[24]

> Hail, Ra! Let every voice unite.
> Bend, bend the knee to Ra, each morn.
> Ra, who by his creative might,
> With each new day, springs forth newborn.
>
> All hail to thee, thou mighty One!
> Source of all life! Thou tak'st thy way,
> 'Neath the blue vault of Heaven, thy throne,
> And all earth's creatures own thy sway.
>
> Hail, Guardian, by whose gentle light
> The pure have life and blessings given,
> E'en gods, with rapture infinite
> Thrill, when thou'rt near, Ra, child of Heaven.[*]

This hymn brought comfort with it, and as she

---

[24]. From an inscription on a tomb in the Berlin Museum, first treated by E. de Rougé, *Zeitschrift der Deutsch-morgenländischen Gesellschaft* IV. 375.

[*] Translated by Miss M. J. Safford.

gazed on the young light, the rays of which were not yet strong enough to dazzle her, she thought of her childhood, and the tears gathered in her eyes. Then she looked down over the broad plain. There was the Euphrates with his yellow waves looking so like the Nile; the many villages, just as in her own home, peeping out from among luxuriant cornfields and plantations of fig-trees. To the west lay the royal hunting-park; she could see its tall cypresses and nut-trees miles away in the distance. The dew was glistening on every little leaf and blade of grass, and the birds sang deliciously in the shrubberies round her dwelling. Now and then a gentle breath of wind arose, carrying the sweet scent of the roses across to her, and playing in the tops of the slender, graceful palms which grew in numbers on the banks of the river and in the fields around.

She had so often admired these beautiful trees, and compared them to dancing-girls, as she watched the wind seizing their heavy tops and swaying the slender stems backwards and forwards. And she had often said to herself that here must be the home of the Phœnix,* that wonderful bird from the land of palms, who, the priests said, came once in every five hundred years to the temple of Ra in Heliopolis and burnt himself in the sacred incense-flames, only to rise again from his own ashes more beautiful than before, and, after three days, to fly back again to his home in the East. While she was thinking of this bird, and wishing that she too might rise again from the ashes of her unhappiness to a new and still more glorious joy, a large bird with brilliant plumage rose out of the dark cypresses,

* See vol. 1. note 117.

which concealed the palace of the man she loved and who had made her so miserable, and flew towards her. It rose higher and higher, and at last settled on a palm-tree close to her window. She had never seen such a bird before, and thought it could not possibly be a usual one, for a little gold chain was fastened to its foot, and its tail seemed made of sunbeams instead of feathers. It must be Benno,* the bird of Ra! She fell on her knees again and sang with deep reverence the ancient hymn to the Phœnix,[25] never once turning her eyes from the brilliant bird.

> 'The work of an omnipotent Creator,
> Far, far above the heads of men I soar.
> My mighty pinions cleave the waves of air,
> With pride my Maker's glorious pomp I wear,
> My wondrous grace and loveliness of mien,
> Vies with the flow'rets in the meadows green,
> Yet, radiant though I soar in fullest glow
> Of light, my nature, birth-place none may know,
> While I know all—the past—futurity,
> The soul of the eternal Ra am I.'**

The bird listened to her singing, bending his little head with its waving plumes, wisely and inquisitively from side to side, and flew away directly she

25. From the first sentences of chap. 83. of the book of the dead. A picture of the Phœnix stands as vignette at the head of this chapter, which is entitled "the chapter of the transformation into the Benno-bird." In fact the souls are represented in the form of the Phœnix and of other birds. The Benno must be looked at as the soul of the Deity, with which the soul of man, being regarded as a part and emanation of the former, unites itself after earthly death, retaining nevertheless a certain individuality. This union can of course only take place if the soul has been justified and has passed through all the preparatory stages.

* In ancient Egyptian the Phœnix was called Benno. On this bird and the worship paid to him at Heliopolis see vol. 1. note 117., vol. II. note 23. Lepsius, *Chron.* p. 180. and Brugsch., *geogr. Inschrift* l. p. 258.

** Translated by Miss M. J. Safford.

ceased. Nitetis looked after him with a smile. It was really only a bird of paradise that had broken the chain by which he had been fastened to a tree in the park, but to her he was the Phœnix. A strange certainty of deliverance filled her heart; she thought the god Ra had sent the bird to her, and that as a happy spirit she should take that form. So long as we are able to hope and wish, we can bear a great deal of sorrow; if the wished-for happiness does not come, anticipation is at least prolonged and has its own peculiar sweetness. This feeling is of itself enough, and contains a kind of enjoyment which can take the place of reality. Though she was so weary, yet she lay down on her couch with fresh hopes, and fell into a dreamless sleep almost against her will, without having touched the poison.

The rising sun generally gives comfort to sad hearts who have passed the night in weeping, but to a guilty conscience, which longs for darkness, his pure light is an unwelcome guest. While Nitetis slept, Mandane lay awake, tormented by fearful remorse. How gladly she would have held back the sun which was bringing on the day of death to this kindest of mistresses, and have spent the rest of her own life in perpetual night, if only her yesterday's deed could but have been undone!

The good-natured, thoughtless girl called herself a wretched murderess unceasingly, resolved again and again to confess the whole truth and so to save Nitetis; but love of life and fear of death gained the victory over her weak heart every time. To confess was certain death, and she felt as if she had been made for life; she had so many hopes for the future, and the grave seemed so dreadful. She thought she could perhaps have confessed the whole truth, if perpetual imprisonment had been all she had to fear; but death! no, she could not resolve on that. And besides, would her confession really save the already condemned Nitetis?

Had she not sent a message to Bartja herself by that unfortunate gardener's boy? This secret correspondence had been discovered, and that was enough of itself to ruin Nitetis, even if she, Mandane, had done nothing in the matter. We are never so clever as when we have to find excuses for our own sins.

At sunrise, Mandane was kneeling by her mistress's couch, weeping bitterly and wondering that Nitetis could sleep so calmly.

Boges, the eunuch, had passed a sleepless night too, but a very happy one. His hated colleague, Kandaules, whom he had used as a substitute for himself, had been already executed, by the king's command, for negligence, and on the supposition that he had accepted a bribe; Nitetis was not only ruined, but certain to die a shameful death. The influence of the king's mother had suffered a severe shock; and lastly, he had the pleasure of knowing, not only that he had outwitted every one and succeeded in all his plans, but that through his favorite Phædime he might hope once more to become the all-powerful favorite of former days. That sentence of death had been pronounced on Crœsus and the young heroes, was by no means an unwelcome thought either, as they might have been instrumental in bringing his intrigues to light.

In the grey of the morning he left the king's apartment and went to Phædime. The proud Persian had taken no rest. She was waiting for him with feverish anxiety, as a rumor of all that had happened had already reached the harem and penetrated to her apartments.

She was lying on a purple couch in her dressing-room; a thin silken chemise and yellow slippers thickly sown with turquoises and pearls composed her entire dress. Twenty attendants were standing round her, but the moment she heard Boges she sent her slaves away, sprang up to meet him, and overwhelmed him with a stream of incoherent questions, all referring to her enemy Nitetis.

"Gently, gently, my little bird," said Boges, laying his hand on her shoulder. "If you can't make up your mind to be as quiet as a little mouse while I tell my story, and not to ask one question, you won't hear a syllable of it to-day. Yes, indeed, my golden queen, I've so much to tell that I shall not have finished till to-morrow, if you are to interrupt me as often as you like. Ah, my little lamb, and I've still so much to do to-day. First I must be present at an Egyptian donkey-ride; secondly, I must witness an Egyptian execution . . . but I see I am anticipating my story; I must begin at the beginning. I'll allow you to cry, laugh and scream for joy as much as you will, but you're forbidden to ask a single question until I have finished. I think really I have deserved these caresses. There, now I am quite at my ease, and can begin. Once upon a time there was a great king in Persia, who had many wives, but he loved Phædime better than the rest, and set her above all the others. One day the thought struck him that he would ask for the hand of the King of Egypt's daughter in marriage, and he sent a great embassy to Sais, with his own brother to do the wooing for him—"

"What nonsense!" cried Phædime impatiently; "I want to know what has happened now."

"Patience, patience, my impetuous March wind. If you interrupt me again, I shall go away and tell my story to the trees. You really need not grudge me the pleasure of living my successes over again. While I tell this story, I feel as happy as a sculptor when he puts down his hammer and gazes at his finished work."

"No, no!" said Phædime, interrupting him again. "I cannot listen now to what I know quite well already. I am dying of impatience, and every fresh report that the eunuchs and slave-girls bring makes it worse. I am in a perfect fever—I cannot wait. Ask whatever else you like, only deliver me from this awful suspense. Afterwards I will listen to you for days, if you wish."

Boges' smile at these words was one of great satisfaction; he rubbed his hands and answered: "When I was a child I had no greater pleasure than to watch a fish writhing on the hook; now I have got you, my splendid golden carp, at the end of my line, and I can't let you go until I have sated myself on your impatience."

Phædime sprang up from the couch which she had shared with Boges, stamping her foot and behaving like a naughty child. This seemed to amuse the eunuch immensely; he rubbed his hands again and again, laughed till the tears ran down over his fat cheeks, emptied many a goblet of wine to the health of the tortured beauty, and then went on with his tale: "It had not escaped me that Cambyses sent his brother (who had brought Nitetis from Egypt), out to the war with the Tapuri purely from jealousy. That proud woman, who was to take no orders from me, seemed to care as little for the handsome, fair-haired boy as a Jew for pork, or an Egyptian for white beans.[26] But still I resolved to nourish the king's jealousy, and use it as a means of rendering this impudent creature harmless, as she seemed likely to succeed in supplanting us both in his favor. It was long, however, before I could hit on a feasible plan.

"At last the new-year's festival arrived.[*] and all the priests in the kingdom assembled at Babylon. For eight days the city was full of rejoicing, feasting and merry-making. At court it was just the same, and so I had very little time to think of my plans. But just then, when I had hardly any hope of succeeding, the gracious Amescha çpenta[**] sent a youth across my path, who seemed created by Angramainjus himself to suit my plan. Gaumata, the brother of Oropastes, came to Babylon to be present at the great new-year's sacrifice. I saw him first in his brother's house, whither I had been sent on a message from the king, and his likeness to Bartja was so wonderful, that I almost fancied I was looking at an apparition. When I had finished my business with Oropastes the youth accompanied me to my carriage. I showed no signs of astonishment at this remarkable likeness, treated him

---

26. The Egyptians were forbidden to eat beans, probably because of their tendency to cause flatulence. Cicero. *De Divin.* I. 30. Plut. *Isis and Osiris* 9. Pythagoras borrowed this prohibition from the Egyptians. It is possible according to Diodorus (I. 89.) that this command was limited to a portion of the Egyptian nation, as some refrained from eating lentiles, others beans, etc. At the present day, beans, which form the principal food of the lower classes, are rarely absent from Egyptian tables. In the Papyrus Ebers they are mentioned among the medicines.

[*] In March, at the spring equinox.   [**] See Note 17.

however, with immense civility, and begged him to pay me a visit. He came the very same evening. I sent for my best wine, pressed him to drink, and experienced,— not for the first time,—that the juice of the vine has one quality which outweighs all the rest: it can turn even a silent man into a chatter-box. The youth confessed that the great attraction which had brought him to Babylon was, not the sacrifice, but a girl who held the office of upper attendant to the Egyptian Princess. He said he had loved her since he was a child; but his ambitious brother had higher views for him, and in order to get the lovely Mandane out of his way, had procured her this situation. At last he begged me to arrange an interview with her. I listened goodnaturedly, made a few difficulties, and at last asked him to come the next day and see how matters were going on. He came, and I told him that it might be possible to manage it, but only if he would promise to do what I told him without a question. He agreed to everything, returned to Rhagæ at my wish, and did not come to Babylon again until yesterday, when he arrived secretly at my house, where I concealed him. Meanwhile Bartja had returned from the war. The great point now was to excite the king's jealousy again, and ruin the Egyptian at one blow. I roused the indignation of your relations through your public humiliation, and so prepared the way for my plan. Events were wonderfully in my favor. You know how Nitetis behaved at the birthday banquet, but you do not know that that very evening she sent a gardener's boy to the palace with a note for Bartja. The silly fellow managed to get caught and was executed that very night, by command of the king, who was almost mad with rage; and

I took care that Nitetis should be as entirely cut off from all communication with her friends, as if she lived in the nest of the Simurg.²⁷ You know the rest."

"But how did Gaumata escape?"

"Through a trap-door, of which nobody knows but myself, and which stood wide open waiting for him. Everything turned out marvellously; I even succeeded in getting hold of a dagger which Bartja had lost while hunting, and in laying it under Nitetis' window. In order to get rid of the prince during these occurrences, and prevent him from meeting the king or any one else who might be important as a witness, I asked the Greek merchant Kolæus, who was then at Babylon with a cargo of Milesian cloth, and who is always willing to do me a favor, because I buy all the woollen stuffs required for the harem of him, to write a Greek letter, begging Bartja, in the name of her he loved best, to come alone to the first station outside the Euphrates gate at the rising of the Tistar-star. But I had a misfortune with this letter, for the messenger managed the matter clumsily. He declares that he delivered the letter to Bartja; but there can be no doubt that he gave it to some one else, probably to Gaumata, and I was not a little dismayed to hear that Bartja was sitting over the wine with his friends on that very evening. Still what had been done could not be undone, and I knew that the witness of men like your father, Hystaspes, Crœsus and Intaphernes, would far outweigh anything that Darius, Gyges and Araspes could say. The former would testify against their friend, the latter for

27. The Simurg is the fabulous bird of the Persians, and may be compared to the Roc or Griffin. Sal, the father of Rustem, was brought up in its nest. It was not only spoken of as large and strong, but as "wise." See Firdusi, *Book of Kings*. Sal.

him. And so at last everything went as I would have had it. The young gentlemen are sentenced to death and Crœsus, who as usual, presumed to speak impertinently to the king, will have lived his last hour by this time. As to the Egyptian Princess, the secretary in chief has just been commanded to draw up the following order. Now listen and rejoice, my little dove!

"'Nitetis, the adulterous daughter of the King of Egypt, shall be punished for her hideous crimes according to the extreme rigor of the law, thus: She shall be set astride upon an ass and led through the streets of Babylon; and all men shall see that Cambyses knows how to punish a king's daughter, as severely as his magistrates would punish the meanest beggar.—To Boges, chief of the eunuchs, is entrusted the execution of this order.

By command of King Cambyses.

Ariabignes, chief of the Secretaries.'

"I had scarcely placed these lines in the sleeve of my robe, when the king's mother, with her garments rent, and led by Atossa, pressed hastily into the hall. Weeping and lamentation followed; cries, reproaches, curses, entreaties and prayers; but the king remained firm, and I verily believe Kassandane and Atossa would have been sent after Crœsus and Bartja into the other world, if fear of Cyrus's spirit had not prevented the son, even in this furious rage, from laying hands on his father's widow. Kassandane, however, did not say one word for Nitetis. She seems as fully convinced of her guilt as you and I can be. Neither have we anything to fear from the enamored Gaumata. I have hired three men to give him a cool bath in the Euphrates, before he gets back to Rhagæ. Ah, ha! the fishes and worms will have a jolly time!"

Phædime joined in Boges' laughter, bestowed on him all the flattering names which she had caught from his own smooth tongue, and in token of her gratitude, hung a heavy chain studded with jewels round his neck with her own beautiful arms.

CHAPTER V.

BEFORE the sun had reached his mid-day height, the news of what had happened and of what was still to happen had filled all Babylon. The streets swarmed with people, waiting impatiently to see the strange spectacle which the punishment of one of the king's wives, who had proved false and faithless, promised to afford. The whip-bearers were forced to use all their authority to keep this gaping crowd in order. Later on in the day the news that Bartja and his friends were soon to be executed arrived among the crowd; they were under the influence of the palm-wine, which was liberally distributed on the king's birthday and the following days, and could not control their excited feelings; but these now took quite another form.

Bands of drunken men paraded the streets, crying: "Bartja, the good son of Cyrus, is to be executed!" The women heard these words in their quiet apartments, eluded their keepers, forgot their veils, and rushing forth into the streets, followed the excited and indignant men with cries and yells. Their pleasure in the thought of seeing a more fortunate sister humbled, vanished at the painful news that their beloved prince was condemned to death. Men, women and children raged, stormed and cursed, exciting one another to louder and louder bursts of indignation. The workshops were emptied, the merchants closed their warehouses, and the school-boys and servants, who had a week's holiday on occasion of the king's birthday, used their freedom to scream louder than any one else, and often to groan and yell without in the least knowing why.

At last the tumult was so great that the whip-bearers were insufficient to cope with it, and a detachment of the body-guard was sent to patrol the streets. At the sight of their shining armor and long lances, the crowd retired into the side streets, only, however, to reassemble in fresh numbers when the troops were out of sight.

At the gate, called the Bel gate, which led to the great western high-road, the throng was thicker than at any other point, for it was said that through this gate, the one by which she had entered Babylon, the Egyptian Princess was to be led out of the city in shame and disgrace. For this reason a larger number of whip-bearers were stationed here, in order to make way for travellers entering the city. Very few people indeed left the city at all on this day, for curiosity was stronger than either business or pleasure; those, on the other hand, who arrived from the country, took up their stations near the gate on hearing what had drawn the crowd thither.

It was nearly mid-day, and only wanted a few hours to the time fixed for Nitetis' disgrace, when a caravan approached the gate with great speed. The first carriage was a so-called *harmamaxa*,* drawn by four horses decked out with bells and tassels; a two-wheeled cart followed, and last in the train was a baggage-wagon drawn by mules. A fine, handsome man of about fifty, dressed as a Persian courtier, and another, much older, in long white robes, occupied the first carriage. The cart was filled by a number of slaves in simple blouses, and broad-brimmed felt hats, wearing the hair cut close to the head. An old man, dressed as a Persian servant, rode by the side of the cart. The driver of the first carriage had great difficulty in making way for his gaily-ornamented horses through the crowd; he was obliged to come to a halt before the gate and call some whip-bearers to his assistance. "Make way for us!" he cried to the captain of the police who came up with some of his men; "the royal post has no time to lose, and I am driving some one, who will make you repent every minute's delay."

"Softly, my son," answered the official. "Don't you see that it's easier to-day to get out of Babylon, than to come in? Whom are you driving?"

"A nobleman, with a passport from the king. Come, be quick and make way for us."

"I don't know about that; your caravan does not look much like royalty."

"What have you to do with that? The pass . . ."

"I must see it, before I let you into the city."

These words were half meant for the traveller, whom he was scrutinizing very suspiciously.

While the man in the Persian dress was feeling in his sleeve for the passport, the whip-bearer turned to some comrades who had just come up, and pointed out

* See vol. 1. note at foot of page 204.

the scanty retinue of the travellers, saying: "Did you ever see such a queer cavalcade? There's something odd about these strangers, as sure as my name's Giw. Why, the lowest of the king's carpet-bearers travels with four times as many people, and yet this man has a royal pass and is dressed like one of those who sit at the royal table."

At this moment the suspected traveller handed him a little silken roll scented with musk,[28] sealed with the royal seal, and containing the king's own handwriting.

The whip-bearer took it and examined the seal. "It is all in order," he murmured, and then began to study the characters. But no sooner had he deciphered the first letters than he looked even more sharply than before at the traveller, and seized the horses' bridles, crying out: "Here, men, form a guard round the carriage! this is an impostor."

When he had convinced himself that escape was impossible, he went up to the stranger again and said:

"You are using a pass which does not belong to you. Gyges, the son of Crœsus, the man you give yourself out for, is in prison and is to be executed to-day. You are not in the least like him, and you will have reason to repent having tried to pass for him. Get out of your carriage and follow me."

The traveller, however, instead of obeying, began to speak in broken Persian, and begged the officer rather to take a seat by him in the carriage, for that he had very important news to communicate. The man hesitated a moment; but on seeing a fresh band of

---

28. From Firdusi:
"And now he wrote on silken stuff so fine
A letter breathing fragrance musk and wine."

whip-bearers come up, he nodded to them to stand before the impatient, chafing horses, and got into the carriage.

The stranger looked at him with a smile and said: "Now, do I look like an impostor?"

"No; your language proves that you are not a Persian, but yet you look like a nobleman."

"I am a Greek, and have come hither to render Cambyses an important service. Gyges is my friend, and lent me his passport when he was in Egypt, in case I should ever come to Persia. I am prepared to vindicate my conduct before the king, and have no reason for fear. On the contrary, the news I bring gives me reason to expect much from his favor. Let me be taken to Crœsus, if this is your duty; he will be surety for me, and will send back your men, of whom you seem to stand in great need to-day. Distribute these gold pieces among them, and tell me without further delay what my poor friend Gyges has done to deserve death, and what is the reason of all this crowd and confusion."

The stranger said this in bad Persian, but there lay so much dignity and confidence in his tone, and his gifts were on such a large scale, that the cringing and creeping servant of despotism felt sure he must be sitting opposite to a prince, crossed his arms reverentially, and, excusing himself from his many pressing affairs, began to relate rapidly. He had been on duty in the great hall during the examination of the prisoners the night before, and could therefore tell all that had happened with tolerable accuracy. The Greek followed his tale eagerly, with many an incredulous shake of his handsome head, however, when the daughter of Amasis and the son of Cyrus were spoken of as having been disloyal and false. That sentence of death had been pronounced, especially on Crœsus, distressed him visibly, but the sadness soon vanished from his quickly-changing features, and gave place to thought; this in its turn was quickly followed by a joyful look, which could only betoken that the thinker had arrived at a satisfactory result. His dignified gravity vanished in a moment; he laughed aloud, struck his forehead merrily, seized the hand of the astonished captain, and said:

"Should you be glad, if Bartja could be saved?"

"More than I can say."

"Very well, then I will vouch for it, that you shall receive at least two talents,* if you can procure me an interview with the king before the first execution has taken place."

"How can you ask such a thing of me, a poor captain? . . ."

"Yes, you must, you must!"

"I cannot."

"I know well that it is very difficult, almost impossible, for a stranger to obtain an audience of your king; but my errand brooks no delay, for I can prove that Bartja and his friends are not guilty. Do you hear? I can *prove* it. Do you think now, you can procure me admittance?"

"How is it possible?"

"Don't ask, but act. Didn't you say Darius was one of the condemned?"

"Yes."

"I have heard, that his father is a man of very high rank."

* £450.

"He is the first in the kingdom, after the sons of Cyrus."

"Then take me to him at once. He will welcome me when he hears I am able to save his son."

"Stranger, you are a wonderful being. You speak with so much confidence that . . ."

"That you feel you may believe me. Make haste then, and call some of your men to make way for us, and escort us to the palace."

There is nothing, except a doubt, which runs more quickly from mind to mind, than a hope that some cherished wish may be fulfilled, especially when this hope has been suggested to us by some one we can trust.

The officer believed this strange traveller, jumped out of the carriage, flourishing his scourge and calling to his men: "This nobleman has come on purpose to prove Bartja's innocence, and must be taken to the king at once. Follow me, my friends, and make way for him!"

Just at that moment a troop of the guards appeared in sight. The captain of the whip-bearers went up to their commander, and, seconded by the shouts of the crowd, begged him to escort the stranger to the palace.

During this colloquy the traveller had mounted his servant's horse, and now followed in the wake of the Persians.

The good news flew like wind through the huge city. As the riders proceeded, the crowd fell back more willingly, and louder and fuller grew the shouts of joy until at last their march was like a triumphal procession.

In a few minutes they drew up before the palace; but before the brazen gates had opened to admit them, another train came slowly into sight. At the head rode a grey-headed old man; his robes were brown, and rent, in token of mourning, the mane and tail of his horse had been shorn off and the creature colored blue.[29] It was Hystaspes, coming to entreat mercy for his son.

The whip-bearer, delighted at this sight, threw himself down before the old man with a cry of joy, and with crossed arms told him what confidence the traveller had inspired him with.

Hystaspes beckoned to the stranger; he rode up, bowed gracefully and courteously to the old man, without dismounting, and confirmed the words of the whip-bearer. Hystaspes seemed to feel fresh confidence too after hearing the stranger, for he begged him to follow him into the palace and to wait outside the door of the royal apartment, while he himself, conducted by the head chamberlain, went in to the king.

When his old kinsman entered, Cambyses was lying on his purple couch, pale as death. A cup-bearer was kneeling on the ground at his feet, trying to collect the broken fragments of a costly Egyptian drinking-cup which the king had thrown down impatiently because its contents had not pleased his taste. At some distance stood a circle of court-officials, in whose faces it was easy to read that they were afraid of their ruler's wrath, and preferred keeping as far from him as possible. The dazzling light and oppressive heat of a Baby-

---

29. From the mourning for Iredsch. Firdusi. *Book of Kings*. The brown mourning garment is from Rosenmüller, *Das alte und neue Morgenland*. l. p. 179.

Ionian May day came in through the open windows, and not a sound was to be heard in the great room, except the whining of a large dog of the Epirote breed, which had just received a tremendous kick from Cambyses for venturing to fawn on his master, and was the only being that ventured to disturb the solemn stillness. Just before Hystaspes was led in by the chamberlain, Cambyses had sprung up from his couch. This idle repose had become unendurable, he felt suffocated with pain and anger. The dog's howl suggested a new idea to his poor tortured brain, thirsting for forgetfulness.

"We will go out hunting!" he shouted to the poor startled courtiers. The master of the hounds, the equerries, and huntsmen hastened to obey his orders. He called after them, "I shall ride the unbroken horse Reksch;[30] get the falcons ready, let all the dogs out and order every one to come, who can throw a spear. We'll clear the preserves!"

He then threw himself down on his divan again, as if these words had quite exhausted his powerful frame, and did not see that Hystaspes had entered, for his sullen gaze was fixed on the motes playing in the sunbeams that glanced through the window.

Hystaspes did not dare to address him; but he stationed himself in the window so as to break the stream of motes and thus draw attention to himself.

At first Cambyses looked angrily at him and his rent garments, and then asked with a bitter smile ; "What do you want?"

"Victory to the king! Your poor servant and uncle has come to entreat his ruler's mercy."

---

30. The celebrated war-horse of Rustem had the same name. It signifies "Lightning."

"Then rise and go! You know, that I have no mercy for perjurers and false swearers. 'Tis better to have a dead son than a dishonorable one."

"But if Bartja should not be guilty, and Darius . . ."

"You dare to question the justice of my sentence?"

"That be far from me. Whatever the king does is good, and cannot be gainsaid; but still . . ."

"Be silent! I will not hear the subject mentioned again. You are to be pitied as a father; but have these last few hours brought me any joy? Old man, I grieve for you, but I have as little power to rescind his punishment as you to recall his crime."

"But if Bartja really should not be guilty—if the gods . . ."

"Do you think the gods will come to the help of perjurers and deceivers?"

"No, my King; but a fresh witness has appeared."

"A fresh witness? Verily, I would gladly give half my kingdom, to be convinced of the innocence of men so nearly related to me."

"Victory to my lord, the eye of the realm! A Greek is waiting outside, who seems, to judge by his figure and bearing, one of the noblest of his race."

The king laughed bitterly: "A Greek! Ah, ha! perhaps some relation to Bartja's faithful fair one! What can this stranger know of my family affairs? I know these beggarly Ionians well. They are impudent enough to meddle in everything, and think they can cheat us with their sly tricks. How much have you had to pay for this new witness, uncle? A Greek is as ready with a lie as a Magian with his spells, and I know they'll do anything for gold. I'm really curious to see your witness. Call him in. But if he wants to deceive me, he had better remember that where the head of a son of Cyrus is about to fall, a Greek head has but very little chance." And the king's eyes flashed with anger as he said these words. Hystaspes, however, sent for the Greek.

Before he entered, the chamberlains fastened the usual cloth before his mouth, and commanded him to cast himself on the ground before the king. The Greek's bearing, as he approached, under the king's penetrating glance, was calm and noble; he fell on his face, and, according to the Persian custom, kissed the ground.

His agreeable and handsome appearance, and the calm and modest manner in which he bore the king's gaze, seemed to make a favorable impression on the latter; he did not allow him to remain long on the earth, and asked him in a by no means unfriendly tone:

"Who are you?"

"I am a Greek nobleman. My name is Phanes, and Athens is my home. I have served ten years as commander of the Greek mercenaries in Egypt, and not ingloriously."

"Are you the man, to whose clever generalship the Egyptians were indebted for their victories in Cyprus?"

"I am."

"What has brought you to Persia?"

"The glory of your name, Cambyses, and the wish to devote my arms and experience to your service."

"Nothing else? Be sincere, and remember that one single lie may cost your life. We Persians have different ideas of truth from the Greeks."

"Lying is hateful to me too, if only, because, as a

distortion and corruption of what is noblest. it seems unsightly in my eyes."

"Then speak."

"There was certainly a third reason for my coming hither, which I should like to tell you later. It has reference to matters of the greatest importance, which it will require a longer time to discuss; but to-day . . ."

"Just to-day I should like to hear something new. Accompany me to the chase. You come exactly at the right time, for I never had more need of diversion than now."

"I will accompany you with pleasure, if . . ."

"No conditions to the king! Have you had much practice in hunting?"

"In the Libyan desert I have killed many a lion."

"Then come, follow me."

In the thought of the chase the king seemed to have thrown off all his weakness and roused himself to action; he was just leaving the hall, when Hystaspes once more threw himself at his feet, crying with up-raised hands: "Is my son—is your brother, to die innocent? By the soul of your father, who used to call me his truest friend, I conjure you to listen to this noble stranger."

Cambyses stood still. The frown gathered on his brow again, his voice sounded like a menace and his eyes flashed as he raised his hand and said to the Greek: "Tell me what you know; but remember that in every untrue word, you utter your own sentence of death."

Phanes heard this threat with the greatest calmness, and answered, bowing gracefully as he spoke: "From the sun and from my lord the king, nothing can be hid.

What power has a poor mortal to conceal the truth from one so mighty? The noble Hystaspes has said, that I am able to prove your brother innocent. I will only say, that I wish and hope I may succeed in accomplishing anything so great and beautiful. The gods have at least allowed me to discover a trace which seems calculated to throw light on the events of yesterday; but you yourself must decide whether my hopes have been presumptuous and my suspicions too easily aroused. Remember, however, that throughout, my wish to serve you has been sincere, and that if I have been deceived, my error is pardonable; that nothing is perfectly certain in this world, and every man believes that to be infallible which seems to him the most probable."

"You speak well, and remind me of . . . curse her! there, speak and have done with it! I hear the dogs already in the court."

"I was still in Egypt when your embassy came to fetch Nitetis. At the house of Rhodopis, my delightful, clever and celebrated countrywoman, I made the acquaintance of Crœsus and his son; I only saw your brother and his friends once or twice, casually; still I remembered the young prince's handsome face so well, that some time later, when I was in the workshop of the great sculptor Theodorus at Samos, I recognized his features at once."

"Did you meet him at Samos?"

"No, but his features had made such a deep and faithful impression on Theodorus' memory, that he used them to beautify the head of an Apollo, which the Alkmæonidæ had ordered for the new temple of Delphi."

"Your tale begins, at least, incredibly enough. How is it possible to copy features so exactly, when you have not got them before you?"

"I can only answer that Theodorus has really completed this master-piece, and if you wish for a proof of his skill would gladly send you a second likeness of . . ."

"I have no desire for it. Go on with your story."

"On my journey hither, which, thanks to your father's excellent arrangements, I performed in an incredibly short time, changing horses every sixteen or seventeen miles . . ."

"Who allowed you, a foreigner, to use the post-horses?"

"The pass drawn out for the son of Crœsus, which came by chance into my hands, when once, in order to save my life, he forced me to change clothes with him."

"A Lydian can outwit a fox, and a Syrian a Lydian, but an Ionian is a match for both," muttered the king, smiling for the first time; "Crœsus told me this story—poor Crœsus!" and then the old gloomy expression came over his face and he passed his hand across his forehead, as if trying to smooth the lines of care away. The Athenian went on: "I met with no hindrances on my journey till this morning at the first hour after midnight, when I was detained by a strange occurrence."

The king began to listen more attentively, and reminded the Athenian, who spoke Persian with difficulty, that there was no time to lose.

"We had reached the last station but one," continued he, "and hoped to be in Babylon by sunrise. I was thinking over my past stirring life, and was so haunted by the remembrance of evil deeds unrevenged that I could not sleep; the old Egyptian at my side, however, slept and dreamt peacefully enough, lulled by the monotonous tones of the harness bells, the sound of the horses' hoofs and the murmur of the Euphrates. It was a wonderfully still, beautiful night; the moon and stars were so brilliant, that our road and the landscape were lighted up almost with the brightness of day. For the last hour we had not seen a single vehicle, foot-passenger, or horseman; we had heard that all the neighboring population had assembled in Babylon to celebrate your birthday, gaze with wonder at the splendor of your court, and enjoy your liberality. At last the irregular beat of horses' hoofs, and the sound of bells struck my ear, and a few minutes later I distinctly heard cries of distress. My resolve was taken at once; I made my Persian servant dismount, sprang into his saddle, told the driver of the cart in which my slaves were sitting not to spare his mules, loosened my dagger and sword in their scabbards, and spurred my horse towards the place from whence the cries came. They grew louder and louder. I had not ridden a minute, when I came on a fearful scene. Three wild-looking fellows had just pulled a youth, dressed in the white robes of a Magian, from his horse, stunned him with heavy blows, and, just as I reached them, were on the point of throwing him into the Euphrates, which at that place washes the roots of the palms and fig-trees bordering the high-road. I uttered my Greek war-cry, which has made many an enemy tremble before now, and rushed on the murderers. Such fellows are always cowards; the moment they saw one of their accomplices mortally wounded, they fled. I did not pursue them, but stooped down to examine the poor boy, who was severely wounded. How can I describe my horror at seeing, as I believed, your brother Bartja? Yes, they were the very same features that I had seen, first at Naukratis and then in Theodorus' workshop, they were ... ."

"Marvellous!" interrupted Hystaspes.

"Perhaps a little too much so to be credible," added the king. "Take care, Hellene! remember my arm reaches far. I shall have the truth of your story put to the proof."

"I am accustomed," answered Phanes bowing low, "to follow the advice of our wise philosopher Pythagoras, whose fame may perhaps have reached your ears, and always, before speaking, to consider whether what I am going to say may not cause me sorrow in the future."

"That sounds well; but, by Mithras, I knew some one who often spoke of that great teacher, and yet in her deeds turned out to be a most faithful disciple of Angramainjus. You know the traitress, whom we are going to extirpate from the earth like a poisonous viper to-day."

"Will you forgive me," answered Phanes, seeing the anguish expressed in the king's features, "if I quote another of the great master's maxims?"

"Speak."

"Blessings go as quickly as they come. Therefore bear thy lot patiently. Murmur not, and remember that the gods never lay a heavier weight on any man than he can bear. Hast thou a wounded heart? touch it as seldom as thou wouldst a sore eye. There are only two remedies for heart-sickness:—hope and patience."

Cambyses listened to this sentence, borrowed from

the golden maxims of Pythagoras, and smiled bitterly at the word "patience." Still the Athenian's way of speaking pleased him, and he told him to go on with his story.

Phanes made another deep obeisance, and continued: "We carried the unconscious youth to my carriage, and brought him to the nearest station. There he opened his eyes, looked anxiously at me, and asked who I was and what had happened to him? The master of the station was standing by, so I was obliged to give the name of Gyges in order not to excite his suspicions by belying my pass, as it was only through this that I could obtain fresh horses.

"This wounded young man seemed to know Gyges, for he shook his head and murmured: 'You are not the man you give yourself out for.' Then he closed his eyes again, and a violent attack of fever came on.

"We undressed, bled him and bound up his wounds. My Persian servant, who had served as overlooker in Amasis' stables and had seen Bartja there, assisted by the old Egyptian who accompanied me, was very helpful, and asserted untiringly that the wounded man could be no other than your brother. When we had cleansed the blood from his face, the master of the station too swore that there could be no doubt of his being the younger son of your great father Cyrus. Meanwhile my Egyptian companion had fetched a potion from the travelling medicine-chest,[31] without which an Egyptian does not care to leave his native

---

[31]. A similar travelling medicine-chest is to be seen in the Egyptian Museum at Berlin. It is prettily and compendiously fitted up, and must be very ancient, for the inscription on the chest, which contained it stated that it was made in the 11th dynasty (end of the third century B. C.) in the reign of King Mentuhotep.

country. The drops worked wonders; in a few hours the fever was quieted, and at sunrise the patient opened his eyes once more. We bowed down before him, believing him to be your brother, and asked if he would like to be taken to the palace in Babylon. This he refused vehemently, and asseverated that he was not the man we took him for, but, . . ."

"Who can be so like Bartja? tell me quickly," interrupted the king, "I am very curious to know this."

"He declared that he was the brother of your high-priest, that his name was Gaumata, and that this would be proved by the pass which we should find in the sleeve of his Magian's robe. The landlord found this document and, being able to read, confirmed the statement of the sick youth; he was, however, soon seized by a fresh attack of fever, and began to speak incoherently."

"Could you understand him?"

"Yes, for his talk always ran on the same subject. The hanging-gardens seemed to fill his thoughts. He must have just escaped some great danger, and probably had had a a lover's meeting there with a woman called Mandane."

"Mandane, Mandane," said Cambyses in a low voice; "if I do not mistake, that is the name of the highest attendant on Amasis' daughter."

These words did not escape the sharp ears of the Greek. He thought a moment and then exclaimed with a smile; "Set the prisoners free, my King; I will answer for it with my own head, that Bartja was not in the hanging-gardens."

The king was surprised at this speech but not angry. The free, unrestrained, graceful manner of this Athenian towards himself produced the same impression, that a fresh sea-breeze makes when felt for the first time. The nobles of his own court, even his nearest relations, approached him bowing and cringing, but this Greek stood erect in his presence; the Persians never ventured to address their ruler without a thousand flowery and flattering phrases, but the Athenian was simple, open and straightforward. Yet his words were accompanied by such a charm of action and expression, that the king could understand them, notwithstanding the defective Persian in which they were clothed, better than the allegorical speeches of his own subjects. Nitetis and Phanes were the only human beings, who had ever made him forget that he was a king. With them he was a man speaking to his fellow-man, instead of a despot speaking with creatures whose very existence was the plaything of his own caprice. Such is the effect produced by real manly dignity, superior culture and the consciousness of a right to freedom, on the mind even of a tyrant. But there was something beside all this, that had helped to win Cambyses' favor for the Athenian. This man's coming seemed as if it might possibly give him back the treasure he had believed was lost and more than lost. But how could the life of such a foreign adventurer be accepted as surety for the sons of the highest Persians in the realm? The proposal, however, did not make him angry. On the contrary, he could not help smiling at the boldness of this Greek, who in his eagerness had freed himself from the cloth which hung over his mouth and beard, and exclaimed: "By Mithras, Greek, it really seems as if you were to prove a messenger of good for us! I accept your offer. If the prisoners, notwithstanding your supposition, should still prove guilty you are bound to pass your whole life at my court and in my service, but if, on the contrary, you are able to prove what I so ardently long for, I will make you richer than any of your countrymen."

Phanes answered by a smile which seemed to decline this munificent offer, and asked: "Is it permitted me to put a few questions to yourself and to the officers of your court?"

"You are allowed to say and ask whatever you wish."

At this moment the master of the huntsmen, one of those who daily ate at the king's table, entered, out of breath from his endeavors to hasten the preparations, and announced that all was ready.

"They must wait," was the king's imperious answer. "I am not sure, that we shall hunt at all to-day. Where is Bischen, the captain of police?"

Datis, the so-called "eye of the king,"[32] who held the office filled in modern days by a minister of police, hurried from the room, returning in a few minutes with the desired officer. These moments Phanes made use of for putting various questions on important points to the nobles who were present.

"What news can you bring of the prisoners?" asked the king, as the man lay prostrate before him.

"Victory to the king! They await death with calmness, for it is sweet to die by thy will."

"Have you heard anything of their conversation?"

"Yes, my Ruler."

"Do they acknowledge their guilt, when speaking to each other?"

"Mithras alone knows the heart; but you, my prince, if you could hear them speak, would believe in

[32]. See Vol. I. note 239.

their innocence, even as I the humblest of your servants."

The captain looked up timidly at the king, fearing lest these words should have excited his anger; Cambyses, however, smiled kindly instead of rebuking him. But a sudden thought darkened his brow again directly, and in a low voice he asked: "When was Crœsus executed?"

The man trembled at this question; the perspiration stood on his forehead, and he could scarcely stammer the words: "He is . . . he has . . . we thought . . ."

"What did you think?" interrupted Cambyses, and a new light of hope seemed to dawn in his mind. "Is it possible, that you did not carry out my orders at once? Can Crœsus still be alive? Speak at once, I must know the whole truth."

The captain writhed like a worm at his lord's feet, and at last stammered out, raising his hands imploringly towards the king: "Have mercy, have mercy, my Lord the king! I am a poor man, and have thirty children, fifteen of whom . . ."

"I wish to know if Crœsus is living or dead."

"He is alive! He has done so much for me, and I did not think I was doing wrong in allowing him to live a few hours longer, that he might . . ."

"That is enough," said the king breathing freely. "This once your disobedience shall go unpunished, and the treasurer may give you two talents, as you have so many children.—Now go to the prisoners,—tell Crœsus to come hither, and the others to be of good courage, if they are innocent."

"My King is the light of the world, and an ocean of mercy."

"Bartja and his friends need not remain any longer in confinement; they can walk in the court of the palace, and you will keep guard over them. You, Datis, go at once to the hanging-gardens and order Boges to defer the execution of the sentence on the Egyptian Princess; and further, I wish messengers sent to the post-station mentioned by the Athenian, and the wounded man brought hither under safe escort."

The "king's eye" was on the point of departure, but Phanes detained him, saying: "Does my King allow me to make one remark?"

"Speak."

"It appears to me, that the chief of the eunuchs could give the most accurate information. During his delirium the youth often mentioned his name in connection with that of the girl he seemed to be in love with."

"Go at once, Datis, and bring him quickly."

"The high-priest Oropastes, Gaumata's brother, ought to appear too; and Mandane, whom I have just been assured on the most positive authority, is the principal attendant of the Egyptian Princess."

"Fetch her, Datis."

"If Nitetis herself could . . ."

At this the king turned pale and a cold shiver ran through his limbs. How he longed to see his darling again! But the strong man was afraid of this woman's reproachful looks; he knew the captivating power that lay in her eyes. So he pointed to the door, saying: "Fetch Boges and Mandane; the Egyptian Princess is to remain in the hanging-gardens, under strict custody."

The Athenian bowed deferentially; as if he would

say: "Here no one has a right to command but the king."

Cambyses looked well pleased, seated himself again on the purple divan, and resting his forehead on his hand, bent his eyes on the ground and sank into deep thought. The picture of the woman he loved so dearly refused to be banished; it came again and again, more and more vividly, and the thought that these features could not have deceived him—that Nitetis must be innocent—took a firmer root in his mind; he had already begun to hope. If Bartja could be cleared, there was no error that might not be conceivable; in that case he would go to the hanging-gardens, take her hand and listen to her defence. When love has once taken firm hold of a man in riper years, it runs and winds through his whole nature like one of his veins, and can only be destroyed with his life.

The entrance of Crœsus roused Cambyses from his dream; he raised the old man kindly from the prostrate position at his feet, into which he had thrown himself on entering, and said: "You offended me, but I will be merciful; I have not forgotten that my father, on his dying bed, told me to make you my friend and adviser. Take your life back as a gift from me, and forget my anger as I wish to forget your want of reverence. This man says he knows you; I should like to hear your opinion of his conjectures."

Crœsus turned away much affected, and after having heartily welcomed the Athenian, asked him to relate his suppositions and the grounds on which they were founded.

The old man grew more and more attentive as the Greek went on, and when he had finished raised his hands to heaven, crying: "Pardon me, oh ye eternal gods, if I have ever questioned the justice of your decrees. Is not this marvellous, Cambyses? My son once placed himself in great danger to save the life of this noble Athenian, whom the gods have brought hither to repay the deed tenfold. Had Phanes been murdered in Egypt, this hour might have seen our sons executed."

And as he said this he embraced Hystaspes; both shared one feeling; their sons had been as dead and were now alive.

The king, Phanes, and all the Persian dignitaries watched the old men with deep sympathy, and though the proofs of Bartja's innocence were as yet only founded on conjecture, not one of those present doubted it one moment longer. Wherever the belief in a man's guilt is but slight, his defender finds willing listeners.

CHAPTER VI.

THE sharp-witted Athenian saw clearly how matters lay in this sad story; nor did it escape him that malice had had a hand in the affair. How could Bartja's dagger have come into the hanging-gardens except through treachery?

While he was telling the king his suspicions, Oropastes was led into the hall.

The king looked angrily at him and without one preliminary word, asked: "Have you a brother?"

"Yes, my King. He and I are the only two left out of a family of six. My parents . . ."

"Is your brother younger or older than yourself?"

"I was the eldest of the family; my brother, the youngest, was the joy of my father's old age."

"Did you ever notice a remarkable likeness between him and one of my relations?"

"Yes, my King. Gaumata is so like your brother Bartja, that in the school for priests at Rhagæ, where he still is, he was always called 'the prince.'"

"Has he been at Babylon very lately?"

"He was here for the last time at the New Year's festival."

"Are you speaking the truth?"

"The sin of lying would be doubly punishable in one who wears my robes, and holds my office."

The king's face flushed with anger at this answer and he exclaimed: "Nevertheless you are lying; Gaumata was here yesterday evening. You may well tremble."

"My life belongs to the king, whose are all things; nevertheless I swear—I, the high-priest—by the most high God, whom I have served faithfully for thirty years, that I know nothing of my brother's presence in Babylon yesterday."

"Your face looks as if you were speaking the truth."

"You know that I was not absent from your side the whole of that high holiday."

"I know it."

Again the doors opened; this time they admitted the trembling Mandane. The high-priest cast such a look of astonishment and enquiry on her, that the king saw she must be in some way connected with him, and therefore, taking no notice of the trembling girl who lay at his feet, he asked: "Do you know this woman?"

"Yes, my King. I obtained for her the situation of upper attendant to the—may Auramazda forgive her!—King of Egypt's daughter."

"What led you,—a priest,—to do a favor to this girl?"

"Her parents died of the same pestilence, which carried off my brothers. Her father was a priest, respected, and a friend of our family; so we adopted the little girl, remembering the words: 'If thou withhold help from the man who is pure in heart and from his widow and orphans, then shall the pure, subject earth cast thee out unto the stinging-nettles, to painful sufferings and to the most fearful regions!' Thus I became her foster-father, and had her brought up with my youngest brother until he was obliged to enter the school for priests."

The king exchanged a look of intelligence with Phanes, and asked: "Why did not you keep the girl longer with you?"

"When she had received the ear-rings* I, as priest, thought it more suitable to send such a young girl away from my house, and to put her in a position to earn her own living."

"Has she seen your brother since she has been grown up?"

"Yes, my King. Whenever Gaumata came to see me I allowed him to be with her as with a sister; but on discovering later that the passionate love of youth had begun to mingle with the childish friendship of

---

* See vol. I. note 236.

former days, I felt strengthened in my resolution to send her away."

"Now we know enough," said the king, commanding the high-priest by a nod to retire. He then looked down on the prostrate girl, and said imperiously: "Rise!"

Mandane rose, trembling with fear. Her fresh young face was pale as death, and her red lips were blue from terror.

"Tell all you know about yesterday evening; but remember, a lie and your death are one and the same."

The girl's knees trembled so violently that she could hardly stand, and her fear entirely took away the power of speaking.

"I have not much patience," exclaimed Cambyses.

Mandane started, grew paler still, but could not speak. Then Phanes came forward and asked the angry king to allow him to examine the girl, as he felt sure that fear alone had closed her lips and that a kind word would open them.

Cambyses allowed this, and the Athenian's words proved true; no sooner had he assured Mandane of the good-will of all present, laid his hand on her head and spoken kindly to her, than the source of her tears was unlocked, she wept freely, the spell which had seemed to chain her tongue, vanished, and she began to tell her story, interrupted only by low sobs. She hid nothing, confessed that Boges had given her his sanction and assistance to the meeting with Gaumata, and ended by saying: "I know that I have forfeited my life, and am the worst and most ungrateful creature in the world; but none of all this would have happened, if Oropastes had allowed his brother to marry me."

The serious audience, even the king himself, could not resist a smile at the longing tone in which these words were spoken and the fresh burst of sobs which succeeded them.

And this smile saved her life. But Cambyses would not have smiled, after hearing such a story, if Mandane, with that instinct which always seems to stand at a woman's command in the hour of her greatest danger, had not known how to seize his weak side, and use it for her own interests, by dwelling much longer than was necessary, on the delight which Nitetis had manifested at the king's gifts.

"A thousand times" cried she, "did my mistress kiss the presents which were brought from you, O King; but oftenest of all did she press her lips to the nosegay which you plucked with your own hands for her, some days ago. And when it began to fade, she took every flower separately, spread out the petals with care, laid them between woollen cloths, and, with her own hands, placed her heavy, golden ointment-box upon them, that they might dry and so she might keep them always as a remembrance of your kindness."

Seeing Cambyses' awful features grow a little milder at these words, the girl took fresh courage, and at last began to put loving words into her mistress's mouth which the latter had never uttered, professing that she herself had heard Nitetis a hundred times murmur the word "Cambyses" in her sleep with indescribable tenderness. She ended her confession by sobbing and praying for mercy.

The king looked down at her with infinite contempt,

though without anger, and pushing her away with his foot said: "Out of my sight, you dog of a woman! Blood like yours would soil the executioner's axe. Out of my sight!"

Mandane needed no second command to depart. The words "out of my sight" sounded like sweet music in her ears. She rushed through the courts of the palace, and out into the streets, crying like a mad woman: "I am free! I am free!"

She had scarcely left the hall, when Datis "the king's eye" reappeared with the news that the chief of the eunuchs was nowhere to be found. He had vanished from the hanging-gardens in an unaccountable manner; but he, Datis, had left word with his subordinates that he was to be searched for and brought, dead or alive.

The king went off into another violent fit of passion at this news, and threatened the officer of police, who prudently concealed the excitement of the crowd from his lord, with a severe punishment, if Boges were not in their hands by the next morning.

As he finished speaking, a eunuch was brought into the hall, sent by the king's mother to ask an interview for herself with her son.

Cambyses prepared at once to comply with his mother's wish, at the same time giving Phanes his hand to kiss, a rare honor, only shown to those that ate at the king's table, and saying: "All the prisoners are to be set at liberty. Go to your sons, you anxious, troubled fathers, and assure them of my mercy and favor. I think we shall be able to find a satrapy a-piece for them, as compensation for to-night's undeserved imprisonment. To you, my Greek friend, I am deeply indebted. In discharge of this debt, and as a means of retaining you at my court, I beg you to accept one hundred talents* from my treasury."

"I shall scarcely be able to use so large a sum," said Phanes, bowing low.

"Then abuse it," said the king with a friendly smile, and calling out to him, "We shall meet again at supper," he left the hall accompanied by his court.

In the meantime there had been sadness and mourning in the apartments of the queen-mother. Judging from the contents of the letter to Bartja, Kassandane had made up her mind that Nitetis was faithless, and her own beloved son innocent. But in whom could she ever place confidence again, now that this girl, whom she had looked upon as the very embodiment of every womanly virtue, had proved reprobate and faithless—now that the noblest youths in the realm had proved perjurers?

Nitetis was more than dead for her; Bartja, Crœsus, Darius, Gyges, Araspes, all so closely allied to her by relationship and friendship, as good as dead. And yet she durst not indulge her sorrow; she had to restrain the despairing outbursts of grief of her impetuous child.

Atossa behaved like one deprived of her senses when she heard of the sentences of death. The self-control which she had learnt from Nitetis gave way, and her old impetuosity burst forth again with double vehemence.

* £22,500.

Nitetis, her only friend,—Bartja, the brother whom she loved with her whole heart,—Darius, whom she felt now she not only looked up to as her deliverer, but loved with all the warmth of a first affection—Crœsus to whom she clung like a father,—she was to lose every one she loved in one day.

She tore her dress and her hair, called Cambyses a monster, and every one who could possibly believe in the guilt of such people, infatuated or insane. Then her tears would burst out afresh, she would utter imploring supplications to the gods for mercy, and a few minutes later, begin conjuring her mother to take her to the hanging-gardens, that they might hear Nitetis' defence of her own conduct.

Kassandane tried to soothe the violent girl, and assured her every attempt to visit the hanging-gardens would be in vain. Then Atossa began to rage again, until at last her mother was forced to command silence, and as morning had already began to dawn, sent her to her sleeping-room.

The girl obeyed, but instead of going to bed, seated herself at a tall window looking towards the hanging-gardens. Her eyes filled with tears again, as she thought of her friend—her sister—sitting in that palace alone, forsaken, banished, and looking forward to an ignominious death. Suddenly her tearful, weary eyes lighted up as if from some strong purpose, and instead of gazing into the distance, she fixed them on a black speck which flew towards her in a straight line from Nitetis' house, becoming larger and more distinct every moment; and finally settling on a cypress before her window. The sorrow vanished at once from her lovely face and with a deep sigh of relief she sprang up, exclaiming:

"Oh, there is the Homaï,[33] the bird of good fortune! Now everything will turn out well."

It was the same bird of paradise which had brought so much comfort to Nitetis that now gave poor Atossa fresh confidence.

She bent forward to see whether any one was in the garden; and finding that she would be seen by no one but the old gardener, she jumped out, trembling like a fawn, plucked a few roses and cypress twigs and took them to the old man, who had been watching her performances with a doubtful shake of the head.

She stroked his cheeks coaxingly, put her flowers in his brown hand, and said: "Do you love me, Sabaces?"

"O, my mistress!" was the only answer the old man could utter, as he pressed the hem of her robe to his lips.

"I believe you, my old friend, and I will show you how I trust my faithful, old Sabaces. Hide these flowers carefully and go quickly to the king's palace. Say that you had to bring fruit for the table. My poor brother Bartja, and Darius, the son of the noble Hystaspes, are in prison, near the guard-house of the Immortals. You must manage that these flowers reach them, with a warm greeting from me, but mind, the message must be given with the flowers."

"But the guards will not allow me to see the prisoners."

"Take these rings, and slip them into their hands."

"I will do my best."

"I knew you loved me, my good Sabaces. Now make haste, and come back soon."

---

33. The bird of paradise is called in Persian Homaï. See Malcolm, *Persia*, *p.* 53.

The old man went off as fast as he could. Atossa looked thoughtfully after him, murmuring to herself: "Now they will both know, that I loved them to the last. The rose means, 'I love you,' and the evergreen cypress, 'true and steadfast.'" The old man came back in an hour; bringing her Bartja's favorite ring, and from Darius an Indian handkerchief dipped in blood.

Atossa ran to meet him; her eyes filled with tears as she took the tokens, and seating herself under a spreading plane-tree, she pressed them by turns to her lips, murmuring: "Bartja's ring means that he thinks of me; the blood-stained handkerchief that Darius is ready to shed his heart's blood for me."

Atossa smiled as she said this, and her tears, when she thought of her friends and their sad fate, were quieter, if not less bitter, than before.

A few hours later a messenger arrived from Crœsus with news that the innocence of Bartja and his friends had been proved, and that Nitetis was, to all intents and purposes, cleared also.

Kassandane sent at once to the hanging-gardens, with a request that Nitetis would come to her apartments. Atossa, as unbridled in her joy as in her grief, ran to meet her friend's litter and flew from one of her attendants to the other crying: "They are all innocent; we shall not lose one of them—not one!"

When at last the litter appeared and her loved one, pale as death, within it, she burst into loud sobs, threw her arms round Nitetis as she descended, and covered her with kisses and caresses till she perceived that her friend's strength was failing, that her knees gave way, and she required a stronger support than Atossa's girlish strength could give.

The Egyptian girl was carried insensible into the queen-mother's apartments. When she opened her eyes, her head—more like a marble piece of sculpture than a living head—was resting on the blind queen's lap, she felt Atossa's warm kisses on her forehead, and Cambyses, who had obeyed his mother's call, was standing at her side.

She gazed on this circle, including all she loved best, with anxious, perplexed looks, and at last, recognizing them one by one, passed her hand across her pale forehead as if to remove a veil, smiled at each, and closed her eyes once more. She fancied Isis had sent her a beautiful vision, and wished to hold it fast with all the powers of her mind.

Then Atossa called her by her name, impetuously and lovingly. She opened her eyes again, and again she saw those loving looks that she fancied had only been sent her in a dream. Yes, that was her own Atossa—this her motherly friend, and there stood, not the angry king, but the man she loved. And now his lips opened too, his stern, severe eyes rested on her so beseechingly, and he said: "O Nitetis, awake! you must not—you cannot possibly be guilty!" She moved her head gently with a look of cheerful denial and a happy smile stole across her features, like a breeze of early spring over fresh young roses.

"She is innocent! by Mithras, it is impossible that she can be guilty," cried the king again, and forgetful of the presence of others, he sank on his knees.

A Persian physician came up and rubbed her forehead with a sweet-scented oil, and Nebenchari approached, muttering spells, felt her pulse, shook his head, and administered a potion from his portable medicine-chest. This restored her to perfect consciousness; she raised herself with difficulty into a sitting posture, returned the loving caresses of her two friends, and then turning to Cambyses, asked: " How could you believe such a thing of me, my King ?" There was no reproach in her tone, but deep sadness, and Cambyses answered softly, " Forgive me."

Kassandane's blind eyes expressed her gratitude for this self-renunciation on the part of her son, and she said: " My daughter, I need your forgiveness too."

" But *I* never once doubted you," cried Atossa, proudly and joyfully kissing her friend's lips.

" Your letter to Bartja shook my faith in your innocence," added Kassandane.

" And yet it was all so simple and natural," answered Nitetis. "Here, my mother, take this letter from Egypt. Crœsus will translate it for you. It will explain all. Perhaps I was imprudent. Ask your mother to tell you what you would wish to know, my King. Pray do not scorn my poor, ill sister. When an Egyptian girl once loves, she cannot forget. But I feel so frightened. The end must be near. The last hours have been so very, very terrible. That horrible man, Boges, read me the fearful sentence of death, and it was that which forced the poison into my hand. Ah, my heart !"

And with these words she fell back into the arms of Kassandane.

Nebenchari rushed forward, and gave her some more drops, exclaiming: " I thought so ! She has taken poison and her life cannot be saved, though this antidote may possibly prolong it for a few days."

Cambyses stood by, pale and rigid, following the physician's slightest movements, and Atossa bathed her friend's forehead with her tears.

"Let some milk be brought," cried Nebenchari, "and my large medicine-chest; and let attendants be called to carry her away, for quiet is necessary, above all things."

Atossa hastened into the adjoining room; and Cambyses said to the physician, but without looking into his face: "Is there no hope?"

"The poison which she has taken results in certain death."

On hearing this the king pushed Nebenchari away from the sick girl, exclaiming: "She *shall* live. It is my will. Here, eunuch! summon all the physicians in Babylon—assemble the priests and Mobeds![34] She is not to die; do you hear? she must live, I am the king, and I command it."

Nitetis opened her eyes as if endeavoring to obey her lord. Her face was turned towards the window, and the bird of paradise with the gold chain on its foot, was still there, perched on the cypress-tree. Her eyes fell first on her lover, who had sunk down at her side and was pressing his burning lips to her right hand. She murmured with a smile: "O, this great happiness!" Then she saw the bird, and pointed to it with her left hand, crying: "Look, look, there is the Phœnix, the bird of Ra!"

After saying this she closed her eyes and was soon seized by a violent attack of fever.

---

[34]. Mobeds are priests. They are not mentioned in the Avesta. Spiegel derives the name from *nmâna paiti*. Rogge prefers, with Tiele, Haug's derivation from *magu pat*, Lord of the Magi.

CHAPTER VII.

PREXASPES, the king's messenger, and one of the highest officials at court, had brought Gaumata, Mandane's lover, whose likeness to Bartja was really most wonderful, to Babylon, sick and wounded as he was. He was now awaiting his sentence in a dungeon, while Boges, the man who had led him into crime, was nowhere to be found, notwithstanding all the efforts of the police. His escape had been rendered possible by the trap-door in the hanging-gardens, and greatly assisted by the enormous crowds assembled in the streets. Immense treasures were found in his house. Chests of gold and jewels, which his postion had enabled him to obtain with great ease, were restored to the royal treasury. Cambyses, however, would gladly have given ten times as much treasure to secure possession of the traitor.

To Phædime's despair the king ordered all the inhabitants of the harem, except his mother, Atossa and the dying Nitetis, to be removed to Susa, two days after the accused had been declared innocent. Several eunuchs of rank were deposed from their offices. The entire caste was to suffer for the sins of him who had escaped punishment.

Oropastes, who had already entered on his duties as regent of the kingdom, and had clearly proved his non-participation in the crime of which his brother had been proved guilty, bestowed the vacant places exclusively on the Magi. The demonstration made by the people in favor of Bartja did not come to the king's ears until the crowd had long dispersed. Still, occupied as he was, almost entirely, by his anxiety for Nitetis, he caused exact information of this illegal manifestation to be furnished him, and ordered the ringleaders to be severely punished. He fancied it was a proof that Bartja had been trying to gain favor with the people, and Cambyses would perhaps have shown his displeasure by some open act, if a better impulse had not told him that he, not Bartja, was the brother who stood in need of forgiveness. In spite of this, however, he could not get rid of the feeling that Bartja, had been, though innocent,—the cause of the sad events which had just happened, nor of his wish to get him out of the way as far as might be; and he therefore gave a ready consent to his brother's wish to start at once for Naukratis.

Bartja took a tender farewell of his mother and sister, and started two days after his liberation. He was accompanied by Gyges, Zopyrus, and a numerous retinue charged with splendid presents from Cambyses for Sappho. Darius remained behind, kept back by his love for Atossa. The day too was not far distant, when, by his father's wish, he was to marry Artystone, the daughter of Gobryas.

Bartja parted from his friend with a heavy heart, advising him to be very prudent with regard to Atossa. The secret had been confided to Kassandane, and she had promised to take Darius' part with the king.

If any one might venture to raise his eyes to the daughter of Cyrus, assuredly it was the son of Hystaspes; he was closely connected by marriage with the royal family, belonged like Cambyses to the Pasargadæ, and his family was a younger branch of the reigning dynasty.[35] His father called himself the highest noble in the realm, and as such, governed the province of Persia proper, the mother-country, to which this enormous world-empire and its ruler owed their origin. Should the family of Cyrus become extinct, the descendants of Hystaspes would have a well-grounded right to the Persian throne. Darius therefore, apart from his personal advantages, was a fitting claimant for Atossa's hand. And yet no one dared to ask the king's consent. In the gloomy state of mind into which he had been brought by the late events, it was likely that he might refuse it, and such an answer would have to be regarded as irrevocable. So Bartja was obliged to leave Persia in anxiety about the future of these two who were very dear to him.

Crœsus promised to act as mediator in this case also, and before Bartja left, made him acquainted with Phanes.

The youth had heard such a pleasant account of the Athenian from Sappho, that he met him with great cordiality, and soon won the fancy of the older and more experienced man, who gave him many a useful hint, and a letter to Theopompus, the Milesian, at Naukratis.[36] Phanes concluded by asking for a private interview.

35. In the inscription of Behistân there is a pedigree of the family of Darius, which can be reconciled with the one for which we are principally indebted to Herodotus. *Inscription of Behistûn* I. §. II.

36. It is clear from different passages in the classics, that the ancient Greeks were accustomed to take introductions with them on their journeys. These consisted sometimes of letters, sometimes merely of the impression of a seal. Even as early as the Iliad, Glaukus mentions such a Symbolon. Compare Plutarch. *Artaxerxes*, XVIII., and especially Böckh, *Corp. Inscr.* I. p. 126. *Marmor. Oxon.* II. 24. In this inscription mention is made of the letter of recom-

Bartja returned to his friends looking grave and thoughtful; soon, however, he forgot his cause of anxiety and joked merrily with them over a farewell cup. Before he mounted his horse the next morning, Nebenchari asked to be allowed an audience. He was admitted, and begged Bartja to take the charge of a large written roll for king Amasis. It contained a detailed account of Nitetis' sufferings, ending with these words: "Thus the unhappy victim of your ambitious plans will end her life in a few hours by poison, to the use of which she was driven by despair. The arbitrary caprices of the mighty can efface all happiness from the life of a human creature, just as we wipe a picture from the tablet with a sponge. Your servant Nebenchari is pining in a foreign land, deprived of home and property, and the wretched daughter of a king of Egypt dies a miserable and lingering death by her own hand. Her body will be torn to pieces by dogs and vultures, after the manner of the Persians. Woe unto them who rob the innocent of happiness here and of rest beyond the grave!"

mendation or token (σύμβολα) which Strato, the king of Sidon, might give, say, to his ambassadors to Athens. A passport (σφραγίς) abroad is also spoken of in the Birds of Aristophanes 1212. This was provided with the government seal. The Lokrian seal bore the evening-star; the Samian a lyre, and so on. See Vol. I. note 286.

We will here insert the following letter, found by Passalacqua, with the seal still unbroken, in the wrappings of a mummy belonging to the time of the Ptolemies. It was addressed by a certain Timoxenes to Moschion, introducing a man, whose name is destroyed, and who died on the journey before he could deliver it. The letter he carried was placed in his coffin. It runs as follows: "Timoxenes greets Moschion—M . . . . s, who will give you this letter, is the brother of Philon, Lysis' private secretary. See that no wrong is done him. His father is also here with Petonuris Second. These lines have been given him with the token of my family." This token consisted of a palette, similar to those used by the Egyptian scribes, to which the letter was fastened.

Bartja had not been told the contents of this letter, but promised to take it with him; he then, amid the joyful shouts of the people, set up outside the city-gate the stones which, according to a Persian superstition,[37] were to secure him a prosperous journey, and left Babylon.

Nebenchari, meanwhile, prepared to return to his post by Nitetis' dying-bed.

Just as he reached the brazen gates between the harem-gardens and the courts of the large palace, an old man in white robes came up to him. The sight seemed to fill Nebenchari with terror; he started as if the gaunt old man had been a ghost. Seeing, however, a friendly and familiar smile on the face of the other, he quickened his steps, and, holding out his hand with a heartiness for which none of his Persian acquaintances would have given him credit, exclaimed in Egyptian: "Can I believe my eyes? You in Persia, old Hib?* I should as soon have expected the sky to fall as to have the pleasure of seeing you on the Euphrates. But now, in the name of Osiris, tell me what can have induced you, you old ibis, to leave your warm nest on the Nile and set out on such a long journey eastward."

While Nebenchari was speaking, the old man listened in a bowing posture, with his arms hanging down by his side, and when he had finished, looked up into his face with indescribable joy, touched his breast with trembling fingers, and then, falling on the

---

37. This superstition prevails even to the present day. Morier. *Zweite Reise* in Bertuch's *neuer Bibliothek der Reisebeschreibungen*. See also de Wette, *Archäologie* §. 192.

* In ancient Egyptian Hib signifies an ibis. Many of the ancient Egyptians were called after the sacred animals.

right knee, laying one hand on his heart and raising the other to heaven, cried: "Thanks be unto thee, great Isis, for protecting the wanderer and permitting him to see his master once more in health and safety. Ah, child, how anxious I have been! I expected to find you as wasted and thin as a convict from the quarries; I thought you would have been grieving and unhappy, and here you are as well, and handsome and portly as ever. If poor old Hib had been in your place he would have been dead long ago."

"Yes, I don't doubt that, old fellow. I did not leave home of my own will either, nor without many a heartache. These foreigners are all the children of Seth.* The good and gracious gods are only to be found in Egypt on the shores of the sacred, blessed Nile."

"I don't know much about its being so blessed," muttered the old man.

"You frighten me, father Hib. What has happened then?"

"Happened! Things have come to a pretty pass there, and you'll hear of it soon enough. Do you think I should have left house and grandchildren at my age, —going on for eighty,—like any Greek or Phœnician vagabond, and come out among these godless foreigners (the gods blast and destroy them!), if I could possibly have staid on in Egypt?"

' But tell me what it's all about."

"Some other time, some other time. Now you must take me to your own house, and I won't stir out of it as long as we are in this land of Typhon."

The old man said this with so much emphasis, that

* See vol. 1. note 147.

Nebenchari could not help smiling and saying: "Have they treated you so very badly then, old man?"

"Pestilence and Khamsin!"* blustered the old man. "There's not a more good-for-nothing Typhon's brood on the face of the earth than these Persians. I only wonder they're not all red-haired and leprous. Ah, child, two whole days I have been in this hell already, and all that time I was obliged to live among these blasphemers. They said no one could see you; you were never allowed to leave Nitetis' sick-bed. Poor child! I always said this marriage with a foreigner would come to no good, and it serves Amasis right if his children give him trouble. His conduct to you alone deserves that."

"For shame, old man!"

"Nonsense, one must speak one's mind sometimes. I hate a king, who comes from nobody knows where. Why, when he was a poor boy he used to steal your father's nuts, and wrench the name-plates off the house-doors. I saw he was a good-for-nothing fellow then. It's a shame that such people should be allowed to . . ."

"Gently, gently, old man. We are not all made of the same stuff, and if there was such a little difference between you and Amasis as boys, it is your own fault that, now you are old men, he has outstripped you so far."

"My father and grandfather were both servants in the temple, and of course I followed in their footsteps."[38]

[38]. The son was usually obliged to follow the same profession as his father. Diod. I. 74. Lepsius has discovered some remarkably

* The south-west wind, which does so much injury to the crops in the Nile valley. It is known to us as the Simoom, the wind so perilous to travellers in the desert.

"Quite right; it is the law of caste, and by that rule, Amasis ought never to have become anything higher than a poor army-captain at most."

"It is not every one who's got such an easy conscience as this upstart fellow."

"There you are again! For shame, Hib! As long as I can remember, and that is nearly half a century, every other word with you has been an abusive one. When I was a child your ill-temper was vented on me, and now the king has the benefit of it."

"Serves him right! Ah, if you only knew all! It's now seven months since..."

"I can't stop to listen to you now. At the rising of the seven stars I will send a slave to take you to my rooms. Till then you must stay in your present lodging, for I must go to my patient."

"You must?—Very well,—then go and leave poor old Hib here to die. I can't possibly live another hour among these creatures."

"What would you have me do then?"

"Let me live with you as long as we are in Persia."

"Have they treated you so very roughly?"

"I should think they had indeed. It is loathsome

long family pedigrees, in which every member belonged to the same calling. The genealogies appearing on the monuments, which recorded the names and titles of fathers, mothers, children, etc., have been recently collected and published by Lieblein, *Dictionnaire des noms hiéroglyphiques*. They have become important as a means of calculating the epochs of Egyptian history. But the castes among the Egyptians were not so rigidly circumscribed as in India, for we see from the monuments, that the son of a priest could enter the army, and vice versâ; that sons of the same father could devote themselves to different professions; and also (on which point we have favorable evidence in some hieratic manuscripts, the contents of which are of a didactic character) that young men were allowed to choose their own professions. Without question, however, it was more usual, and considered preferable, to remain in the father's calling. This indeed was the case among all ancient nations, not excepting the Greeks.

to think of. They forced me to eat out of the same pot with them and cut my bread with the same knife. An infamous Persian, who had lived many years in Egypt, and travelled here with us, had given them a list of all the things and actions, which we consider unclean.[39] They took away my knife when I was going to shave myself. A good-for-nothing wench kissed me on the forehead, before I could prevent it. There, you needn't laugh; it will be a month at least before I can get purified from all these pollutions. I took an emetic, and when that at last began to take effect, they all mocked and sneered at me. But that was not all. A cursed cook-boy nearly beat a sacred kitten to death before my very eyes. Then an ointment-mixer, who had heard that I was your servant, made that godless Bubares ask me whether I could cure diseases of the eye too. I said yes, because you know in sixty years it's rather hard if one can't pick up something from one's master. Bubares was interpreter between us, and the shameful fellow told him to say that he was very much disturbed about a dreadful disease in his eyes. I asked what it was, and received for answer that he could not tell one thing from another in the dark!"

"You should have told him that the best remedy for that was to light a candle."

"Oh, I hate the rascals! Another hour among them will be the death of me!"

"I am sure you behaved oddly enough among these foreigners," said Nebenchari smiling, "you must have made them laugh at you, for the Persians are

---

39. On the numerous methods of purification, by washing, shaving, purging, etc., see Herod. II. 37. 41. 47. 77. Plutarch, *Isis and Osiris*, 5. Genesis 41. and 43. Ebers, *Aegypten u. d. Bücher Mose's*, I. p. 350.

generally very polite, well-behaved people.[40] Try them again, only once. I shall be very glad to take you in this evening, but I can't possibly do it before."

"It is as I thought! He's altered too, like everybody else! Osiris is dead and Seth rules the world again."

"Farewell! When the seven stars rise, our old Ethiopian slave, Nebununf, will wait for you here."

"Nebununf, that old rogue? I never want to see him again."

"Yes, the very same."

"Hm—well it's a good thing, when people stay as they were. To be sure I know some people who can't say so much of themselves, and who instead of minding their own business, pretend to heal inward diseases, and when a faithful old servant . . ."

"Hold your tongue, and wait patiently till evening."

These last words were spoken seriously, and produced the desired impression. The old man made another obeisance, and before his master left him, said: "I came here under the protection of Phanes, the former commander of the Greek mercenaries. He wishes very much to speak with you."

"That is his concern. He can come to me."

"You never leave that sick girl, whose eyes are as sound as . . ."

"Hib!"

"For all I care she may have a cataract in both. May Phanes come to you this evening?"

"I wished to be alone with you."

"So did I; but the Greek seems to be in a great hurry, and he knows nearly everything that I have to tell you."

---

40. Herod. I. 134.

"Have you been gossiping then?"

"No—not exactly—but . . ."

"I always thought you were a man to be trusted."

"So I was. But this Greek knows already a great deal of what I know, and the rest . . ."

"Well?"

"The rest he got out of me, I hardly know how myself. If I did not wear this amulet against an evil eye, I should have been obliged . . ."

"Yes, yes, I know the Athenian—I can forgive you. I should like him to come with you this evening. But I see the sun is already high in the heavens. I have no time to lose. Tell me in a few words what has happened."

"I thought this evening . . ."

"No, I must have at least a general idea of what has happened before I see the Athenian. Be brief."

"You have been robbed!"

"Is that all?"

"Is not that enough?"

"Answer me. Is that all?"

"Yes!"

"Then farewell."

"But Nebenchari! . . ."

The physician did not even hear this exclamation; the gates of the harem had already closed behind him.

When the Pleiades had risen, Nebenchari was to be found seated alone in one of the magnificent rooms assigned to his use on the eastern side of the palace, near to Kassandane's apartments. The friendly manner in which he had welcomed his old servant had given place to the serious expression which his face usually wore, and which had led the cheerful Persians to call him a morose and gloomy man.

Nebenchari was an Egyptian priest through and through; a member of that caste which never indulged in a jest, and never for a moment forgot to be dignified and solemn before the public; but when among their relations and their colleagues completely threw off this self-imposed restraint, and gave way at times even to exuberant mirth.

Though he had known Phanes in Sais, he received him with cold politeness, and, after the first greeting was ended, told Hib to leave them alone.

"I have come to you," said the Athenian, "to speak about some very important affairs."

"With which I am already acquainted," was the Egyptian's curt reply.

"I am inclined to doubt that," said Phanes with an incredulous smile.

"You have been driven out of Egypt, persecuted and insulted by Psamtik, and you have come to Persia to enlist Cambyses as an instrument of revenge against my country."

"You are mistaken. I have nothing against your country, but all the more against Amasis and his house."

"In Egypt the state and the king are one, as you very well know."

"On the contrary, my own observations have led me to think that the *priests* considered themselves one with the state."

"In that case you are better informed than I, who have always looked on the kings of Egypt as absolute.'

"So they are; but only in proportion as they know

how to emancipate themselves from the influence of your caste.—Amasis himself submits to the priests now."

"Strange intelligence!"

"With which, however, you have already long been made acquainted."

"Is that your opinion?"

"Certainly it is. And I know with still greater certainty that *once*—you hear me—*once*, he succeeded in bending the will of these rulers of his to his own."

"I very seldom hear news from home, and do not understand what you are speaking of."

"There I believe you, for if you knew what I meant and could stand there quietly without clenching your fist, you would be no better than a dog who only whimpers when he's kicked and licks the hand that torments him."

The physician turned pale. "I know that Amasis has injured and insulted me," he said, "but at the same time I must tell you that revenge is far too sweet a morsel to be shared with a stranger."

"Well said! As to my own revenge, however, I can only compare it to a vineyard where the grapes are so plentiful, that I am not able to gather them all myself."

"And you have come hither to hire good laborers."

"Quite right, and I do not even yet give up the hope of securing you to take a share in my vintage."

"You are mistaken. My work is already done. The gods themselves have taken it in hand. Amasis has been severely enough punished for banishing me from country, friends and pupils into this unclean land."

"You mean by his blindness perhaps?"

"Possibly."

"Then you have not heard that Petammon, one of your colleagues, has succeeded in cutting the skin, which covered the pupil of the eye and so restoring Amasis' sight?"

The Egyptian started and ground his teeth; recovered his presence of mind, however, in a moment, and answered: "Then the gods have punished the father through the children."

"In what way? Psamtik suits his father's present mood very well. It is true that Tachot is ill, but she prays and sacrifices with her father all the more for that; and as to Nitetis, you and I both know that her death will not touch him very closely."

"I really do not understand you."

"Of course not, so long as you fancy that I believe your beautiful patient to be Amasis' daughter."

The Egyptian started again, but Phanes went on without appearing to notice his emotion: "I know more than you suppose. Nitetis is the daughter of Hophra, Amasis' dethroned predecessor. Amasis brought her up as his own child—first, in order to make the Egyptians believe that Hophra had died childless; secondly, in order to deprive her of her rights to the throne; for you know women are allowed to govern on the Nile."[41]

"These are mere suppositions."

"For which, however, I can bring irrefragable proofs. Among the papers which your old servant Hib brought with him in a small box, there must be some letters

---

41. In the lists of kings of Egypt, the names of many queens occur who reigned in their own right, and these are corroborated by the monumental inscriptions. Lauth, indeed, in his Manetho, is of opinion that the divisions of the dynasties are connected with the reigns of the queens.

from a certain Sonnophre, a celebrated accoucheur,[42] your own father, which . . ."

"If that be the case, those letters are my property, and I have not the slightest intention of giving them up; besides which you might search Persia from one end to the other without finding any one who could decipher my father's writing."

"Pardon me, if I point out one or two errors into which you have fallen. First, this box is at present in my hands, and though I am generally accustomed to respect the rights of property, I must assure you that, in the present instance, I shall not return the box until its contents have served my purpose. Secondly, the gods have so ordained, that just at this moment there is a man in Babylon who can read every kind of writing known to the Egyptian priests. Do you perhaps happen to know the name of Onuphis?"

For the third time the Egyptian turned pale. "Are you certain," he said, "that this man is still among the living?"

"I spoke to him myself yesterday. He was formerly, you know, high-priest at Heliopolis, and was initiated into all your mysteries there. My wise countryman, Pythagoras of Samos, came to Egypt, and after

---

42. To judge from the pictures on the monuments and from the 1st Chap. of Exodus, it would seem that in ancient, as in modern Egypt, midwives were usually called in to assist at the birth of children; but it is also certain, that in difficult cases physicians were employed also. In the hieratic medical papyrus in Berlin, women are often spoken of as assisting at such times. In the medical Papyrus Ebers certain portions are devoted to subjects peculiar to women. There were special rooms set aside in private houses for the birth of children, as symbolical ones were reserved in the temples. These chambers were called *meschen*, and from them was derived the name given to midwives, *ta meschennu*.

submitting to some of your ceremonies,[43] was allowed to attend the lessons given in the schools for priests. His remarkable talents won the love of the great Onuphis and he taught him all the Egyptian mysteries,[44] which Pythagoras afterwards turned to account for the benefit of mankind. My delightful friend Rhodopis and I are proud of having been his pupils. When the rest

43. Iamblichus, *De vita Pythagorae*, II. p. 18. ed. Kiessl. Diod. I. 98. Plutarch, *Quaest. conv.* VIII. 8. 2. Onuphis is also called Oinuphis. In connection with this subject much is to be found in Röth, *Geschichte unserer abendländischen Philosophie*. It is a pity that this very clever book, which has been the result of such extended studies, should lose in value by the reckless boldness of its combinations.

44. Notwithstanding all the fables told about the Egyptian mysteries by the later Greek writers, especially the Neo-Platonists, we can get no clear idea of them. Much on this subject has been preserved in the papyri, but unfortunately whenever the mysteries are touched upon, the language of the priestly writers becomes so overburthened with metaphors and is made purposely so obscure, that it is very difficult to discover their meaning. The mysteries seem to have been the exclusive property of the priests, (see also Plut. *Isis and Osiris* 4-11.) and to have comprehended what was symbolized in the sacred ceremonies. The belief in one only god (as the Ritual of the Dead teaches also) seems to have been at the root of these mysteries, and they must have contained much that is noble and beautiful, as the wisest Greek philosophers, Lykurgus, Solon, Thales, Pythagoras, Demokritus, Plato, and many others, borrowed much from them in their teaching on political economy, geometry, astronomy and philosophy. Moses too owed many of his moral and sanitary laws to the acquaintance with these mysteries, which he made as pupil of the Egyptian priests. See Vol. I. note 251. A great deal of erudition has been spent by modern scholars on this subject, with but very small result; as, for instance, by I. G. Bremer, *Symbolische Weisheit der Aegypter*, &c.; R. Howard, *Revelations of Egyptian Mysteries;* F. Nork, *Andeutungen eines Systems der priesterlichen Mysteriosophie und Hierologie*. &c. A thorough understanding of the Ritual of the Dead, (already translated by Birch in his English translation of Bunsen's *Egypt's Place in the History of the World*), and the publication of the existing hieratic papyri, which, in the present advanced state of Egyptian philology, must soon be compelled to yield their secrets to earnest students, will in many ways clear up these mysteries of mysteries, if not do away with them entirely. Much has been already gained in this direction, especially from the inscriptions belonging to the times of the Ptolemies, the 1st, 17th and 125th chapters of the Ritual of the Dead, the Pantheistic text in the tombs of the kings and the temples of the oases, the book of Athem, and many manuscripts, whose text can be restored by comparison.

of your caste heard that Onuphis had betrayed the sacred mysteries, the ecclesiastical judges determined on his death. This was to be caused by a poison extracted from peach-kernels. The condemned man, however, heard of their machinations, and fled to Naukratis, where he found a safe asylum in the house of Rhodopis, whom he had heard highly praised by Pythagoras, and whose dwelling was rendered inviolable by the king's letter. Here he met Antimenidas the brother of the poet Alcæus* of Lesbos, who, having been banished by Pittakus, the wise ruler of Mitylene, had gone to Babylon, and there taken service in the army of Nebuchadnezzar, the King of Assyria. Antimenidas gave him letters to the Chaldæans. Onuphis travelled to the Euphrates, settled there, and was obliged to seek for some means of earning his daily bread, as he had left Egypt a poor man. He is now supporting himself in his old age, by the assistance which his superior knowledge enables him to render the Chaldæans in their astronomical observations from the tower of Bel. Onuphis is nearly eighty, but his mind is as clear as ever, and when I saw him yesterday and asked him to help me, his eyes brightened as he promised to do so. Your father was one of his judges, but he bears you no malice and sends you a greeting."

Nebenchari's eyes were fixed thoughtfully on the ground during this tale. When Phanes had finished, he gave him a penetrating look and said: "Where are my papers?"

"They are in Onuphis' hands. He is looking among them for the document I want."

"I expected to hear that. Be so good as to tell me

* See vol. 1. note 15. (Alcæus).

what the box is like, which Hib thought proper to bring over to Persia?"

"It is a small ebony trunk, with an exquisitely-carved lid. In the centre is a winged beetle, and on the four corners . . ."

"That contains nothing but a few of my father's notices and memorandums," said Nebenchari, drawing a deep breath of relief.

"They will very likely be sufficient for my purpose. I do not know whether you have heard, that I stand as high as possible in Cambyses' favor."

"So much the better for you. I can assure you, however, that the papers which would have been most useful to you have all been left behind in Egypt."

"They were in a large chest made of sycamore-wood and painted in colors."

"How do you know that?"

"Because—now listen well to what I am going to say, Nebenchari—because I can tell you (I do not swear, for our great master Pythagoras forbade oaths), that *this very chest*, with all it contained, was burnt in the grove of the temple of Neith, in Sais, by order of the king."

Phanes spoke slowly, emphasizing every syllable, and the words seemed to strike the Egyptian like so many flashes of lightning. His quiet coolness and deliberation gave way to violent emotion; his cheeks glowed and his eyes flashed. But only for one single minute; then the strong emotion seemed to freeze, his burning cheeks grew pale. "You are trying to make me hate my friends, in order to gain me as your ally," he said, coldly and calmly. "I know you Greeks very well. You are so intriguing and artful, that there is no lie, no fraud, too base, if it will only help to gain your purpose."

"You judge me and my countrymen in true Egyptian fashion; that is, they are foreigners, and therefore *must* be bad men. But this time your suspicions happen to be misplaced. Send for old Hib; he will tell you whether I am right or not."

Nebenchari's face darkened, as Hib came into the room.

"Come nearer," said he in a commanding tone to the old man.

Hib obeyed with a shrug of the shoulders.

"Tell me, have you taken a bribe from this man? Yes or no? I must know the truth; it can influence my future for good or evil. You are an old and faithful servant, to whom I owe a great deal, and so I will forgive you if you were taken in by his artifices, but I must know the truth. I conjure you to tell me by the souls of your fathers gone to Osiris!"

The old man's sallow face turned ashy pale as he heard these words. He gulped and wheezed some time before he could find an answer, and at last, after choking down the tears which had forced their way to his eyes, said, in a half-angry, half-whining tone: "Didn't I say so? they've bewitched him, they've ruined him in this wicked land. Whatever a man would do himself, he thinks others are capable of. Aye, you may look as angry as you like; it matters but little to me. What can it matter indeed to an old man, who has served the same family faithfully and honestly for sixty years, if they call him at last a rogue, a knave, a traitor, nay even a murderer, if it should take their fancy."

And the scalding tears flowed down over the old man's cheeks, sorely against his will.

The easily-moved Phanes clapped him on the

shoulder and said, turning to Nebenchari: "Hib is a faithful fellow. I give you leave to call me a rascal, if he has taken one single obolus from me."

The physician did not need Phanes' assurance; he had known his old servant too well and too long not to be able to read his simple, open features, on which his innocence was written as clearly as in the pages of an open book. "I did not mean to reproach you, old Hib," he said kindly, coming up to him. "How can any one be so angry at a simple question?"

"Perhaps you expect me to be pleased at such a shameful suspicion?"

"No, not that; but at all events now you can tell me what has happened at our house since I left."

"A pretty story that is! Why only to think of it makes my mouth as bitter, as if I were chewing wormwood."

"You said I had been robbed."

"Yes indeed: no one was ever so robbed before. There would have been some comfort if the knaves had belonged to the thieves' caste,[45] for then we should have got the best part of our property back again, and should not after all have been worse off than many another; but when . . ."

---

[45] The cunning son of the architect, who robbed the treasure-house of Rhampsinitus was, according to Herodotus, (II. 120), severely punished; but in Diod. I. 80. and Aul. Gell. XI. 18. we see that when thieves acknowledged themselves to the authorities to be such, they were not punished, though a strict watch was set over them. According to Diodorus, there was a president of the thieves' caste, from whom the stolen goods could be reclaimed on relinquishment of a fourth part of the same. This strange rule possibly owed its rise to the law, which compelled every Egyptian to appear once in each year before the authorities of his district and give an account of his means of subsistence. Those who made false statements were punished with death. Diod. I. 77. Thus no one who valued his life could escape the watchful eye of the police, and the thief sacrificed the best part of his gains in order to save his life.

"Keep to the point, for my time is limited."

"You need not tell me that; I see old Hib can't do anything right here in Persia. Well, be it so, you're master; you must give orders; I am only the servant, I must obey. I won't forget it. Well, as I was saying, it was just at the time when the great Persian embassy came over to Sais to fetch Nitetis, and made everybody stare at them as if they were monsters or prodigies, that this shameful thing happened. I was sitting on the mosquito-tower just as the sun was setting, playing with my little grandson, my Baner's* eldest boy—he's a fine strapping little lad now, wonderfully sharp and strong for his age. The rogue was just telling me how his father,—the Egyptians do that when their wives leave the children too much alone—had hidden his mother's shoes,[46] and I was laughing heartily, because my Baner won't let any of the little ones live with me, she always says I spoil them, and so I was glad she should have the trick played her—when all of a sudden there was such a loud knocking at the house-door, that I thought there must be a fire and let the child drop off my lap. Down the stairs I ran, three steps at a time, as fast as my long legs would carry me, and unbarred the door. Before I had time to ask them what they wanted, a whole crowd of temple-servants and policemen—there must have been at least fifteen of them—forced their

---

46. Plutarch writes that to walk barefoot in the streets was considered improper among the Egyptians. To make their wives domestic, therefore, the husbands hid their shoes. It was the women's duty, however, according to Herod. II. 35. to buy at market, which seems natural enough to us, but not at all so to the Greeks, as in their native country this duty was performed by the men.

* Baner signifies a palm-tree. Lepsius, *Denkm* IV. 74 c.

way into the house. Pichi,—you know, that impudent fellow from the temple of Neith,—pushed me back, barred the door inside and told the police to put me in fetters if I refused to obey him. Of course I got angry and did not use very civil words to them—you know that's my way when I'm put out—and what does that bit of a fellow do—by our god Thoth, the protector of knowledge who must know all, I'm speaking the truth—but order them to bind my hands, forbid me —me, old Hib—to speak, and then tell me that he had been told by the high-priest to order me five-and-twenty strokes, if I refused to do his bidding. He showed me the high-priest's ring, and so I knew there was nothing for it but to obey the villain, whether I would or no. And what was his modest demand? Why, nothing less than to give him all the written papers you had left behind. But old Hib is not quite so stupid as to let himself be caught in that way, though some people, who ought to know better, do fancy he can be bribed and is no better than the son of an ass. What did I do then? I pretended to be quite crushed into submission by the sight of the signet-ring, begged Pichi as politely as I could to unfasten my hands, and told him I would fetch the keys. They loosened the cords, I flew up the stairs five steps at a time, burst open the door of your sleeping-room, pushed my little grandson, who was standing by it, into the room and barred it within. Thanks to my long legs, the others were so far behind that I had time to get hold of the black box which you had told me to take so much care of, put it into the child's arms, lift him through the window on to the balcony which runs round the house towards the inner court. and tell him to put it at once into the pigeon-house. Then I opened the door as if nothing had happened, told Pichi the child had had a knife in his mouth, and that that was the reason I had run upstairs in such a hurry, and had put him out on the balcony to punish him. That brother of a hippopotamus was easily taken in, and then he made me show him over the house. First they found the great sycamore-chest which you had told me to take great care of too, then the papyrus-rolls on your writing-table, and so by degrees every written paper in the house. They made no distinction, but put all together into the great chest and carried it downstairs; the little black box, however, lay safe enough in the pigeon-house. My grandchild is the sharpest boy in all Sais!

"When I saw them really carrying the chest downstairs, all the anger I'd been trying so hard to keep down burst out again. I told the impudent fellows I would accuse them before the magistrates, nay, even before the king if necessary, and if those confounded Persians, who were having the city shown them, had not come up just then and made everybody stare at them, I could have roused the crowd to take my side. The same evening I went to my son-in-law—he is employed in the temple of Neith too, you know,—and begged him to make every effort to find out what had become of the papers. The good fellow has never forgotten the handsome dowry you gave my Baner when he married her, and in three days he came and told me he had seen your beautiful chest and all the rolls it contained burnt to ashes. I was so angry that I fell ill of the jaundice, but that did not hinder me from sending in a written accusation to the magistrates. The wretches,—I suppose only because they were priests too,—refused to take any notice of me or my complaint. Then I sent in a petition to the king, and was turned away there too with the shameful threat, that I should be considered guilty of high treason if I mentioned the papers again. I valued my tongue too much to take any further steps,[47] but the ground burnt under my feet; I could not stay in Egypt, I wanted to see you, tell you what they had done to you, and call on you, who are more powerful than your poor servant, to revenge yourself. And besides, I wanted to see the black box safe in your hands, lest they should take that from me too. And so, old man as I am, with a sad heart I left my home and my grandchildren to go forth into this foreign Typhon's land. Ah, the little lad was too sharp! As I was kissing him, he said: 'Stay with us, grandfather. If the foreigners make you unclean, they won't let me kiss you any more.' Baner sends you a hearty greeting, and my son-in-law told me to say he had found out that Psamtik, the crown-prince, and your rival, Petammon, had been the sole causes of this execrable deed. I could not make up my mind to trust myself on that Typhon's sea, so I travelled with an Arabian trading caravan as far as Tadmor, the Phoenician palm-tree station in the wilderness,[48] and then on to

47. The Egyptian law decreed the cutting out of the tongue as punishment for high treason. Diod. I. 78.

48. Tadmor, afterwards called Palmyra, was probably built by Solomon, though the Arabian legends give it a still earlier date. Schultens, *Index geogr.* Solomon's attention, as a wise king and enterprising trader, was more likely directed to this oasis in the midst of the Syrian deserts as a resting-place for his caravans, than as a place of defence against the attacks of the Syrians and Arabians, as Winer imagines in the third edition of his *Biblischen Realwörterbuch.* Palmyra rose quickly from small beginnings to great splendor, and to this day travellers are astonished at the size and beauty of its ruins. See R. Wood, *The Ruins of Palmyra.*—Carchemish on the Euphrates, famous for the battle between Necho and Nebuchadnezzar, Jerem. 46. 2.—the Circesium of later times—is named as the principal station on the road to Babylon by Palmyra. Josephus, *Ant.* VIII. 6. X. 6. Movers. *Das phönizische Alterthum,* II. 40. Ritter, *Erdkunde,* XI. *p.* 690. See also Maspero's treatise on this city.

Carchemish, on the Euphrates, with merchants from Sidon. The roads from Sardis and from Phœnicia meet there, and, as I was sitting very weary in the little wood before the station, a traveller arrived with the royal post-horses, and I saw at once that it was the former commander of the Greek mercenaries."

"And I," interrupted Phanes, "recognized just as soon in you, the longest and most quarrelsome old fellow that had ever come across my path. Oh, how often I've laughed to see you scolding the children, as they ran after you in the street whenever you appeared behind your master with the medicine-chest. The minute I saw you too I remembered a joke which the king once made in his own way, as you were both passing by. 'The old man,' he said, 'reminds me of a fierce old owl followed by a flight of small teazing birds, and Nebenchari looks as if he had a scolding wife, who will some day or other reward him for healing other people's eyes by scratching out his own!'"

"Shameful!" said the old man, and burst into a flood of execrations.

Nebenchari had been listening to his servant's tale in silence and thought. He had changed color from time to time and on hearing that the papers which had cost him so many nights of hard work had been burnt, his fists clenched and he shivered as if seized by biting frost.

Not one of his movements escaped the Athenian. He understood human nature; he knew that a jest is often much harder to bear than a grave affront, and therefore seized this opportunity to repeat the inconsiderate joke which Amasis had, it is true, allowed himself to make in one of his merry moods. Phanes had calculated rightly, and had the pleasure of seeing, that as he uttered the last words Nebenchari pressed his hand on a rose which lay on the table before him, and crushed it to pieces. The Greek suppressed a smile of satisfaction, and did not even raise his eyes from the ground, but continued speaking: "Well, now we must bring the travelling adventures of good old Hib to a close. I invited him to share my carriage. At first he refused to sit on the same cushion with such a godless foreigner, as I am, gave in, however, at last, had a good opportunity at the last station of showing the world how many clever processes of manipulation he had learnt from you and your father, in his treatment of Oropastes' wounded brother; he reached Babylon at last safe and sound, and there, as we could not get sight of you, owing to the melancholy poisoning of your country-woman, I succeeded in obtaining him a lodging in the royal palace itself. The rest you know already."

Nebenchari bowed assent and gave Hib a sign to leave the room, which the old man obeyed, grumbling and scolding in a low tone as he departed. When the door had closed on him, Nebenchari, the man whose calling was to heal, drew nearer to the soldier Phanes, and said: "I am afraid we cannot be allies after all, Greek."

"Why not?"

"Because I fear, that your revenge will prove far too mild when compared with that which I feel bound to inflict."

"On that head there is no need for solicitude," answered the Athenian. "May I call you my ally then?"

"Yes," answered the other; "but only on one condition."

"And that is—?"

"That you will procure me an opportunity of seeing our vengeance with my own eyes."

"That is as much as to say you are willing to accompany Cambyses' army to Egypt?"

"Certainly I am; and when I see my enemies pining in disgrace and misery I will cry unto them, 'Ah ha, ye cowards, the poor despised and exiled physician, Nebenchari, has brought this wretchedness upon you!' Oh,. my books, my books! They made up to me for my lost wife and child. Hundreds were to have learnt from them how to deliver the blind from the dark night in which he lives, and to preserve to the seeing the sweetest gift of the gods, the greatest beauty of the human countenance, the receptacle of light, the seeing eye. Now that my books are burnt I have lived in vain; the wretches have burnt me in burning my works. O my books, my books!" And he sobbed aloud in his agony. Phanes came up and took his hand, saying: "The Egyptians have struck you, my friend, but me they have maltreated and abused—thieves have broken into your granaries, but my hearth and home have been burnt to ashes by incendiaries. Do you know, man, what I have had to suffer at their hands? In persecuting me, and driving me out of Egypt, they only did what they had a right to do; by their law I was a condemned man; and I could have forgiven all they did to me personally, for I loved Amasis, as a man loves his friend. The wretch knew that, and yet he suffered them to commit a monstrous, an incredible act—an act that a man's brain refuses to take in. They stole like wolves by night into a helpless woman's house—they seized my children, a girl and boy, the pride, the joy and comfort of my homeless, wandering life. And how think you, did they treat them? The girl they kept in confinement, on the pretext that by so doing they should prevent me from betraying Egypt to Cambyses. But the boy—my beautiful, gentle boy—my only son—has been murdered by Psamtik's orders, and possibly with the knowledge of Amasis. My heart was withered and shrunk with exile and sorrow, but I feel that it expands—it beats more joyfully now that there is a hope of vengeance."

Nebenchari's sullen but burning glance met the flashing eye of the Athenian as he finished his tale; he gave him his hand and said: "We are allies."

The Greek clasped the offered hand and answered: "Our first point now is to make sure of the king's favor."

"I will restore Kassandane's sight."

"Is that in your power?"

"The operation which removed Amasis' blindness was my own discovery. Petammon stole it from my burnt papers."

"Why did you not exert your skill earlier?"

"Because I am not accustomed to bestow presents on my enemies."

Phanes shuddered slightly at these words, recovered himself, however, in a moment, and said: "And I am certain of the king's favor too. The Massagetan envoys have gone home to-day; peace has been granted them and . . ."

While he was speaking the door was burst open and one of Kassandane's eunuchs rushed into the room crying: "The Princess Nitetis is dying! Follow me at once, there is not a moment to lose."

The physician made a parting sign to his confederate,

and followed the eunuch to the dying-bed of the royal bride.

CHAPTER VIII.

THE sun was already trying to break a path for his rays through the thick curtains, that closed the window of the sick-room, but Nebenchari had not moved from the Egyptian girl's bedside. Sometimes he felt her pulse, or spread sweet-scented ointments on her forehead or chest, and then he would sit gazing dreamily into vacancy. Nitetis seemed to have sunk into a deep sleep after an attack of convulsions. At the foot of her bed stood six Persian doctors, murmuring incantations under the orders of Nebenchari, whose superior science they acknowledged, and who was seated at the bed's head.

Every time he felt the sick girl's pulse he shrugged his shoulders, and the gesture was immediately imitated by his Persian colleagues. From time to time the curtain was lifted and a lovely head appeared, whose questioning blue eyes fixed at once on the physician, but were always dismissed with the same melancholy shrug. It was Atossa. Twice she had ventured into the room, stepping so lightly as hardly to touch the thick carpet of Milesian wool, had stolen to her friend's bedside and lightly kissed her forehead, on which the pearly dew of death was standing, but each time a severe and reproving glance from Nebenchari had sent her back again into the next room, where her mother Kassandane was lying, awaiting the end.

Cambyses had left the sick-room at sunrise, on seeing that Nitetis had fallen asleep; he flung himself on to his horse, and accompanied by Phanes, Prexaspes, Otanes, Darius, and a number of courtiers, only just aroused from their sleep, took a wild ride through the game-park. He knew by experience, that he could best overcome or forget any violent mental emotion when mounted on an unmanageable horse.

Nebenchari started on hearing the sound of horses' hoofs in the distance. In a waking dream he had seen Cambyses enter his native land at the head of immense hosts; he had seen its cities and temples on fire, and its gigantic pyramids crumbling to pieces under the powerful blows of his mighty hand. Women and children lay in the smouldering ruins, and plaintive cries arose from the tombs in which the very mummies moved like living beings; and all these—priests, warriors, women, and children—the living and the dead—all had uttered his,—Nebenchari's,—name, and had cursed him as a traitor to his country. A cold shiver struck to his heart; it beat more convulsively than the blood in the veins of the dying girl at his side. Again the curtain was raised; Atossa stole in once more and laid her hand on his shoulder. He started and awoke. Nebenchari had been sitting three days and nights with scarcely any intermission by this sick-bed, and such dreams were the natural consequence.

Atossa slipped back to her mother. Not a sound broke the sultry air of the sick-room, and Nebenchari's thoughts reverted to his dream. He told himself that he was on the point of becoming a traitor and a criminal, the visions he had just beheld passed before him again, but this time it was another, and a different one which gained the foremost place. The forms of Amasis,—

who had laughed at and exiled him,—of Psamtik and the priests,—who had burnt his works,—stood near him; they were heavily fettered and besought mercy at his hands. . His lips moved, but this was not the place in which to utter the cruel words which rose to them. And then the stern man wiped away a tear as he remembered the long nights, in which he had sat with the reed in his hand, by the dull light of the lamp, carefully painting every sign of the fine hieratic character in which he committed his ideas and experience to writing. He had discovered remedies for many diseases of the eye, spoken of in the sacred books of Thoth and the writings of a famous old physician of Byblos as incurable, but, knowing that he should be accused of sacrilege by his colleagues, if he ventured on a correction or improvement of the sacred writings, he had entitled his work, "Additional writings on the treatment of diseases of the eye, by the great god Thoth,[49] newly discovered by the oculist Nebenchari."[50]

49. The discovery of nearly every science is attributed to the ibis-headed god Thoth, the writer or clerk of heaven, whom the Greeks compared to their god Hermes. (See Pietschmänn, *Hermes Trismegistos*, L. 1875.) He is second in rank to Osiris, the logos, the reason, whose counsels aid the creative power. Thoth, the "thrice greatest" (Trismegistos) was said to have written six books on the healing art, in which anatomy, the doctrine of disease, and the use of medicines are said to have been treated, besides diseases of the eye. The book on the use of medicine has been preserved to the present day in the Papyrus Ebers. Clem. Alex. *Strom.* VI. 260. See Iamblichus, *De Myst. Aegypt.* VI. 4. Isis also was glorified as a healing divinity and in later times Serapis. Diod. I. 25. Tacit. *Hist.* IV. 81,

50. In the writings of the ancient Egyptians which have come down to us, we read constantly of books and documents, which had been found under this or that statue of a god. This was certainly intended as a proof of their sanctity and divine authorship. It is true that in some works the name of the author is given; as for instance the Legend of the two brothers (Papyr. d'Orbiney) the author of which was named Anana. In the Papyrus Anastasi IV. seven other authors are named: Kagabu, Hora, Merapu, Bek en Ptah, Amen Mes, Sun-

He had resolved on bequeathing his works to the library at Thebes,[51] that his experience might be useful to his successors and bring forth fruit for the whole body of sufferers. This was to be his reward for the long nights which he had sacrificed to science—recognition after death, and fame for the caste to which he belonged. And there stood his old rival Petammon,

ro, and Mer Ptah. One of the hermetic books was devoted entirely to diseases of the eye, to which a large portion of the Papyrus Ebers was also allotted. The "book on the eyes" commences p. 56, line 1. The first prescription is for the alleviation of inflammation in the eye. Other remedies are given for watering of the eyes, blear-eyes, etc. Page 56, line 7 treats of iridectomy; page 57, lines 2-4 contains a remedy for contraction of the pupil; p. 57, lines 5-6 has a cure for white spots (albugo) in the eyes. Granulation, fatty matter in the visual organs, etc., are also mentioned. Page 63, line 8, gives a prescription for the eyes taken from the directions of a Semite from Byblos. It was in Alexandria too, in the third century B. C., that Herophilus of Chalcedon discovered and named the retina of the eye. In the Papyrus Ebers the physician Nebsecht and the priest Chui are mentioned.

51. The library of Thebes, which according to Diodorus bore the inscription ψυχῆς ἰατρεῖον, "place of healing for the soul," contained, according to Iamblichus, De Myst. Aegypt. VIII, 1., 20,000 hermetic or sacerdotal books. It was in the Ramesseum, which, according to Diodorus of Osymandyas, was erected to Rameses Miamun, ("the beloved of Ammon") of the monuments, in the fourteenth century B. C. Champollion discovered what must formerly have been the space occupied by the library in the ruins of the Ramesseum. At the entrance were representations of Thoth, the god of wisdom, and Safech, the goddess of history. Many of the hieratic papyri which we possess are dated from this library and it is often mentioned in the Egyptian books. Lepsius even discovered at Thebes the tombs of two of the librarians under Rameses Miamun. Their possessors were father and son, this office, like most others, having been hereditary. They were called "governors of the books," and "presidents of the books." See Lepsius, Chronologie Einleitung, p. 39. The libraries seem always to have belonged to the temples. At Dendera, Edfu, and especially at Philœ, the inscriptions state in which rooms of the temples the manuscripts were preserved. Thus in the Ritual of the Dead, 17. 47. 48. we read of the library of Osiris Seb; Galen speaks of a library belonging to the temple of Ptah at Memphis, where medical manuscripts had also been preserved. Gal. De comp. med. sec. gen. V. 2. and we know that there was one attached to the Serapeum at Alexandria. See Parthey's Monograph, das Alexandrinische Museum. Fr. Richtel, with the ingenuity peculiar to him, ascertained the number of works preserved in the Alexandrine library.

by the side of the crown-prince in the grove of Neith, and stirred the consuming fire, after having stolen his discovery of the operation of couching. Their malicious faces were tinged by the red glow of the flames, which rose with their spiteful laughter towards heaven, as if demanding vengeance. A little further off he saw in his dream Amasis receiving his father's letters from the hands of the high-priest. Scornful and mocking words were being uttered by the king; Neithotep looked exultant.—In these visions Nebenchari was so lost, that one of the Persian doctors was obliged to point out to him that his patient was awake. He nodded in reply, pointing to his own weary eyes with a smile, felt the sick girl's pulse, and asked her in Egyptian how she had slept.

"I do not know," she answered, in a voice that was hardly audible. "It seemed to me that I was asleep, and yet I saw and heard everything that had happened in the room. I felt so weak that I hardly knew whether I was awake or asleep. Has not Atossa been here several times?"

"Yes."

"And Cambyses stayed with Kassandane until sunrise; then he went out, mounted his horse Reksch, and rode into the game-park."

"How do you know that?"

"I saw it."

Nebenchari looked anxiously into the girl's shining eyes. She went on: "A great many dogs have been brought into the court behind this house."

"Probably the king has ordered a hunt, in order to deaden the pain which he feels at seeing you suffer."

"Oh, no. I know better what it means. Oropastes

taught me, that whenever a Persian dies dogs[52] are brought in, that the Divs may enter into them."

"But you are living, my mistress, and . . ."

"Oh, I know very well that I shall die. I knew that I had not many hours more to live, even if I had not seen how you and the other physicians shrugged your shoulders whenever you looked at me. That poison is deadly."

"You are speaking too much, my mistress, it will hurt you."

"Oh let me speak, Nebenchari! I must ask you to do something for me before I die."

"I am your servant."

"No, Nebenchari, you must be my friend and priest. You are not angry with me for having prayed to the Persian gods? Our own Hathor was always my best friend still. Yes, I see by your face that you forgive me. Then you must promise not to allow my corpse to be torn in pieces by dogs and vultures.* The thought is so very dreadful. You will promise to embalm my body and ornament it with amulets?"

"If the king allows."

"Of course he will. How could Cambyses possibly refuse my last request?"

"Then my skill is at your service."

"Thank you; but I have still something else to ask."

---

52. As soon as a Persian was dead, the *Drukhs Naçus*, or unclean demon of death, rushed to the spot in the form of a fly and seated himself on the corpse and on one of the living who were present, bringing destruction and taint. *Vendid.* Farg. VII. 2-24; Even to this day, the Parsees hold dogs before dying people. Ritter, *Erdkunde* IV. p. 1092. Possibly they do this in hopes that the spectre of death may enter into the animals; but the eyes of two especially spotted dogs were said to have the power of scaring the evil Drukhs. The latter remark is from the Dutch translator. See also Tiele, *Godsd. v. Zarath. p.* 184.

* See vol. I. note 110.

"You must be brief. My Persian colleagues are already making signs to me, to enjoin silence on you."

"Can't you send them away for a moment?"

"I will try to do so."

Nebenchari then went up and spoke to the Magi for a few minutes, and they left the room. An important incantation, at which no one but the two concerned might be present, and the application of a new and secret antidotal poison were the pretexts which he had used in order to get rid of them.

When they were alone, Nitetis drew a breath of relief and said: "Give me your priestly blessing on my long journey into the nether world, and prepare me for my pilgrimage to Osiris."

Nebenchari knelt down by her bed and in a low voice repeated hymns, Nitetis making devotional responses.

The physician represented Osiris, the lord of the nether world—Nitetis the soul, justifying itself before him.*

When these ceremonies were ended the sick girl breathed more freely. Nebenchari could not but feel moved in looking at this young suicide. He felt confident that he had saved a soul for the gods of his native land, had cheered the last sad and painful hours of one of God's good creatures. During these last moments, compassion and benevolence had excluded every bitter feeling; but when he remembered that this lovely creature owed all her misery to Amasis too, the old black cloud of thought darkened his mind again.—Nitetis, after lying silent for some time, turned to her new friend with a

* See vol. 1. note 251.

pleasant smile, and said: "I shall find mercy with the judges of the dead now, shall not I?"

"I hope and believe so."

"Perhaps I may find Tachot before the throne of Osiris, and my father . . ."

"Your father and mother are waiting for you there. Now in your last hour bless those who begot you, and curse those who have robbed you of your parents, your crown and your life."

"I do not understand you."

"Curse those who robbed you of your parents, crown and life, girl!" cried the physician again, rising to his full height, breathing hard as he said the words, and gazing down on the dying girl. "Curse those wretches, girl! that curse will do more in gaining mercy from the judges of the dead, than thousands of good works!" And as he said this he seized her hand and pressed it violently.

Nitetis looked up uneasily into his indignant face, and stammered in blind obedience, "I curse."

"Those who robbed my parents of their throne and lives!"

"Those who robbed my parents of their throne and their lives," she repeated after him, and then crying, "Oh, my heart!" sank back exhausted on the bed.

Nebenchari bent down, and before the royal physicians could return, kissed her forehead gently, murmuring: "She dies my confederate. The gods hearken to the prayers of those who die innocent. By carrying the sword into Egypt, I shall avenge king Hophra's wrongs as well as my own."

When Nitetis opened her eyes once more, a few hours later, Kassandane was holding her right hand, Atossa kneeling at her feet, and Crœsus standing at the head of her bed, trying, with the failing strength of old age, to support the gigantic frame of the king, who was so completely overpowered by his grief, that he staggered like a drunken man. The dying girl's eyes lighted up as she looked round on this circle. She was wonderfully beautiful. Cambyses came closer and kissed her lips; they were growing cold in death. It was the first kiss he had ever given her,—and the last. Two large tears sprang to her eyes; their light was fast growing dim; she murmured Cambyses' name softly, fell back in Atossa's arms, and died.

We shall not give a detailed account of the next few hours: it would be an unpleasant task to describe how, at a signal from the principal Persian doctor, every one, except Nebenchari and Crœsus, hastily left the room;— how dogs were brought in and their sagacious heads turned towards the corpse in order to scare the demon of death;*—how, directly after Nitetis' death, Kassandane, Atossa and their entire retinue moved into another house in order to avoid defilement;—how fire was extinguished throughout the dwelling, that the pure element might be removed from the polluting spirits of death;[53] how spells and exorcisms were muttered,[54] and how every person and thing, which had approached or been brought into contact with the dead body, was subjected to numerous purifications with water and pungent fluids.

53. In winter fire might be brought back to the deceased's dwelling nine days after the death, in summer not until a month had passed. *Vendid.* Farg. V. 130.

54. The entire tenth Fargard of the Vendidad is devoted to these spells.

* See note 52.

The same evening Cambyses was seized by one of his old epileptic attacks. Two days later he gave Nebenchari permission to embalm Nitetis' body in the Egyptian manner, according to her last wish. The king gave way to the most immoderate grief; he tore the flesh of his arms, rent his clothes and strewed ashes on his head, and on his couch. All the magnates of his court were obliged to follow his example. The troops mounted guard with rent banners and muffled drums. The cymbals and kettle-drums of the "Immortals" were bound round with crape. The horses which Nitetis had used, as well as all which were then in use by the court, were colored blue and deprived of their tails; the entire court appeared in mourning robes of dark brown, rent to the girdle,* and the Magi were compelled to pray three days and nights unceasingly for the soul of the dead,[55] which was supposed to be awaiting its sentence for eternity at the bridge Chinvat** on the third night.

Neither the king, Kassandane, nor Atossa shrank from submitting to the necessary purifications; they repeated, as if for one of their nearest relations, thirty prayers for the dead, while, in a house outside the city gates, Nebenchari began to embalm her body in the most costly manner, and according to the strictest rules of his art.[56]

55. The number of prayers to be said according to the degrees of relationship with the deceased are to be found *Vendidad* Farg. XII. 1.

56. Embalming was practised in three different ways. The first cost a talent of silver (£225.); the second 20 Minae (£60.) and the third was very inexpensive. Herod. II. 86-88. Diod. I. 91. The brain was first drawn out through the nose and the skull filled with spices. The intestines were then taken out, and the body filled in like manner with aromatic spices. When all was finished, the corpse was left 70 days in a solution of soda, and then wrapped in bandages of

* See note 29. ** See note 15.

For nine days Cambyses remained in a condition, which seemed little short of insanity. At times furious, at others dull and stupefied, he did not even allow his relations or the high-priest to approach him. On the morning of the tenth day he sent for the chief of the seven judges and commanded, that as lenient a sentence as possible should be pronounced on Gaumata. Nitetis, on her dying-bed, had begged him to spare the life of this unhappy youth.

One hour later the sentence was submitted to the king for ratification. It ran thus: "Victory to the king! Inasmuch as Cambyses, the eye of the world and the sun of righteousness, hath, in his great mercy, which is as broad as the heavens and as inexhaustible as the great deep, commanded us to punish the crime of the son of the Magi, Gaumata, with the indulgence of a mother instead of with the severity of a judge, we, the seven judges of the realm, have determined to grant his forfeited life. Inasmuch, however, as by the folly of this youth the lives of the noblest and best in this realm have been imperilled, and it may reasonably

byssus spread over with gum. The microscopical examinations of mummy-bandages made by Dr. Ure and Prof. Czermak have proved that byssus is linen, not cotton. The manner of embalming just described is the most expensive, and the latest chemical researches prove that the description given of it by the Greeks was tolerably correct. L. Penicher maintains that the bodies were first somewhat dried in ovens, and that then resin of the cedar-tree, or asphalte, was poured into every opening. *Traité sur les embaumements selon les anciens et les modernes.* Paris 1699. According to Herodotus, female corpses were embalmed by women. Herod. II. 89. The subject is treated in great detail by Pettigrew, *History of Egyptian Mummies.* London. 1834. Czermak's microscopical examinations of Egyptian mummies show how marvellously the smallest portions of the bodies were preserved, and confirm the statements of Herodotus on many points. The monuments also contain much information in regard to embalming, and we now know the purpose of nearly all the amulets placed with the dead.

be apprehended that he may again abuse the marvellous likeness to Bartja, the noble son of Cyrus, in which the gods have been pleased in their mercy to fashion his form and face, and thereby bring prejudice upon the pure and righteous, we have determined to disfigure him in such wise, that in the time to come it will be a light matter to discern between this, the most worthless subject of the realm, and him who is most worthy. We therefore, by the royal will and command, pronounce sentence, that both the ears of Gaumata be cut off, for the honor of the righteous and shame of the impure."

Cambyses confirmed this sentence at once, and it was excuted the same day.

Oropastes did not dare to intercede for his brother, though this ignominious punishment mortified his ambitious mind more than even a sentence of death could have done. As he was afraid that his own influence and consideration might suffer through this mutilated brother, he ordered him to leave Babylon at once for a country-house of his own on Mount Arakadris.[57]

During the few days which had just passed, a shabbily-dressed and closely-veiled woman had watched day and night at the great gate of the palace; neither the threats of the sentries nor the coarse jests of the palace-servants could drive her from her post. She never allowed one of the less important officials to pass without eagerly questioning him, first as to the state of the

---

57. This mountain is mentioned in the inscription of Behistân I. §. IX. With reference to Gaumata's punishment, the same which Herodotus says was inflicted on the pretended Smerdis, we would observe that even Persians of high rank were sometimes deprived of their ears. In the Behistân inscription (Spiegel p. 15 and 21.) the ears, tongue and nose of the man highest in rank among the rebels, Fravartis, (Phraortes) were cut off. Similar punishments are quoted by Brisson. *De regn Persar.* II. p. 334-5.

Egyptian Princess, and then what had become of Gaumata. When his sentence was told her as a good joke by a chattering lamp-lighter, she went off into the strangest excitement, and astonished the poor man so much by kissing his robe, that he thought she must be crazed, and gave her an alms. She refused the money, but remained at her post, subsisting on the bread which was given her by the compassionate distributors of food. Three days later Gaumata himself, with his head bound up, was driven out in a closed *harmamaxa*. She rushed to the carriage and ran screaming by the side of it, until the driver stopped his mules and asked what she wanted. She threw back her veil and showed the poor, suffering youth her pretty face covered with deep blushes. Gaumata uttered a low cry as he recognized her, collected himself, however, in a moment, and said: "What do you want with me, Mandane?"

The wretched girl raised her hands beseechingly to him, crying: "Oh, do not leave me, Gaumata! Take me with you! I forgive you all the misery you have brought on me and my poor mistress. I love you so much, I will take care of you and nurse you as if I were the lowest servant-girl."

A short struggle passed in Gaumata's mind. He was just going to open the carriage-door and clasp Mandane—his earliest love—in his arms, when the sound of horses' hoofs coming nearer struck on his ear, and looking round he saw a carriage full of Magi, among whom were several who had been his companions at the school for priests. He felt ashamed and afraid of being seen by the very youths, whom he had often treated proudly and haughtily because he was the brother of the high-priest, threw Mandane a purse of gold, which his brother had given him at parting, and ordered the driver to go on as fast as possible. The mules galloped off. Mandane kicked the purse away, rushed after the carriage and clung to it firmly. One of the wheels caught her dress and dragged her down. With the strength of despair she sprang up, ran after the mules, overtook them on a slight ascent which had lessened their speed, and seized the reins. The driver used his three-lashed whip, or scourge, the creatures reared, pulled the girl down and rushed on. Her last cry of agony pierced the wounds of the mutilated man like a sharp lance-thrust.

On the twelfth day after Nitetis' death Cambyses went out hunting, in the hope that the danger and excitement of the sport might divert his mind. The magnates and men of high rank at his court received him with thunders of applause, for which he returned cordial thanks. These few days of grief had worked a great change in a man so unaccustomed to suffering as Cambyses. His face was pale, his raven-black hair and beard had grown grey, and the consciousness of victory which usually shone in his eyes was dimmed. Had he not, only too painfully, experienced that there was a stronger will than his own, and that, easily as he could destroy, it did not lie in his power to preserve the life of the meanest creature? Before starting, Cambyses mustered his troop of sportsmen, and calling Gobryas, asked why Phanes was not there.

"My King did not order . . ."

"He is my guest and companion, once for all; call him and follow us."

Gobryas bowed, dashed back to the palace, and in

half an hour reappeared among the royal retinue with Phanes.

The Athenian was warmly welcomed by many of the group, a fact which seems strange when we remember that courtiers are of all men the most prone to envy, and a royal favorite always the most likely object to excite their ill will. But Phanes seemed a rare exception to this rule. He had met the Achæmenidæ in so frank and winning a manner, had excited so many hopes by the hints he had thrown out of an expected and important war, and had aroused so much merriment by well-told jests, such as the Persians had never heard before, that there were very few who did not welcome his appearance gladly, and when—in company with the king—he separated from the rest in chase of a wild ass, they openly confessed to one another, that they had never before seen so perfect a man. The clever way in which he had brought the innocence of the accused to light, the finesse which he had shown in securing the king's favor, and the ease with which he had learnt the Persian language in so short a time, were all subjects of admiration. Neither was there one even of the Achæmenidæ themselves, who exceeded him in beauty of face or symmetry of figure. In the chase he proved himself a perfect horseman, and in a conflict with a bear an exceptionally courageous and skilful sportsman. On the way home, as the courtiers were extolling all the wonderful qualities possessed by the king's favorite, old Araspes exclaimed, "I quite agree with you that this Greek, who by the way has proved himself a better soldier than anything else, is no common man, but I am sure you would not praise him half as much, if he were not a foreigner and a novelty."

Phanes happened to be only separated from the speaker by some thick bushes, and heard these words. When the other had finished, he went up and said, smiling: "I understood what you said and feel obliged to you for your kind opinion. The last sentence, however, gave me even more pleasure than the first, because it confirmed my own idea that the Persians are the most generous people in the world—they praise the virtues of other nations as much, or even more, than their own."

His hearers smiled, well pleased at this flattering remark, and Phanes went on: "How different the Jews are now, for instance! They fancy themselves the exclusive favorites of the gods, and by so doing incur the contempt of all wise men, and the hatred of the whole world. And then the Egyptians! You have no idea of the perversity of that people. Why, if the priests could have their way entirely, (and they have a great deal of power in their hands) not a foreigner would be left alive in Egypt, nor a single stranger allowed to enter the country. A true Egyptian would rather starve, than eat out of the same dish with one of us. There are more strange, astonishing and wonderful things to be seen in that country than anywhere else in the world. And yet, to do it justice, I must say that Egypt has been well spoken of as the richest and most highly cultivated land under the sun. The man who possesses that kingdom need not envy the very gods themselves. It would be mere child's play to conquer that beautiful country. Ten years there gave me a perfect insight into the condition of things, and I know that their entire military caste would not be sufficient to resist one such troop as your Immortals. Well, who knows what the future may bring! Perhaps we may all make a little trip together to the Nile some day. In my opinion, your good swords have been rather long idle."

These well-calculated words were received with such shouts of applause, that the king turned his horse to enquire the cause. Phanes answered quickly that the Achæmenidæ were rejoicing in the thought that a war might possibly be near at hand.

"What war?" asked the king, with the first smile that had been seen on his face for many days.

"We were only speaking in general of the possibility of such a thing," answered Phanes carelessly; then, riding up to the king's side, his voice took an impressive tone full of feeling, and looking earnestly into his face, he began: "It is true, my Sovereign, that I was not born in this beautiful country as one of your subjects, nor can I boast of a long acquaintance with the most powerful of monarchs, but yet I cannot resist the presumptuous, perhaps criminal thought, that the gods at my birth appointed me to be your real friend. It is not your rich gifts that have drawn me to you. I did not need them, for I belong to the wealthier class of my countrymen, and I have no son,—no heir,—to whom I can bequeath my treasures. Once I had a boy—a beautiful, gentle child; . . but I was not going to speak of that,—I . . . Are you offended at my freedom of speech, my Sovereign?"

"What is there to offend me?" answered the king, who had never been spoken to in this manner before, and felt strongly attracted to the original foreigner.

"Till to-day I felt that your grief was too sacred to be disturbed, but now the time has come to rouse you from it and to make your heart glow once more.

You will have to hear what must be very painful to you."

"There is nothing more now, that can grieve me."

"What I am going to tell you will not give you pain; on the contrary, it will rouse your anger."

"You make me curious."

"You have been shamefully deceived; you and that lovely creature, who died such an early death a few days ago."

Cambyses' eyes flashed a demand for further information.

"Amasis, the King of Egypt, has dared to make sport of you, the lord of the world. That gentle girl was not his daughter, though she herself believed that she was; she . . ."

"Impossible!"

"It would seem so, and yet I am speaking the simple truth. Amasis spun a web of lies, in which he managed to entrap, not only the whole world, but you too, my Sovereign. Nitetis, the most lovely creature ever born of woman, was the daughter of a king, but not of the usurper Amasis. Hophra, the rightful king of Egypt, was the father of this pearl among women. You may well frown, my Sovereign. It is a cruel thing to be betrayed by one's friends and allies."

Cambyses spurred his horse, and after a silence of some moments, kept by Phanes purposely, that his words might make a deeper impression, cried, "Tell me more! I wish to know everything."

"Hophra had been living twenty years[58] in easy

---

58. According to Herodotus, II. 169. Amasis treated his dethroned predecessor with great lenity, and spared his life until the Egyptians fell upon him and hung him. On account of Nitetis' age, we are obliged to allow Hophra twenty years of life after his dethrone-

captivity in Sais after his dethronement, when his wife, who had borne him three children and buried them all, felt that she was about to give birth to a fourth. Hophra, in his joy, determined to offer a sacrifice of thanksgiving in the temple of Pacht,* the Egyptian goddess supposed to confer the blessing of children, when, on his way thither, a former magnate of his court, named Patarbemis,[59] whom, in a fit of unjust anger, he had ignominiously mutilated, fell upon him with a troop of slaves and massacred him. Amasis had the unhappy widow brought to his palace at once, and assigned her an apartment next to the one occupied by his own queen Ladice, who was also expecting soon to give birth to a child. A girl was born to Hophra's widow, but the mother died in the same hour, and two days later Ladice bore a child also.—But I see we are in the court of the palace. If you allow, I will have the report of the physician, by whom this imposture was effected, read before you. Several of his notes have, by a remarkable conjuncture of circumstances, which I will explain to you later, fallen into my hands. A former high-priest of Heliopolis, Onuphis, is now living in Babylon, and understands all the different styles of writing in use among his countrymen.[60] Nebenchari will, of course,

---

ment. It is the only way in which we can rescue Herodotus' narrative, which forms the basis of our tale. Amasis would scarcely have dared to send Cambyses a bride of forty; for it must be remembered that on the Nile a woman of forty is older than one of sixty in Europe. This subject has already been mentioned in our preface.

59. Herod. II. 162.

60. The three Egyptian styles of writing existed already at the time of Amasis, though the demotic or popular style used for correspondence, does not seem much older than the dynasty to which he belonged, (the 26th).

* See vol. I. note 53.

refuse to help in disclosing an imposture, which must inevitably lead to the ruin of his country."

"In an hour I expect to see you here with the man you have just spoken of. Crœsus, Nebenchari, and all the Achæmenidæ who were in Egypt, will have to appear also. I must have certainty before I can act, and your testimony alone is not sufficient, because I know from Amasis, that you have cause to feel a grudge against his house."

At the time appointed all were assembled before the king in obedience to his command.

Onuphis, the former high-priest, was an old man of eighty. A pair of large, clear, intelligent, grey eyes looked out of a head so worn and wasted, as to be more like a mere skull than the head of a living man. He held a large papyrus-roll in his gaunt hand, and was seated in an easy chair, as his paralyzed limbs did not allow of his standing, even in the king's presence. His dress was snow-white, as beseemed a priest, but there were patches and rents to be seen here and there. His figure might perhaps once have been tall and slender, but it was now so bent and shrunk by age, privation and suffering, as to look unnatural and dwarfish, in comparison with the size of his head.

Nebenchari, who revered Onuphis, not only as a high-priest deeply initiated in the most solemn mysteries, but also on account of his great age,[61] stood by his side and arranged his cushions. At his left stood Phanes, and then Crœsus, Darius and Prexaspes.

The king sat upon his throne. His face was dark

---

61. Among the Egyptians it was a sacred duty to honor the aged. Herod. II. 80. Cicero, *De Senectute*, 18. The Egyptian remains testify to the same. In the Prisse Papyrus, the fifth commandment of the Mosaic law exists, even including the annexed promise.

and stern as he broke the silence with the following words: "This noble Greek, who, I am inclined to believe, is my friend, has brought me strange tidings. He says that I have been basely deceived by Amasis,— that my deceased wife was not his, but his predecessor's daughter."

A murmur of astonishment ran through the assembly.

"This old man is here to prove the imposture."

Onuphis gave a sign of assent.

"Prexaspes, my first question is to you. When Nitetis was entrusted to your care, was it expressly said that she was the daughter of Amasis?"

"Expressly. Nebenchari had, it is true, praised Tachot to the noble Kassandane as the most beautiful of the twin sisters; but Amasis insisted on sending Nitetis to Persia. I imagined that, by confiding his most precious jewel to your care, he meant to put you under a special obligation; and as it seemed to me that Nitetis surpassed her sister, not only in beauty but in dignity of character, I ceased to sue for the hand of Tachot. In his letter to you too, as you will remember, he spoke of confiding to you his most beautiful, his dearest child."

"Those were his words."

"And Nitetis was, without question, the more beautiful and the nobler of the two sisters," said Crœsus in confirmation of the envoy's remark. "But it certainly did strike me that Tachot was her royal parents' favorite."

"Yes," said Darius, "without doubt. Once, at a revel, Amasis joked Bartja in these words: 'Don't look too deep into Tachot's eyes, for if you were a god, I could not allow you to take her to Persia!' Psamtik was evidently annoyed at this remark and said to the king, 'Father, remember Phanes,'"

"Phanes!"

"Yes, my Sovereign," answered the Athenian. "Once, when he was intoxicated, Amasis let out his secret to me, and Psamtik was warning him not to forget himself a second time."

"Tell the story as it occurred."

"On my return from Cyprus to Sais as a conqueror, a great entertainment was given at court. Amasis distinguished me in every way, as having won a rich province for him, and even, to the dismay of his own countrymen, embraced me. His affection increased with his intoxication, and at last, as Psamtik and I were leading him to his private apartments, he stopped at the door of his daughter's room, and said: "The girls sleep there. If you will put away your own wife, Athenian, I will give you Nitetis. I should like to have you for a son-in-law. There's a secret about that girl, Phanes; she's not my own child.' Before his drunken father could say more, Psamtik laid his hand before his mouth, and sent me roughly away to my lodging, where I thought the matter over and conjectured what I now, from reliable sources, know to be the truth. I entreat you, command this old man to translate those parts of the physician Sonnophre's journal, which allude to this story."

Cambyses nodded his consent, and the old man began to read in a voice far louder than any one could have supposed possible from his infirm appearance: "On the fifth day of the month Thoth,[62] I was sent for

---

62. The month of Thoth or Taut lasted from August 29 till September 27. The 5th of Thoth was therefore equal to our 2nd of September.

by the king. I had expected this, as the queen was near her confinement. With my assistance she was easily and safely delivered of a child—a weakly girl. As soon as the nurse had taken charge of this child, Amasis led me behind a curtain which ran across his wife's sleeping-apartment. There lay another infant, which I recognized as the child of Hophra's widow, who herself had died under my hands on the third day of the same month. The king then said, pointing to this strong child, 'This little creature has no parents, but, as it is written in the law that we are to show mercy to the desolate orphans,[63] Ladice and I have determined to bring her up as our own daughter. We do not, however, wish that this deed should be made known, either to the world or to the child herself, and I ask you to keep the secret and spread a report that Ladice has given birth to twins. If you accomplish this according to our wish, you shall receive to-day five thousand rings of gold,* and the fifth part of this sum yearly, during your life.' I made my obeisance in silence, ordered every one to leave the sick room, and, when I again called them in, announced that Ladice had given birth to a second girl. Amasis' real child received the name of Tachot,—the spurious one was called Nitetis."

At these words Cambyses rose from his seat, and strode through the hall; but Onuphis continued, with-

---

63. We gather, not only from the Ritual of the Dead, but from many others of the Egyptian documents, that charity, especially towards widows and orphans, was commanded by their religion. Thus, for instance, a governor of high rank boasts on his tomb at Beni-hassan (Lepsius, *Denkmäler* II. Vol. 22.) that he has never injured a weak child (orphan is perhaps meant) nor done evil to a widow.

* See vol. I. note 172.

out allowing himself to be disturbed: "Sixth day of the month Thoth. This morning I had just lain down to rest after the fatigues of the night, when a servant appeared with the promised gold and a letter from the king, asking me to procure a dead child, to be buried with great ceremony as the deceased daughter of King Hophra. After a great deal of trouble I succeeded, an hour ago, in obtaining one from a poor girl who had given birth to a child secretly in the house of the old woman, who lives at the entrance to the City of the Dead. The little one had caused her shame and sorrow enough, but she would not be persuaded to give up the body of her darling, until I promised that it should be embalmed and buried in the most splendid manner. We put the little corpse into my large medicine-chest, my son Nebenchari carried it this time instead of my servant Hib, and so it was introduced into the room where Hophra's widow had died. The poor girl's baby will receive a magnificent funeral. I wish I might venture to tell her, what a glorious lot awaits her darling after death. Nebenchari has just been sent for by the king."

At the second mention of this name, Cambyses stopped in his walk, and said: "Is our oculist Nebenchari the man whose name is mentioned in this manuscript?"

"Nebenchari," returned Phanes, "is the son of this very Sonnophre who changed the children."

The physician did not raise his eyes; his face was gloomy and sullen.

Cambyses took the roll of papyrus out of Onuphis' hand, looked at the characters with which it was covered, shook his head, went up to Nebenchari and said:

"Look at these characters and tell me if it is your father's writing."

Nebenchari fell on his knees and raised his hands.

"I ask, did your father paint these signs?"

"I do not know—whether . . . Indeed . . ."

"I will know the truth. Yes or no?"

"Yes, my King; but . . ."

"Rise, and be assured of my favor. Faithfulness to his ruler is the ornament of a subject; but do not forget that I am your king now. Kassandane tells me, that you are going to undertake a delicate operation to-morrow in order to restore her sight. Are you not venturing too much?"

"I can depend on my own skill, my Sovereign."

"One more question. Did you know of this fraud?"

"Yes."

"And you allowed me to remain in error?"

"I had been compelled to swear secrecy, and an oath . . ."

"An oath is sacred. Gobryas, see that both these Egyptians receive a portion from my table. Old man, you seem to require better food."

"I need nothing beyond air to breathe, a morsel of bread and a draught of water to preserve me from dying of hunger and thirst, a clean robe, that I may be pleasing in the eyes of the gods and in my own, and a small chamber for myself, that I may be a hindrance to no man. I have never been richer than to-day."

"How so?"

"I am about to give away a kingdom."

"You speak in enigmas."

"By my translation of to-day I have proved, that your deceased consort was the child of Hophra. Now, our law allows the daughter of a king to succeed to the throne, when there is neither son nor brother* living; if she should die childless, her husband becomes her legitimate successor. Amasis is a usurper, but the throne of Egypt is the lawful birthright of Hophra and his descendants. Psamtik forfeits every right to the crown the moment that a brother, son, daughter or son-in-law of Hophra appears. I can, therefore, salute my present sovereign as the future monarch of my own beautiful native land."

Cambyses smiled self-complacently, and Onuphis went on: "I have read in the stars too, that Psamtik's ruin and your own accession to the throne of Egypt have been fore-ordained."

"We'll show that the stars were right," cried the king, "and as for you, you liberal old fellow, I command you to ask me any wish you like."

"Give me a conveyance, and let me follow your army to Egypt. I long to close my eyes on the Nile."

"Your wish is granted. Now, my friends, leave me, and see that all those who usually eat at my table are present at this evening's revel. We will hold a council of war over the luscious wine. Methinks a campaign in Egypt will pay better than a contest with the Massagetæ."

He was answered by a joyful shout of "Victory to the king!" They all then left the hall, and Cambyses, summoning his dressers, proceeded for the first time to exchange his mourning garments for the splendid royal robes.

---

* See note 41.

Crœsus and Phanes went into the green and pleasant garden lying on the eastern side of the royal palace, which abounded in groves of trees, shrubberies, fountains and flower-beds. Phanes was radiant with delight; Crœsus full of care and thought.

"Have you duly reflected," said the latter, "on the burning brand that you have just flung out into the world?"

"It is only children and fools that act without reflection," was the answer.

"You forget those who are deluded by passion."

"I do not belong to that number."

"And yet revenge is the most fearful of all the passions."

"Only when it is practised in the heat of feeling. My revenge is as cool as this piece of iron; but I know my duty."

"The highest duty of a good man, is to subordinate his own welfare to that of his country."

"That I know."

"You seem to forget, however, that with Egypt you are delivering your own country over to the Persians."

"I do not agree with you there."

"Do you believe, that when all the rest of the Mediterranean coasts belong to Persia, she will leave your beautiful Greece untouched?"

"Certainly not, but I know my own countrymen; I believe them fully capable of a victorious resistance to the hosts of the barbarians, and am confident that their courage and greatness will rise with the nearness of the danger. It will unite our divided tribes into one great nation, and be the ruin of the tyrants."

"I cannot argue with you, for I am no longer

acquainted with the state of things in your native country, and besides, I believe you to be a wise man— not one who would plunge a nation into ruin merely for the gratification of his own ambition. It is a fearful thing that entire nations should have to suffer for the guilt of one man, if that man be one who wears a crown. And now, if my opinion is of any importance to you, tell me what the deed was which has roused your desire of vengeance."

"Listen then, and never try again to turn me from my purpose. You know the heir to the Egyptian throne, and you know Rhodopis too. The former was, for many reasons, my mortal enemy, the latter the friend of every Greek, but mine especially. When I was obliged to leave Egypt, Psamtik threatened me with his vengeance; your son Gyges saved my life. A few weeks later my two children came to Naukratis, in order to follow me out to Sigeum. Rhodopis took them kindly under her protection, but some wretch had discovered the secret and betrayed it to the prince. The very next night her house was surrounded and searched, —my children found and taken captive. Amasis had meanwhile become blind, and allowed his miserable son to do what he liked; the wretch dared to . . ."

" Kill your only son ?"
" You have said it."
" And your other child ?"
" The girl is still in their hands."
" They will do her an injury when they hear . . ."
" Let her die. Better go to one's grave childless, than unrevenged."
" I understand. I cannot blame you any longer. The boy's blood must be revenged."

And so saying, the old man pressed the Athenian's right hand. The latter dried his tears, mastered his emotion, and cried: "Let us go to the council of war now. No one can be so thankful for Psamtik's infamous deeds as Cambyses. That man with his hasty passions was never made to be a prince of peace."

"And yet it seems to me the highest duty of a king is to work for the inner welfare of his kingdom. But human beings are strange creatures; they praise their butchers more than their benefactors. How many poems have been written on Achilles! but did any one ever dream of writing songs on the wise government of Pittakus?"*

"More courage is required to shed blood, than to plant trees."

"But much more kindness and wisdom to heal wounds, than to make them.—I have still one question which I should very much like to ask you, before we go into the hall. Will Bartja be able to stay at Naukratis when Amasis is aware of the king's intentions?"

"Certainly not. I have prepared him for this, and advised his assuming a disguise and a false name."

"Did he agree?"

"He seemed willing to follow my advice."

"But at all events it would be well to send a messenger to put him on his guard."

"We will ask the king's permission."

"Now we must go. I see the wagons containing the viands of the royal household just driving away from the kitchen."

"How many people are maintained from the king's table daily?"

* See vol. I. notes 15, 16.

"About fifteen thousand."[64]

"Then the Persians may thank the gods, that their king only takes one meal a day."

CHAPTER IX.

Six weeks after these events a little troop of horsemen might have been seen riding towards the gates of Sardis.

The horses and their riders were covered with sweat and dust. The former knew that they were drawing near a town, where there would be stables and mangers, and exerted all their remaining powers; but yet their pace did not seem nearly fast enough to satisfy the impatience of two men, dressed in Persian costume, who rode at the head of the troop.

The well-kept royal road ran through fields of good black, arable land, planted with trees of many different kinds. It crossed the outlying spurs of the Tmolus range of mountains. At their foot stretched rows of olive, citron and plane-trees, plantations of mulberries and vines; at a higher level grew firs, cypresses and nut-tree copses. Fig-trees and date-palms, covered with fruit, stood sprinkled over the fields; and the woods and meadows were carpeted with brightly-colored and sweetly-scented flowers. The road led over ravines and brooks, now half dried up by the heat of summer, and here and there the traveller came upon a well at the side of the road, carefully enclosed, with seats for the weary, and sheltering shrubs. Oleanders bloomed in the more

---

64. This immense royal household is said to have cost 400 talents, that is £90,000, daily. Athenæus, *Deipn. p.* 607.

damp and shady places; slender palms waved wherever the sun was hottest. Over this rich landscape hung a deep blue, perfectly cloudless sky, bounded on its southern horizon by the snowy peaks of the Tmolus mountains, and on the west by the Sipylus range of hills, which gave a bluish shimmer in the distance.

The road went down into the valley, passing through a little wood of birches, the stems of which, up to the very tree-top, were twined with vines covered with bunches of grapes.

The horsemen stopped at a bend in the road, for there, before them, in the celebrated valley of the Hermus, lay the golden Sardis, formerly the capital of the Lydian kingdom and residence of its king, Crœsus.[65]

Above the reed-thatched roofs of its numerous houses rose a black, steep rock; the white marble buildings on its summit could be seen from a great distance. These buildings formed the citadel, round the threefold walls of which, many centuries before, King Meles had carried a lion in order to render them impregnable.[66] On its southern side the citadel-rock was not so steep, and houses had been built upon it. Crœsus' former palace lay to the north, on the golden-sanded Pactolus. This reddish-colored river flowed above the market-place, (which, to our admiring travellers, looked like a barren spot in the midst of a blooming meadow), ran on in a westerly direction, and then entered a narrow mountain valley, where it washed the walls of the temple of Cybele.

Large gardens stretched away towards the east, and in the midst of them lay the lake Gygæus, covered with

65. Aeschylus, *Pers.* v. 45.
66. Herod. I. 84 and 94. V. 101.

gay boats and snowy swans, and sparkling like a mirror.

A short distance from the lake were a great number of artificial mounds, three of which were especially noticeable from their size and height.[67]

"What can those strange-looking earth-heaps mean?" said Darius, the leader of the troop, to Prexaspes, Cambyses' envoy, who rode at his side.

"They are the graves of former Lydian kings," was the answer. "The middle one is in memory of the princely pair Panthea and Abradatas,* and the largest, that one to the left, was erected to the father of Crœsus, Alyattes. It was raised by the tradesmen, mechanics, and girls, to their late king, and on the five columns, which stand on its summit, you can read how much each of these classes contributed to the work. The girls were the most industrious.[68] Gyges' grandfather is said to have been their especial friend."

---

67. The lake of Gygæa was known as early as Homer's day. *Iliad.* II. 863. XX. 386, 392. According to Prokesch, it is 3 leagues long and one broad. See also Hamilton's *Asia Minor*, I. p. 145. Herodotus (I. 93.) calls the tombs of the Lydian kings the largest works of human hands, next to the Egyptian and Babylonian. These cone-shaped hills can be seen to this day, standing near the ruins of Sardis, not far from the lake of Gygæa. Hamilton (*Asia Minor*, I. p. 45.) counted some sixty of them, and could not ride round the hill of Alyattes in less than ten minutes. Prokesch saw 100 such tumuli *(Denkwürdigkeiten und Erinnerungen aus dem Orient).* The largest, the tomb of Alyattes, still measures 3400 feet in circumference, and the height of its slope is 650 feet. According to Prokesch, gigantic Phallus columns lie on some of these graves. Spiegelthal, the Prussian consul at Smyrna, discovered a separate chamber in the tumulus of Alyattes. *Monatsberichte der Berliner Akademie der Wisssenschaften,* Dec. 1854. p. 700. Farther particulars by E. Curtius. *Beitrage zur Geschichte und Topographie Kleinasiens. Abhandl. d. k. A. d. Wissenschaften zu Berlin.* 1872. Ph-h. Kl. page 84 and following.

68. Herod. I. 93.

* See note 22.

"Then the grandson must have degenerated very much from the old stock."

"Yes, and that seems the more remarkable, because Crœsus himself in his youth was by no means averse to women, and the Lydians generally are devoted to such pleasures. You see the white walls of that temple yonder in the midst of its sacred grove. That is the temple of the goddess of Sardis,[69] Cybele or Ma, as they call her. In that grove there is many a sheltered spot where the young people of Sardis meet, as they say, in honor of their goddess."

"Just as in Babylon, at the festival of Mylitta."[70]

"There is the same custom too on the coast of

---

69. The Greeks of Asia Minor adopted the worship of this goddess, and represented her either as riding on a lion or attended by lions. O. Müller, *Archäol*, §. 395. 387. In her hand she carried a tambourine, which, according to Pindar, in Strabo p. 470, was struck at her wild festivals. In his *Thekla*, Paul Heyse has given a beautiful description of a Cybele-festival. This goddess was the personification of nature's productiveness and fertility, and the worship offered her was of a voluptuous character. Among the Greeks, this mother of the inhabitants of Asia Minor was the wife of Kronos, the mother of Zeus, and the grandmother of the gods. The myth of Cybele, or the fruitful earth, probably lies at the root of the story of Niobe, who is robbed of her children every autumn, M. Duncker. *Geschichte des Altherthums*. I. p. 252. The stone of Niobe looks, as Pausanias tells us (I. 21.) like a weeping woman. On the 4th Nov. 1862, v. Olfers laid some photographs before the Archæological Society at Berlin, which prove that this figure of a woman had in some measure been obtained by the assistance of art. Dr. A. Stietz, who saw it, found a relief rudely executed on the rock. Cybele was worshipped at Pessinus in the form of a middle-sized stone, which a man could lift. This stone was brought to Rome at the end of the third century, B. C. by command of the Sibylline books, and used to test the suspected chastity of the vestal virgins. Livius XXIX. 14. Its priests were eunuchs from Phrygia. The two last-named circumstances, in connection with other information, prove that two different divinities (the one friendly, th other hostile to production) must have been denoted by the nam Cybele. Duncker very justly sees in her a union of the Syrian Astarte and Aschera.

70. Herod. I. 199. Book of Baruch VI. 43. Strabo 1058.

Cyprus.[71] When I landed there on the way back from Egypt, I was met by a troop of lovely girls, who, with songs, dances, and the clang of cymbals, conducted me to the sacred grove of their goddess."

"Well, Zopyrus will not grumble at Bartja's illness."

"He will spend more of his time in the grove of Cybele, than at his patient's bedside. How glad I shall be to see that jolly fellow again!"

"Yes, he'll keep you from falling into those melancholy fits that you have been so subject to lately."

"You are quite right to blame me for those fits, and I must not yield to them, but they are not without ground. Crœsus says we only get low-spirited, when we are either too lazy or too weak to struggle against annoyances, and I believe he is right. But no one shall dare to accuse Darius of weakness or idleness. If I can't rule the world, at least I will be my own master."

And as he said these words, the handsome youth drew himself up, and sat erect in his saddle. His companion gazed in wonder at him.

"Really, you son of Hystaspes," he said, "I believe you must be meant for something great. It was not by chance that, when you were still a mere child, the gods sent their favorite Cyrus that dream which induced him to order you into safe keeping."

"And yet my wings have never appeared."

"No bodily ones, certainly; but mental ones, likely enough. Young man, young man, you're on a dangerous road."

"Have winged creatures any need to be afraid of precipices?"

71. Herod. I. 199. Justin XVIII. 5. Mövers, *Religion der Phœnizier a. a. O.*

"Certainly; when their strength fails them."

"But I am strong."

"Stronger creatures than you will try to break your pinions."

"Let them. I want nothing but what is right, and shall trust to my star."

"Do you know its name?"

"It ruled in the hour of my birth, and its name is Anahita."[72]

"I think I know better. A burning ambition is the sun, whose rays guide all your actions. Take care; I tried that way myself once; it leads to fame or to disgrace, but very seldom to happiness. Fame to the ambitious is like salt water to the thirsty; the more he gets, the more he wants. I was once only a poor soldier, and am now Cambyses' ambassador. But you, what can you have to strive for? There is no man in the kingdom greater than yourself, after the sons of Cyrus . . . Do my eyes deceive me? Surely those two men riding to meet us with a troop of horsemen must be Gyges and Zopyrus. The Angare, who left the inn before us, must have told them of our coming."

"To be sure. Look at that fellow Zopyrus, how he's waving and beckoning with that palm-leaf."

"Here, you fellows, cut us a few twigs from those bushes—quick. We'll answer his green palm-leaf with a purple pomegranate-branch."

In a few minutes the friends had embraced one another, and the two bands were riding together into the populous town, through the gardens surrounding the lake Gygæus, the Sardians' place of recreation. It was

---

72. The planet Venus. Vullers, *Fragmente über die Religion des Zoroaster.*

now near sunset, a cooler breeze was beginning to blow, and the citizens were pouring through the gates to enjoy themselves in the open air. Lydian and Persian warriors, the former wearing richly-ornamented helmets, the latter tiaras in the form of a cylinder, were following girls who were painted and wreathed. Children were being led to the lake by their nurses, to see the swans fed. An old blind man was seated under a plane-tree, singing sad ditties to a listening crowd and accompanying them on the Magadis, the twenty-stringed Lydian lute. Youths were enjoying themselves at games of ball, ninepins, and dice,[73] and half-grown girls screaming with fright, when the ball hit one of their group or nearly fell into the water.

The travellers scarcely noticed this gay scene, though at another time it would have delighted them. They were too much interested in enquiring particulars of Bartja's illness and recovery.

At the brazen gates of the palace which had formerly belonged to Crœsus, they were met by Oroetes, the satrap of Sardis, in a magnificent court-dress overloaded with ornaments. He was a stately man, whose small penetrating black eyes looked sharply out from beneath a bushy mass of eyebrow. His satrapy was one of the most important and profitable in the entire kingdom, and his household could bear a comparison with that of Cambyses in richness and splendor. Though he possessed fewer wives and attendants than the king, it was no inconsiderable troop of guards, slaves, eunuchs and

---

73. The Lydians are said to have invented various games, amongst others dice and balls, but not the game of draughts. Herod. I. 94. This last seems to have originated in Egypt, and it is highly probable, that the game of ball was known on the Nile earlier than in Lydia.

gorgeously-dressed officials, which appeared at the palace-gates to receive the travellers.

The vice-regal palace, which was still kept up with great magnificence, had been, in the days when Crœsus occupied it, the most splendid of royal residences; after the taking of Sardis, however, the greater part of the dethroned king's treasures and works of art had been sent to Cyrus's treasure-house in Pasargadæ. When that time of terror had passed, the Lydians brought many a hidden treasure into the light of day once more, and, by their industry and skill in art during the peaceful years which they enjoyed under Cyrus and Cambyses, recovered their old position so far, that Sardis was again looked upon as one of the wealthiest cities of Asia Minor, and therefore, of the world.

Accustomed as Darius and Prexaspes were to royal splendor, they were still astonished at the beauty and brilliancy of the satrap's palace. The marble work, especially, made a great impression on them, as nothing of the kind was to be found in Babylon, Susa or Ecbatana,[74] where burnt brick and cedar-wood supply the place of the polished marble.

They found Bartja lying on a couch in the great hall; he looked very pale, and stretched out his arms towards them.

The friends supped together at the satrap's table and then retired to Bartja's private room, in order to enjoy an undisturbed conversation.

---

74. The palace of Persepolis did not exist at the date of our story. It was built partly of black stone from Mount Rachmed, and partly of white marble; it was probably begun by Darius. The palace of Susa was built of brick, (Strabo p. 728) that of Ecbatana of wood overlaid with plates of gold of immense value, and roofed with tiles made of the precious metals. Polyb. X. 27.

"Well, Bartja, how did you come by this dangerous illness?" was Darius' first question after they were seated.

"I was thoroughly well, as you know," said Bartja, "when we left Babylon, and we reached Germa, a little town on the Sangarius, without the slightest hindrance. The ride was long and we were very tired, burnt too by the scorching May sun, and covered with dust; the river flows by the station, and its waves looked so clear and bright—so inviting for a bathe—that in a minute Zopyrus and I were off our horses, undressed, and in the water. Gyges told us we were very imprudent, but we felt confident that we were too much inured to such things to get any harm, and very much enjoyed our swim in the cool, green water. Gyges, perfectly calm as usual, let us have our own way, waited till our bath was over, and then plunged in himself.

"In two hours we were in our saddles again, pushing on as if for our very lives, changing horses at every station, and turning night into day.

"We were near Ipsus, when I began to feel violent pains in the head and limbs. I was ashamed to say anything about it and kept upright on my saddle, until we had to take fresh horses at Bagis. Just as I was in the very act of mounting, I lost my senses and strength, and fell down on the ground in a dead faint."

"Yes, a pretty fright you gave us," interrupted Zopyrus, "by dropping down in that fashion. It was fortunate that Gyges was there, for I lost my wits entirely; he, of course, kept his presence of mind, and after relieving his feelings in words not exactly flattering to us two, he behaved like a circumspect general.—A fool of a doctor came running up and protested that it was all over with poor Bart, for which I gave him a good thrashing."

"Which he didn't particularly object to," said the satrap, laughing, "seeing that you told them to lay a gold stater on every stripe."

"Yes, yes, my pugnacity costs me very dear sometimes. But to our story. As soon as Bartja had opened his eyes, Gyges sent me off to Sardis to fetch a good physician and an easy travelling-carriage. That ride won't so soon be imitated. An hour before I reached the gates my third horse knocked up under me, so I had to trust to my own legs, and began running as fast as I could. The people must all have thought me mad. At last I saw a man on horseback—a merchant from Kelænæ—dragged him from his horse, jumped into the saddle, and, before the next morning dawned, I was back again with our invalid, bringing the best physician in Sardis, and Oroetes' most commodious travelling-carriage. We brought him to this house at a slow footpace, and here a violent fever came on, he became delirious, talked all the nonsense that could possibly come into a human brain, and made us so awfully anxious, that the mere remembrance of that time brings the big drops of perspiration to my forehead."

Bartja took his friend's hand: "I owe my life to him and Gyges," said he, turning to Darius. "Till to-day, when they set out to meet you, they have never left me for a minute; a mother could not have nursed her sick child more carefully. And Oroetes, I am much obliged to you too; doubly so because your kindness subjected you to annoyance."

"How could that be?" asked Darius.

"That Polykrates of Samos, whose name we heard

so often in Egypt, has the best physician that Greece has ever produced. While I was lying here ill, Oroetes wrote to this Democedes,* making him immense promises, if he would only come to Sardis directly. The Samian pirates, who infest the whole Ionian coast, took the messenger captive and brought Oroetes' letter to their master Polykrates. He opened it, and sent the messenger back with the answer, that Democedes was in his pay, and that if Oroetes[75] needed his advice he must apply to Polykrates himself. Our generous friend submitted for my sake, and asked the Samian to send his physician to Sardis."

"Well," said Prexaspes, "and what followed?"

"The proud island-prince sent him at once. He cured me, as you see, and left us a few days ago loaded with presents."

"Well," interrupted Zopyrus, "I can quite understand, that Polykrates likes to keep his physician near him. I assure you, Darius, it would not be easy to find his equal. He's as handsome as Minutscher, as clever as Piran Wisa, as strong as Rustem,** and as benevolent and helpful as the god Soma.*** I wish you could have seen how well he threw those round metal plates he calls discs. I am no weakling, but when we wrestled he soon threw me. And then he could tell such famous stories—stories that made a man's heart dance within him."

75. This very Oroetes afterwards succeeded in enticing Polykrates to Sardis and there crucified him. Herod. III. 120—125. Valerius Maximus VI. 9. 5.

* See vol. 1. note 80.

** These are the names of heroes from the oldest of the Persian legends, preserved to us principally in the epic poems of Firdusi.

*** See vol. 1. note 265.

"We know just such a fellow too," said Darius, smiling at his friend's enthusiasm. "That Athenian Phanes, who came to prove our innocence."

"The physician Democedes is from Crotona, a place which must lie somewhere very near the setting sun."

"But is inhabited by Greeks, like Athens." added Oroetes. "Ah, my young friends, you must beware of those fellows; they're as cunning, deceitful, and selfish, as they are strong, clever, and handsome."

"Democedes is generous and sincere," cried Zopyrus.

"And Crœsus himself thinks Phanes not only an able, but a virtuous man," added Darius.

"Sappho too has always, and only spoken well of the Athenian," said Bartja, in confirmation of Darius's remark. "But don't let us talk any more about these Greeks," he went on. "They give Oroetes so much trouble by their refractory and stubborn conduct, that he is not very fond of them."

"The gods know that," sighed the satrap. "It's more difficult to keep one Greek town in order, than all the countries between the Euphrates and the Tigris."

While Oroetes was speaking, Zopyrus had gone to the window. "The stars are already high in the heavens," he said, "and Bartja is tired; so make haste, Darius, and tell us something about home."

The son of Hystaspes agreed at once, and began by relating the events which we have heard already. Bartja, especially, was distressed at hearing of Nitetis' sad end, and the discovery of Amasis' fraud filled them all with astonishment. After a short pause, Darius went on:

"When once Nitetis' descent had been fully proved, Cambyses was like a changed man. He called a council of war, and appeared at table in the royal robes instead of his mourning garments. You can fancy what universal joy the idea of a war with Egypt excited. Even Crœsus, who you know is one of Amasis' well-wishers, and advises peace whenever it is possible, had not a word to say against it. The next morning, as usual, what had been resolved on in intoxication was reconsidered by sober heads; after several opinions had been given, Phanes asked permission to speak, and spoke I should think for an hour. But how well! It was as if every word he said came direct from the gods. He has learnt our language in a wonderfully short time, but it flowed from his lips like honey. Sometimes he drew tears from every eye, at others excited stormy shouts of joy, and then wild bursts of rage. His gestures were as graceful as those of a dancing-girl, but at the same time manly and dignified. I can't repeat his speech; my poor words, by the side of his, would sound like the rattle of a drum after a peal of thunder. But when at last, inspired and carried away by his eloquence, we had unanimously decided on war, he began to speak once more on the best ways and means of prosecuting it successfully."

Here Darius was obliged to stop, as Zopyrus had fallen on his neck in an ecstasy of delight. Bartja, Gyges and Oroetes were not less delighted, and they all begged him to go on with his tale.

"Our army," began Darius afresh, "ought to be at the boundaries of Egypt by the month Farwardin,[76] as

---

[76]. Farwardin can be reckoned as our March, Murdâd as July. Spiegel, *Avesta*, Einleitung p. XCVIII.

the inundation of the Nile, which would hinder the march of our infantry, begins in Murdâd.* Phanes is now on his way to the Arabians to secure their assistance;[77] in hopes that these sons of the desert may furnish our army with water and guides through their dry and thirsty land. He will also endeavor to win the rich island of Cyprus, which he once conquered for Amasis, over to our side. As it was through his mediation that the kings of the island were allowed to retain their crowns, they will be willing to listen to his advice. In short the Athenian leaves nothing uncared for, and knows every road and path as if he were the sun himself. He showed us a picture of the world on a plate of copper."

Oroetes nodded and said, "I have such a picture of the world too. A Milesian named Hekataeus,[78] who spends his life in travelling, drew it, and gave it me in exchange for a free-pass."

"What notions these Greeks have in their heads!" exclaimed Zopyrus, who could not explain to himself what a picture of the world could look like.

77. Herod. III. 5.

78. Hekataeus of Miletus may be called "the father of geography," as Herodotus was "the father of history." He improved the map made by Anaximander, and his great work, "the journey round the world," was much prized by the ancients; but unfortunately, with the exception of some very small fragments, has now perished. Herodotus assures us, (V. 36.) that Hekataeus was intimately acquainted with every part of the Persian empire, and had also travelled over Egypt. He lived at the date of our narrative, having been born at Miletus 550 B. C. He lived to see the fall of his native city in 496 B. C. His map has been restored by Klausen in the *Fragm. Hecat.* and can be seen also in Mure's *Lan. and Lit. of Ancient Greece.* Vol. IV. Maps existed, however, much earlier, the earliest known being one of the gold-mines, drawn very cleverly by an Egyptian priest, and so well sketched as to give a pretty clear idea of the part of the country intended. It is preserved in the Egyptian Museum at Turin.

* *Farwardin,* March. *Murdâd,* July.

"To-morrow I will show you my copper tablet," said Oroetes, "but now we must allow Darius to go on."

"So Phanes has gone to Arabia," continued Darius, "and Prexaspes was sent hither not only to command you, Oroetes, to raise as many forces as possible, especially Ionians and Carians, of whom Phanes has offered to undertake the command, but also to propose terms of alliance to Polykrates."

"To that pirate!" asked Oroetes, and his face darkened.

"The very same," answered Prexaspes, not appearing to notice the change in Oroetes' face. "Phanes has already received assurances from this important naval power, which sound as if we might expect a favorable answer to my proposal."

"The Phœnician, Syrian and Ionian ships of war would be quite sufficient to cope with the Egyptian fleet."

"There you are right; but if Polykrates were to declare against us, we should not be able to hold our own at sea; you say yourself that he is all-powerful in the Ægean."

"Still I decidedly disapprove of entering into treaty with such a robber."

"We want powerful allies, and Polykrates is very powerful at sea. It will be time to humble him, when we have used him to help us in conquering Egypt. For the present I entreat you to suppress all personal feeling, and keep the success of our great plan alone in view. I am empowered to say this in the king's name, and to show his ring in token thereof."

Oroetes made a brief obeisance before this symbol

of despotism, and asked: "What does Cambyses wish me to do?"

"He commands you to use every means in your power to secure an alliance with the Samian; and also to send your troops to join the main army on the plains of Babylon as soon as possible."

The satrap bowed and left the room with a look betraying irritation and defiance.

When the echo of his footsteps had died away among the colonnades of the inner court, Zopyrus exclaimed: "Poor fellow, it's really very hard for him to have to meet that proud man, who has so often behaved insolently to him, on friendly terms. Think of that story about the physician for instance."

"You are too lenient," interrupted Darius. "I don't like this Oroetes. He has no right to receive the king's commands in that way. Didn't you see him bite his lips till they bled, when Prexaspes showed him the king's ring?"

"Yes," cried the envoy, "he's a defiant, perverse man. He left the room so quickly, only because he could not keep down his anger any longer."

"Still," said Bartja, "I hope you will keep his conduct a secret from my brother, for he has been very good to me."

Prexaspes bowed, but Darius said: "We must keep an eye on the fellow. Just here, so far from the king's gate and in the midst of nations hostile to Persia, we want governors who are more ready to obey their king than this Oroetes seems to be. Why, he seems to fancy he is King of Lydia!"

"Do you dislike the satrap?" said Zopyrus."

"Well, I think I do," was the answer. "I always

take an aversion or a fancy to people at first sight, and very seldom find reason to change my mind afterwards. I disliked Oroetes before I heard him speak a word, and I remember having the same feeling towards Psamtik, though Amasis took my fancy."

"There's no doubt that you're very different from the rest of us," said Zopyrus laughing, "but now, to please me, let this poor Oroetes alone. I'm glad he's gone though, because we can talk more freely about home. How is Kassandane? and your worshipped Atossa? Crœsus too, how is he? and what are my wives about? They'll soon have a new companion. To-morrow I intend to sue for the hand of Oroetes' pretty daughter. We've talked a good deal of love with our eyes already. I don't know whether we spoke Persian or Syrian, but we said the most charming things to one another."

The friends laughed, and Darius, joining in their merriment, said: "Now you shall hear a piece of very good news. I have kept it to the last, because it is the best I have. Now, Bartja, prick up your ears. Your mother, the noble Kassandane, has been cured of her blindness! Yes, yes, it is quite true.—Who cured her? Why who should it be, but that crabbed old Nebenchari, who has become, if possible, moodier than ever. Come, now, calm yourselves, and let me go on with my story, or it will be morning before Bartja gets to sleep. Indeed, I think we had better separate now: you've heard the best, and have something to dream about What, you will not? Then, in the name of Mithras, I must go on, though it should make my heart bleed.

"I'll begin with the king. As long as Phanes was in Babylon, he seemed to forget his grief for Nitetis.

The Athenian was never allowed to leave him. They were as inseparable as Reksch and Rustem.* Cambyses had no time to think of his sorrow, for Phanes had always some new idea or other, and entertained us all, as well as the king, marvellously. And we all liked him too; perhaps, because no one could really envy him. Whenever he was alone, the tears came into his eyes at the thought of his boy, and this made his great cheerfulness—a cheerfulness which he always managed to impart to the king, Bartja,—the more admirable. Every morning he went down to the Euphrates with Cambyses and the rest of us, and enjoyed watching the sons of the Achæmenidæ at their exercises.** When he saw them riding at full speed past the sand-hills and shooting the pots placed on them into fragments with their arrows, or throwing blocks of wood at one another and cleverly evading the blows,[79] he confessed that he could not imitate them in these exercises, but at the same time he offered to accept a challenge from any of us in throwing the spear and in wrestling. In his quick way he sprang from his horse, stripped off his clothes—it was really a shame[80]—and, to the delight of the boys, threw their wrestling-master as if he had been a feather. Then he knocked over a number of bragging fellows,

79. Niebuhr, on his journey to Asia, saw several young men at Shiraz playing very eagerly at these games. See also Hyde, *De Ludis Orientalium*.

80. In the East, nudity was, even in those days, held to be disgraceful, while the Greeks thought nothing so beautiful as the naked human body. The Hetaira Phryne was summoned before the judges for an offence against religion. Her defender, seeing that sentence was about to be pronounced against his client, suddenly tore away the garment which covered her bosom. The artifice was successful. The judges pronounced her not guilty, being convinced that such wondrous grace and beauty could only belong to a favorite of Aphrodite. Athen. XIII. p. 590.

* See note 30.　　　　** See vol. I. note 245.

and would have thrown me too if he had not been too
fatigued. I assure you, I am really stronger than he is,
for I can lift greater weights, but he is as nimble as an
eel, and has wonderful tricks by which he gets hold of
his adversary. His being naked too is a great help. If
it were not so indecent, we ought always to wrestle
stripped, and anoint our skins, as the Greeks do, with
the olive-oil. He beat us too in throwing the spear, but
the king, who you know is proud of being the best
archer in Persia, sent his arrow farther. Phanes was
especially pleased with our rule, that in a wrestling-
match the one who is thrown must kiss the hand of his
victor. At last he showed us a new exercise:—boxing.
He refused, however, to try his skill on any one but a
slave, so Cambyses sent for the biggest and strongest
man among the servants—my groom, Bessus—a giant
who can bring the hind legs of a horse together and hold
them so firmly that the creature trembles all over and
cannot stir. This big fellow, taller by a head than
Phanes, shrugged his shoulders contemptuously on hearing that he was to box with the little foreign gentleman.
He felt quite sure of victory, placed himself opposite his
adversary, and dealt him a blow heavy enough to kill
an elephant. Phanes avoided it cleverly, in the same
moment hitting the giant with his naked fist so power-
fully under the eyes, that the blood streamed from his
nose and mouth, and the huge, uncouth fellow fell on
the ground with a yell. When they picked him up his
face looked like a pumpkin of a greenish-blue color.
The boys shouted with delight at his discomfiture; but
we admired the dexterity of this Greek, and were especially glad to see the king in such good spirits; we
noticed this most when Phanes was singing Greek

songs and dance-melodies to him accompanied by the lute.

"Meanwhile Kassandane's blindness had been cured, and this of course tended not a little to disperse the king's melancholy.

"In short it was a very pleasant time, and I was just going to ask for Atossa's hand in marriage, when Phanes went off to Arabia, and everything was changed.

"No sooner had he turned his back on the gates of Babylon than all the evil Divs seemed to have entered into the king. He went about, a moody, silent man, speaking to no one; and to drown his melancholy would begin drinking, even at an early hour in the morning, quantities of the strongest Syrian wine. By the evening he was generally so intoxicated that he had to be carried out of the hall, and would wake up the next morning with headache and spasms. In the day-time he would wander about as if looking for something, and in the night they often heard him calling Nitetis. The physicians became very anxious about his health, but when they sent him medicine he threw it away. It was quite right of Crœsus to say, as he did once 'Ye Magi and Chaldæans! before trying to cure a sick man we must discover the seat of his disease. Do you know it in this case? No? Then I will tell you what ails the king. He has an internal complaint and a wound. The former is called *ennui*, and the latter is in his heart. The Athenian is a good remedy for the first,—but for the second I know of none; such wounds either scar over of themselves, or the patient bleeds to death inwardly.'"

"I know of a remedy for the king though," exclaimed Otanes when he heard these words. "We must persuade him to send for the women, or at least for my daughter Phædime, back from Susa. Love is good for dispersing melancholy, and makes the blood flow faster." We acknowledged that he was right, and advised him to remind the king of his banished wives. He ventured to make the proposal while we were at supper, but got such a harsh rebuff for his pains, that we all pitied him. Soon after this, Cambyses sent one morning for all the Mobeds and Chaldæans, and commanded them to interpret a strange dream which he had had. In his dream he had been standing in the midst of a dry and barren plain: barren as a threshing-floor,— it did not produce a single blade of grass. Displeased at the desert aspect of the place, he was just going to seek other and more fruitful regions, when Atossa appeared, and, without seeing him, ran towards a spring which welled up through the arid soil as if by enchantment. While he was gazing in wonder at this scene, he noticed that wherever the foot of his sister touched the parched soil, graceful terebinths[81] sprang up, changing, as they grew, into cypresses whose tops reached unto heaven. As he was going to speak to Atossa, he awoke.

"The Mobeds and Chaldæans consulted together and interpreted the dream thus: 'Atossa would be successful in all she undertook.'

"Cambyses seemed satisfied with this answer, but, as the next night the vision appeared again, he threatened the wise men with death, unless they could give him another and a different interpretation. They pondered long, and at last answered, 'that Atossa

---

81. The kings of Persia had to eat a terebinth at their coronation. Plutarch, *Artaxerxes* 3.

would become a queen and the mother of mighty princes.'

"This answer really contented the king, and he smiled strangely to himself as he told us his dream.

"The same day Kassandane sent for me and told me to give up all thoughts of her daughter, as I valued my life.

"Just as I was leaving the queen's garden I saw Atossa behind a pomegranate-bush. She beckoned. I went to her; and in that hour we forgot danger and sorrow, but said farewell to each other for ever. Now you know all; and now that I have given her up— now that I know it would be madness even to think of her again—I am obliged to be very stern with myself, lest, like the king, I should fall into deep melancholy for the sake of a woman. And this is the end of the story, the close of which we were all expecting, when Atossa, as I lay under sentence of death, sent me a rose, and made me the happiest of mortals. If I had not betrayed my secret then, when we thought our last hour was near, it would have gone with me to my grave. But what am I talking about? I know I can trust to your secrecy, but pray don't look at me so deplorably. I think I am still to be envied, for I have had one hour of enjoyment that would outweigh a century of misery. Thank you,—thank you: now let me finish my story as quickly as I can.

"'Three days after I had taken leave of Atossa I had to marry Artystone, the daughter of Gobryas. She is beautiful, and would make any other man happy. The day after the wedding the Angare reached Babylon with the news of your illness. My mind was made up at once; I begged the king to let me go to you, nurse you, and warn you of the danger which threatens your life in Egypt—took leave of my bride, in spite of all my father-in-law's protestations, and went off at full speed with Prexaspes, never resting till I reached your side, my dear Bartja. Now I shall go with you and Zopyrus to Egypt, for Gyges must accompany the ambassador to Samos, as interpreter. This is the king's command; he has been in better spirits the last few days; the inspection of the masses of troops coming up to Babylon diverts him, besides which, the Chaldæans have assured him that the planet Adar,[82] which belongs to their war-god Chanon, promises a great victory to the Persian arms. When do you think you shall be able to travel, Bartja?"

"To-morrow, if you like," was the answer. "The doctors say the sea-voyage will do me good, and the journey by land to Smyrna is very short."

"And I can assure you," added Zopyrus, "that Sappho will cure you sooner than all the doctors in the world."

"Then we will start in three days;" said Darius after some consideration, "we have plenty to do before starting. Remember we are going into what may almost be called an enemy's country. I have been thinking the matter over, and it seems to me that Bartja must pass for a Babylonian carpet-merchant, I for his brother, and Zopyrus for a dealer in Sardian red."[83]

"Couldn't we be soldiers?" asked Zopyrus. "It's such an ignominious thing to be taken for cheating pedlers. How would it be, for instance, if we passed

---

82. The Planet Mars. *Chron. Pasch.* I. p. 18. Cedrenus, *Chron.* I. p. 29. Cicero, *De Nat. Deor.* II. 20, 46.

83. A favorite color among the ancients, made from the blossoms of the Sandix tree. Arlstoph. *Acharn.* 113.

ourselves off for Lydian soldiers, escaped from punishment, and seeking service in the Egyptian army?"

"That's not a bad idea," said Bartja, "and I think too that we look more like soldiers than traders."

"Looks and manner are no guide," said Gyges. "Those great Greek merchants and ship-owners go about as proudly as if the world belonged to them. But I don't find Zopyrus' proposal a bad one."

"Then so let it be," said Darius, yielding. "In that case Oroetes must provide us with the uniform of Lydian Taxiarchs."[84]

"You'd better take the splendid dress of the Chiliarchs[84] at once, I think," cried Gyges. "Why, on such young men, that would excite suspicion directly."

"But we can't appear as common soldiers."

"No, but as Hekatontarchs."[84]

"All right," said Zopyrus laughing. "Anything you like except a shop-keeper.—So in three days we are off. I am glad I shall just have time to make sure of the satrap's little daughter, and to visit the grove of Cybele at last. Now, good night, Bartja; don't get up too early. What will Sappho say, if you come to her with pale cheeks?"

---

84. The Persian army was decimally divided. Each division numbered 10,000 men, each regiment 1000, each company 100. The rank of Taxiarch was similar to that of a captain with us, a Hekatontarch commanded 100, and a Chiliarch 1000 men. Indeed later the title of Chiliarch betokened a very high office among the Persians, the holder of which ($\chi\iota\lambda\iota\acute{\alpha}\rho\chi\eta\varsigma$) is said to have been next in rank to the king. Diod. XVIII. 48. Aelian, *Var. Hist.* I. 21.

CHAPTER X.

The sun of a hot midsummer-day had risen on Naukratis. The Nile had already begun to overflow its banks, and the fields and gardens of the Egyptians were covered with water.

The harbor was crowded with craft of all kinds. Egyptian vessels were there, manned by Phœnician colonists from the coasts of the Delta,[85] and bringing fine woven goods from Malta, metals and precious stones from Sardinia, wine and copper from Cyprus: Greek triremes laden with oil, wine and mastic-wood; metal-work and woollen wares from Chalcis, Phœnician and Syrian craft with gaily-colored sails, and freighted with cargoes of purple stuffs, gems, spices, glass-work, carpets and cedar-trees,—used in Egypt, where wood was very scarce, for building purposes,— and taking back gold, ivory, ebony, brightly-plumaged tropical birds, precious stones and black slaves,—the treasures of Ethiopia; but more especially the far-famed Egyptian corn, Memphian chariots, lace from Sais, and the finer sorts of papyrus. The time when commerce was carried on merely by barter was now, however, long past, and the merchants of Naukratis not seldom paid

---

85. In another place (Ebers, Aegypten p. 127.) we have endeavored to prove that Phœnician colonies existed on the coasts of the Delta. Egypto-Phœnician colonies can be proved to have existed in Sardinia, Crete, Malta, Cyprus, and in earlier times in Eubœa and other places. The discoveries which have been made in Sardinia and the treasures found in Cyprus by Cesnola are most instructive. Communicated by Canonicus Spano, Lamarmora, Neigebaur, in Gerhard's *Archäol Zeitung*, in the Bulletino Sardo and the latest by H. v. Malzan.

for their goods in gold coin and carefully-weighed* silver.

Large warehouses stood round the harbor of this Greek colony, and slightly-built dwelling-houses, into which the idle mariners were lured by the sounds of music and laughter, and the glances and voices of painted and rouged damsels.[86] Slaves, both white and colored, rowers and steersmen, in various costumes, were hurrying hither and thither, while the ships' captains, either dressed in the Greek fashion or in Phœnician garments of the most glaring colors, were shouting orders to their crews and delivering up their cargoes to the merchants. Whenever a dispute arose, the Egyptian police with their long staves, and the Greek warders of the harbor were quickly at hand. The latter were appointed by the elders of the merchant-body in this Milesian colony.**

The port was getting empty now, for the hour at which the market opened was near,[87] and none of the free Greeks cared to be absent from the market-place then. This time, however, not a few remained behind, curiously watching a beautifully-built Samian ship, the Okeia,[88] with a long prow like a swan's neck, on the

---

86. Setting aside the fact, that no large seaport of the ancient world was without such houses of amusement, those on the Canopic mouth of the Nile are expressly mentioned by Strabo, 801.

87. The following little story told by Strabo (658), proves how eagerly the Greeks thronged to market. A flute-player at Jasos was forsaken by his audience the moment they heard the sound of the market-bell, one man alone remaining behind. The musician thanked this man for not having allowed the bell to distract his attention. "What!" cried the other, "has it rung already?" and instantly departed too.

88. Ωχεία "the swift." Böckh, *Staatshaushault der Athener* III. 93. Not only the Greek, but also the Phœnician ships were ornamented with likenesses of the gods.

* See vol. 1. note 172.   ** See vol. 1. note 2.

front of which a likeness of the goddess Hera was conspicuous. It was discharging its cargo, but the public attention was more particularly attracted by three handsome youths, in the dress of Lydian officers, who left the ship, followed by a number of slaves carrying chests and packages.

The handsomest of the three travellers, in whom of course our readers recognize their three young friends, Darius, Bartja and Zopyrus, spoke to one of the harbor-police and asked for the house of Theopompus the Milesian, to whom they were bound on a visit.

Polite and ready to do a service, like all the Greeks, the police functionary at once led the way across the market-place,—where the opening of business had just been announced by the sound of a bell,*—to a handsome house, the property of the Milesian, Theopompus, one of the most important and respected men in Naukratis.

The party, however, did not succeed in crossing the market-place without hindrance. They found it easy enough to evade the importunities of impudent fish-sellers, and the friendly invitations of butchers, bakers, sausage and vegetable-sellers, and potters. But when they reached the part allotted[89] to the flower-girls, Zopyrus was so enchanted with the scene, that he clapped his hands for joy.

Three wonderfully-lovely girls, in white dresses of some half-transparent material, with colored borders,

---

89, Separate portions of the market (χύχλοι) were set apart for the sale of different goods. The part appointed for the flower-sellers, who passed in general for no better than they should be, was called the "myrtle-market." Aristoph. *Thesmoph.* 448. Becker, *Charikles,* II. p. 156.

* See note 87.

were seated together on low stools, binding roses, violets and orange-blossoms into one long wreath. Their charming heads were wreathed with flowers too, and looked very like the lovely rosebuds which one of them, on seeing the young men come up, held out to their notice.

"Buy my roses, my handsome gentlemen," she said in a clear, melodious voice, "to put in your sweethearts' hair."

Zopyrus took the flowers, and holding the girl's hand fast in his own, answered, "I come from a far country, my lovely child, and have no sweetheart in Naukratis yet; so let me put the roses in your own golden hair, and this piece of gold in your white little hand."

The girl burst into a merry laugh, showed her sister the handsome present,[90] and answered: "By Eros, such gentlemen as you cannot want for sweethearts. Are you brothers?"

"No."

"That's a pity, for we are sisters."

"And you thought we should make three pretty couples?"

"I may have thought it, but I did not say so."

"And your sisters?"

---

90. This passage was suggested by the following epigram of Dionysius:

"Roses are blooming on thy cheek, with roses thy basket is laden,
    Which dost thou sell? The flowers? Thyself? Or both, my pretty
        maiden?"

Fr. Jacobs, *Gr. Blumenlese*, IX. 51. A piece of gold was very high payment. In the Acharnæ of Aristophanes the slave of Lamachus is supposed to offer an absurdly high price, when he is willing to pay 3 drachmæ (2s. 3d.) for a fat eel from Kopai, and one drachma (ninepence) for a brace of fieldfares.

The girls laughed, as if they were but little averse to such a connection, and offered Bartja and Darius rose-buds too.

The young men accepted them, gave each a gold piece in return, and were not allowed to leave these beauties until their helmets had been crowned with laurel.

Meanwhile the news of the strangers' remarkable liberality had spread among the many girls, who were selling ribbons, wreaths and flowers close by. They all brought roses too and invited the strangers with looks and words to stay with them and buy their flowers.

Zopyrus, like many a young gentleman in Naukratis, would gladly have accepted their invitations, for most of these girls were beautiful, and their hearts were not difficult to win; but Darius urged him to come away, and begged Bartja to forbid the thoughtless fellow's staying any longer. After passing the tables of the money-changers, and the stone seats on which the citizens sat in the open air and held their consultations, they arrived at the house of Theopompus.

The stroke given by their Greek guide with the metal knocker on the house-door was answered at once by a slave. As the master was at the market, the strangers were led by the steward, an old servant grown grey in the service of Theopompus, into the Andronitis,* and begged to wait there until he returned.

They were still engaged in admiring the paintings on the walls, and the artistic carving of the stone floor, when Theopompus, the merchant whom we first learnt to know at the house of Rhodopis, came back from the

* See vol. 1. note 25. The description of Rhodopis' house.

market, followed by a great number of slaves bearing his purchases.[91]

He received the strangers with charming politeness and asked in what way he could be of use to them, on which Bartja, having first convinced himself that no unwished-for listeners were present, gave him the roll he had received from Phanes at parting.

Theopompus had scarcely read its contents, when he made a low bow to the prince, exclaiming: "By Zeus, the father of hospitality, this is the greatest honor that could have been conferred upon my house! All I possess is yours, and I beg you to ask your companions to accept with kindness what I can offer. Pardon my not having recognized you at once in your Lydian dress. It seems to me that your hair is shorter and your beard thicker, than when you left Egypt. Am I right in imagining that you do not wish to be recognized? It shall be exactly as you wish. He is the best host, who allows his guests the most freedom. Ah, now I recognize your friends; but they have disguised themselves and cut their curls also. Indeed, I could almost say that you, my friend, whose name . . ."

"My name is Darius."

"That you, Darius, have dyed your hair black. Yes? Then you see my memory does not deceive me. But that is nothing to boast of, for I saw you several times at Sais, and here too, on your arrival and departure. You ask, my prince, whether you would be generally recognized? Certainly not. The foreign dress, the change in your hair and the coloring of your

---

91. Men of high rank among the Greeks did not disdain to make purchases at market, accompanied by their slaves, but respectable women could not appear there. Female slaves were generally sent to buy what was needed. Becker, *Charikles*, II. p. 150.

eyebrows have altered you wonderfully. But excuse me a moment, my old steward seems to have some important message to give."

In a few minutes Theopompus came back, exclaiming: " No, no, my honored friends, you have certainly not taken the wisest way of entering Naukratis incognito. You have been joking with the flower-girls and paying them for a few roses, not like runaway Lydian Hekatontarchs, but like the great lords you are. All Naukratis knows the pretty, frivolous sisters, Stephanion, Chloris and Irene, whose garlands have caught many a heart, and whose sweet glances have lured many a bright obolus out of the pockets of our gay young men. They're very fond of visiting the flower-girls at market-time, and agreements are entered into then for which more than one gold piece must be paid later; but for a few roses and good words they are not accustomed to be so liberal as you have been. The girls have been boasting about you and your gifts, and showing your good red gold to their stingier suitors. As rumor is a goddess who is very apt to exaggerate and to make a crocodile out of a lizard, it happened that news reached the Egyptian captain on guard at the market, that some newly-arrived Lydian warriors had been scattering gold broadcast among the flower-girls. This excited suspicion, and induced the Toparch* to send an officer here to enquire from whence you come, and what is the object of your journey hither. I was obliged to use a little stratagem to impose upon him, and told him, as I believe you wish, that you were rich young men from Sardis, who had fled on account of having incurred the satrap's ill-will. But I see the government officer

* See vol. I. note 140.

coming, and with him the secretary who is to make out passports which will enable you to remain on the Nile unmolested. I have promised him a handsome reward, if he can help you in getting admitted into the king's mercenaries. He was caught and believed my story. You are so young, that nobody would imagine you were entrusted with a secret mission."

The talkative Greek had scarcely finished speaking when the clerk, a lean, dry-looking man, dressed in white, came in, placed himself opposite the strangers and asked them from whence they came and what was the object of their journey.

The youths held to their first assertion, that they were Lydian Hekatontarchs, and begged the functionary to provide them with passes and tell them in what way they might most easily obtain admittance into the king's troop of auxiliaries.

The man did not hesitate long, after Theopompus had undertaken to be their surety, and the desired documents were made out.

Bartja's pass ran thus:

"Smerdis, the son of Sandon of Sardis, about 22 years of age—figure, tall and slender—face, well-formed: —nose, straight:—forehead, high with a small scar in the middle:—is hereby permitted to remain in those parts of Egypt in which the law allows foreigners to reside, as surety has been given for him.

In the King's name.

Sachons, Clerk.

Darius and Zopyrus received passports similarly worded.[92]

[92]. Similar descriptions have been preserved in the papyri. Wilkinson, in his *Manners and Customs of the Ancient Egyptians*, gives

When the government official had left the house, Theopompus rubbed his hands and said: "Now if you will follow my advice on all points you can stay in Egypt safely enough. Keep these little rolls as if they were the apple of your eye, and never part from them. Now, however, I must beg you to follow me to breakfast and to tell me, if agreeable to you, whether a report which has just been making the round of the market is not, as usual, entirely false. A trireme from Kolophon, namely, has brought the news that your powerful brother, noble Bartja, is preparing to make war with Amasis."

On the evening of the same day, Bartja and Sappho saw each other again. In that first hour surprise and joy together made Sappho's happiness too great for words. When they were once more seated in the acanthus-grove whose blossoming branches had so often seen and sheltered their young love, she embraced him tenderly, but for a long time they did not speak one word. They saw neither moon nor stars moving silently above them, in the warm summer night; they did not even hear the nightingales who were still repeating their favorite, flute-like, Itys-call to one another; nor did they feel the dew which fell as heavily on their fair heads as on the flowers in the grass around them.

At last Bartja, taking both Sappho's hands in his own, looked long and silently into her face, as if to stamp her likeness for ever on his memory. When he

a picture from Thebes in which a man, making obeisance, is being led before another, a clerk or secretary, who appears to be making out a passport for him.

spoke at last, she cast down her eyes, for he said: "In my dreams, Sappho, you have always been the most lovely creature that Auramazda ever created, but now I see you again, you are more lovely even than my dreams."

And when a bright, happy glance from her had thanked him for these words, he drew her closer to him, asking: "Did you often think of me?"

"I thought only of you."

"And did you hope to see me soon?"

"Yes; hour after hour I thought, 'now he must be coming.' Sometimes I went into the garden in the morning and looked towards your home in the East, and a bird flew towards me from thence and I felt a twitching in my right eyelid; or when I was putting my box to rights and found the laurel crown which I put by as a remembrance, because you looked so well in it, —Melitta says such wreaths are good for keeping true love[93]—then I used to clap my hands with joy and think, 'to-day he must come;' and I would run down to the Nile and wave my handkerchief to every passing boat, for every boat I thought must be bringing you to me. But you did not come, and then I went sadly home, and would sit down by the fire on the hearth in the women's room, and sing, and gaze into the fire till grandmother would wake me out of my dream by saying: 'Listen to me, girl; whoever dreams by daylight is in danger of lying awake at night, and getting up in the morning with a sad heart, a tired brain and weary limbs. The day was not given us for sleep, and we

---

93. A bird flying from the right side, and a twitching of the right eye were considered fortunate omens. Theokritus, III. 37. The wreath put by. See Lucian. *Tox*. 30.

must live in it with open eyes, that not a single hour may be idly spent. The past belongs to the dead; only fools count upon the future; but wise men hold fast by the ever young present; by work they foster all the various gifts which Zeus, Apollo, Pallas, Cypris lend; by work they raise, and perfect and ennoble them, until their feelings, actions, words and thoughts become harmonious like a well-tuned lute. You cannot serve the man to whom you have given your whole heart,—to whom in your great love you look up as so much higher than yourself—you cannot prove the steadfastness and faithfulness of that love better, than by raising and improving your mind to the utmost of your power. Every good and beautiful truth that you learn is an offering to him you love best, for in giving your whole self, you give your virtues too. But no one gains this victory in dreams. The dew by which such blossoms are nourished is called the sweat of man's brow.' So she would speak to me, and then I started up ashamed and left the hearth, and either took my lyre to learn new songs, or listened to my loving teacher's words—she is wiser than most men—attentively and still. And so the time passed on; a rapid stream, just like our river Nile, which flows unceasingly, and brings such changing scenes upon its waves,—sometimes a golden boat with streamers gay,—sometimes a fearful, ravenous crocodile."

"But now we are sitting in the golden boat. Oh, if time's waves would only cease to flow! If this one moment could but last for aye. You lovely girl, how perfectly you speak,—how well you understand and remember all this beautiful teaching and make it even more beautiful by your way of repeating it. Yes, Sappho, I am very proud of you. In you I have a treasure which makes me richer than my brother, though half the world belongs to him."

"You proud of me? you, a king's son, the best and handsomest of your family?"

"The greatest worth that I can find in myself is, that you think me worthy of your love."

"Tell me, ye gods, how can this little heart hold so much joy without breaking? 'Tis like a vase that's overfilled with purest, heaviest gold?"

"Another heart will help you to bear it; and that is my own, for mine is again supported by yours, and with that help I can laugh at every evil that the world or night may bring."

"Oh, don't excite the envy of the gods; human happiness often vexes them. Since you left us we have passed some very, very sad days. The two poor children of our kind Phanes—a boy as beautiful as Eros, and a little girl as fair and rosy as a summer morning's cloud just lit up by the sun,—came for some happy days to stay with us. Grandmother grew quite glad and young again while looking on these little ones, and as for me I gave them all my heart, though really it is your's and your's alone. But hearts, you know, are wonderfully made; they're like the sun who sends his rays everywhere, and loses neither warmth nor light by giving much, but gives to all their due. I loved those little ones so very much. One evening we were sitting quite alone with Theopompus in the women's room, when suddenly we heard a loud, wild noise. The good old Knakias, our faithful slave, just reached the door as all the bolts gave way, and, rushing through the entrance-hall into the peristyle, the andronitis, and so on to us, crashing the door between, came a troop of soldiers. Grandmother showed them the letter by which Amasis secured our house from all attack and made it a sure refuge, but they laughed the writing to scorn and showed us on their side a document with the crown-prince's seal, in which we were sternly commanded to deliver up Phanes' children at once to this rough troop of men. Theopompus reproved the soldiers for their roughness, telling them that the children came from Corinth and had no connection with Phanes; but the captain of the troop defied and sneered at him, pushed my grandmother rudely away, forced his way into her own apartment, where among her most precious treasures, at the head of her own bed, the two children lay sleeping peacefully, dragged them out of their little beds and took them in an open boat through the cold night-air to the royal city. In a few days we heard the boy was dead. They say he has been killed by Psamtik's orders; and the little girl, so sweet and dear, is lying in a dismal dungeon, and pining for her father and for us. Oh, dearest, isn't it a painful thing that sorrows such as these should come to mar our perfect happiness? My eyes weep joy and sorrow in the same moment, and my lips, which have just been laughing with you, have now to tell you this sad story."

"I feel your pain with you, my child, but it makes my hand clench with rage instead of filling my eyes with tears. That gentle boy whom you loved, that little girl who now sits weeping in the dark dungeon, shall both be revenged. Trust me; before the Nile has risen again, a powerful army will have entered Egypt, to demand satisfaction for this murder."

"Oh, dearest, how your eyes are glowing! I never

saw you look so beautiful before. Yes, yes, the boy must be avenged, and none but you must be his avenger."

"My gentle Sappho is becoming warlike too."

"Yes, women must feel warlike when wickedness is so triumphant; women rejoice too when such crimes are punished. Tell me has war been declared already?"

"Not yet; but hosts on hosts are marching to the valley of the Euphrates to join our main army."

"My courage sinks as quickly as it rose. I tremble at the word, the mere word, war. How many childless mothers Ares makes, how many young fair heads must wear the widow's veil, how many pillows are wet through with tears when Pallas takes her shield."

"But a man developes in war; his heart expands, his arm grows strong. And none rejoice more than you when he returns a conqueror from the field. The wife of a Persian, especially, ought to rejoice in the thought of battle, for her husband's honor and fame are dearer to her than his life."

"Go to the war. I shall pray for you there."

"And victory will be with the right. First we will conquer Pharaoh's host, then release Phanes' little daughter . . ."

"And then Aristomachus, the brave old man who succeeded Phanes when he fled. He has vanished, no one knows whither, but people say that the crown-prince has either imprisoned him in a dismal dungeon on account of his having uttered threats of retaliating the cruelty shown to Phanes' children, or—what would be worse—has had him dragged off to some distant quarry. The poor old man was exiled from his home, not for his own fault, but by the malice of his enemies, and the very day on which we lost sight of him an embassy arrived here from the Spartan people recalling Aristomachus to the Eurotas with all the honors Greece could bestow, because his sons had brought great glory to their country. A ship wreathed with flowers was sent to fetch the honored old man, and at the head of the deputation was his own brave, strong son, now crowned with glory and fame."

"I know him. He's a man of iron. Once he mutilated himself cruelly to avoid disgrace. By the Anahita star,* which is setting so beautifully in the east, he shall be revenged!"

"Oh, can it be so late? To me the time has gone by like a sweet breeze, which kissed my forehead and passed away. Did not you hear some one call? They will be waiting for us, and you must be at your friend's house in the town before dawn. Good-bye, my brave hero."

"Good-bye, my dearest one. In five days we shall hear our marriage-hymn. But you tremble as if we were going to battle instead of to our wedding."

"I'm trembling at the greatness of our joy; one always trembles in expectation of anything unusually great."

"Hark, Rhodopis is calling again; let us go. I have asked Theopompus to arrange everything about our wedding with her according to the usual custom; and I shall remain in his house incognito until I can carry you off as my own dear wife."

"And I will go with you."

---

* See note 72.

The next morning, as the three friends were walking with their host in his garden, Zopyrus exclaimed: "Why, Bartja, I've been dreaming all night of your Sappho. What a lucky fellow you are! Why I fancied my new wife in Sardis was no end of a beauty until I saw Sappho, and now when I think of her she seems like an owl. If Araspes could see Sappho he would be obliged to confess that even Panthea had been outdone at last. Such a creature was never made before. Auramazda is an awful spendthrift; he might have made three beauties out of Sappho. And how charmingly it sounded when she said 'good-night' to us in Persian."

"While I was away," said Bartja, "she has been taking a great deal of trouble to learn Persian from the wife of a Babylonian carpet-merchant, a native of Susa, who is living at Naukratis, in order to surprise me."

"Yes, she is a glorious girl," said Theopompus. "My late wife loved the little one as if she had been her own child. She would have liked to have had her as a wife for our son who manages the affairs of my house at Miletus, but the gods have ordained otherwise! Ah, how glad she would have been to see the wedding garland at Rhodopis' door!"

"Is it the custom here to ornament a bride's house with flowers?" said Zopyrus.

"Certainly," answered Theopompus. "When you see a door hung with flowers you may always know that house contains a bride; an olive-branch is a sign that a boy has just come into the world, and a strip of woollen cloth hanging over the gate that a girl has been born; but a vessel of water before the door is the token of death.[94]—But business-hour at the market is very near, my friends, and I must leave you, as I have affairs of great importance to transact."

"I will accompany you," said Zopyrus, "I want to order some garlands for Rhodopis' house."

"Aha," laughed the Milesian. "I see, you want to talk to the flower-girls again. Come, it's of no use to deny. Well, if you like you can come with me, but don't be so generous as you were yesterday, and don't forget that if certain news of war should arrive, your disguise may prove dangerous."

The Greek then had his sandals fastened on by his slaves and started for the market, accompanied by Zopyrus. In a few hours he returned with such a serious expression on his usually cheerful face, that it was easy to see something very important had happened.

"I found the whole town in great agitation," he said to the two friends who had remained at home; "there is a report that Amasis is at the point of death. We had all met on the place of exchange[95] in order to settle our business, and I was on the point of selling all my stored goods at such high prices as to secure me a first-rate profit, with which, when the prospect of an important war had lowered prices again, I could have bought in fresh goods—you see it stands me in good stead to know your royal brother's intentions so early—when suddenly the Toparch appeared among us, and announced that Amasis was not only seriously ill, but that the physicians had given up all hope, and he himself felt he was very

---

94. Schömann, *Privatalterthümer.* Water before a house. Schol. Arist. *Nub.* v. 837.

95. On the so-called δεῖγμα of the exchange the Greek wholesale merchants were accustomed to sell their wares by samples. Böckh, *Staatshaushaltung der Athener* I. p. 84. 85.

near death. We must hold ourselves in readiness for this at any moment, and for a very serious change in the face of affairs. The death of Amasis is the severest loss that could happen to us Greeks; he was always our friend, and favored us whenever he could, while his son is our avowed enemy and will do his utmost to expel us from the country. If his father had allowed, and he himself had not felt so strongly the importance and value of our mercenary troops, he would have turned us hateful foreigners out long ago. Naukratis and its temples are odious to him. When Amasis is dead our town will hail Cambyses' army with delight, for I have had experience already, in my native town Miletus, that you are accustomed to show respect to those who are not Persians and to protect their rights."

"Yes," said Bartja, "I will take care that all your ancient liberties shall be confirmed by my brother and new ones granted you."

"Well, I only hope he will soon be here," exclaimed the Greek, "for we know that Psamtik, as soon as he possibly can, will order our temples, which are an abomination to him, to be demolished. The building of a place of sacrifice for the Greeks at Memphis has long been put a stop to."

"But here," said Darius, "we saw a number of splendid temples as we came up from the harbor."

"Oh, yes, we have several.*—Ah, there comes Zopyrus; the slaves are carrying a perfect grove of garlands behind him. He's laughing so heartily, he must have amused himself famously with the flower-girls.— Good-morning, my friend. The sad news which fills all Naukratis does not seem to disturb you much."

* See vol. 1. note 2.

"Oh, for anything I care, Amasis may go on living a hundred years yet. But if he dies now, people will have something else to do beside looking after us. When do you set off for Rhodopis' house, friends?"

"At dusk."

"Then please, ask her to accept these flowers from me. I never thought I could have been so taken by an old woman before. Every word she says sounds like music, and though she speaks so gravely and wisely it's as pleasant to the ear as a merry joke. But I shan't go with you this time, Bartja; I should only be in the way. Darius, what have you made up your mind to do?"

"I don't want to lose one chance of a conversation with Rhodopis."

"Well, I don't blame you. You're all for learning and knowing everything, and I'm for enjoying. Friends, what do you say to letting me off this evening? You see . . ."

"I know all about it," interrupted Bartja laughing: "You've only seen the flower-girls by daylight as yet, and you would like to know how they look by lamplight."

"Yes, that's it," said Zopyrus, putting on a grave face. "On that point I am quite as eager after knowledge as Darius."

"Well, we wish you much pleasure with your three sisters."

"No, no, not all three, if you please; Stephanion, the youngest, is my favorite."

Morning had already dawned when Bartja, Darius

and Theopompus left Rhodopis' house. Syloson,[96] a Greek noble who had been banished from his native land by his own brother, Polykrates the tyrant, had been spending the evening with them, and was now returning in their company to Naukratis, where he had been living many years.

This man, though an exile, was liberally supplied with money by his brother, kept the most brilliant establishment in Naukratis, and was as famous for his extravagant hospitality as for his strength and cleverness. Syloson was a very handsome man too, and so remarkable for the good taste and splendor of his dress, that the youth of Naukratis prided themselves on imitating the cut and hang of his robes. Being unmarried, he spent many of his evenings at Rhodopis' house, and had been told the secret of her granddaughter's betrothal.

On that evening it had been settled, that in four days the marriage should be celebrated with the greatest privacy. Bartja had formally betrothed himself to Sappho by eating a quince with her, on the same day on which she had offered sacrifices to Zeus, Hera, and the other deities who protected marriage.[97] The wedding-banquet was to be given at the house of Theopompus, which was looked upon as the bridegroom's.[98] The prince's costly

96. Herod. III. 39. 139. 141.

97. Zeus and Hera are the only divinities mentioned by Diodorus (V. 73.) as receiving marriage-offerings. Plutarch says (Solon. 20.) that the Athenian brides were bound by one of Solon's laws to eat a quince before the nuptial ceremony. The quince ($\mu\tilde{\eta}\lambda o\nu$ $\kappa\nu\delta\omega\nu\iota o\nu$) seems in other respects also to have had significance for lovers. That a period of betrothal existed among the Greeks, as with ourselves, is certain. As an instance we need only remind our readers of Sophocles' Antigone, and her betrothal with Haemon.

98. See Böttiger, *Aldobr. Hochzeit* p. 142. where the nuptial hymn or Hymenaeus is sung accompanied by the flute. It cannot be clearly

bridal presents had been entrusted to Rhodopis' care, and Bartja had insisted on renouncing the paternal inheritance which belonged to his bride and on transferring it to Rhodopis, notwithstanding her determined resistance.

Syloson accompanied the friends to Rhodopis' house, and was just about to leave them, when a loud noise in the streets broke the quiet stillness of the night, and soon after, a troop of the watch passed by, taking a man to prison. The prisoner seemed highly indignant, and the less his broken Greek oaths and his utterances in some other totally unintelligible language were understood by the Egyptian guards, the more violent he became.

Directly Bartja and Darius heard the voice they ran up, and recognized Zopyrus at once.

Syloson and Theopompus stopped the guards, and asked what their captive had done. The officer on duty recognized them directly; indeed every child in Naukratis knew the Milesian merchant and the brother of the tyrant Polykrates by sight; and he answered at once, with a respectful salutation, that the foreign youth they were leading away had been guilty of murder.

Theopompus then took him on one side and endeavored, by liberal promises, to obtain the freedom of the prisoner. The man, however, would concede nothing

---

determined, who carried the bridal torches. K. F. Hermann, *Privatalterthümer* §. 31. It is also uncertain whether the marriage-feast was held in the house of the bride or the bridegroom, as passages can be quoted to prove both. For want of the bridegroom's house we have been unable to describe all the customs usual at a marriage, as for instance the procession thither, when the carriage conveying the bride was accompanied by a chorus singing the "carriage-song" ἁρμάτειον μέλος) and preceded by female attendants carrying lighted torches.

but a permission to speak with his captive. Meanwhile his friends begged Zopyrus to tell them at once what had happened, and heard the following story: The thoughtless fellow had visited the flower-girls at dusk and remained till dawn. He had scarcely closed their house-door on his way home, when he found himself surrounded by a number of young men, who had probably been lying in wait for him, as he had already had a quarrel with one of them, who called himself the betrothed lover of Stephanion, on that very morning. The girl had told her troublesome admirer to leave her flowers alone, and had thanked Zopyrus for threatening to use personal violence to the intruder. When the young Achæmenide found himself surrounded, he drew his sword and easily dispersed his adversaries, as they were only armed with sticks, but chanced to wound the jealous lover, who was more violent than the rest, so seriously, that he fell to the ground. Meanwhile the watch had come up, and as Zopyrus' victim howled "thieves" and "murder" incessantly, they proceeded to arrest the offender. This was not so easy. His blood was up, and rushing on them with his drawn sword, he had already cut his way through the first troop when a second came up. He was not to be daunted, attacked them too, split the skull of one, wounded another in the arm and was taking aim for a third blow, when he felt a cord round his neck. It was drawn tighter and tighter till at last he could not breathe and fell down insensible. By the time he came to his senses he was bound, and notwithstanding all his appeals to his pass and the name of Theopompus, was forced to follow his captors.

When the tale was finished the Milesian did not attempt to conceal his strong disapprobation, and told

Zopyrus that his most unseasonable love of fighting might be followed by the saddest consequences. After saying this, he turned to the officer and begged him to accept his own personal security for the prisoner. The other, however, refused gravely, saying he might forfeit his own life by doing so, as a law existed in Egypt by which the concealer of a murder was condemned to death.[59] He must, he assured them, take the culprit to Sais and deliver him over to the Nomarch* for punishment. "He has murdered an Egyptian," were his last words, and must therefore be tried by an Egyptian supreme court. In any other case I should be delighted to render you any service in my power."

During this conversation Zopyrus had been begging his friends not to take any trouble about him. "By Mithras," he cried, when Bartja offered to declare himself to the Egyptians as a means of procuring his freedom, "I vow I'll stab myself without a second thought, if you give yourselves up to those dogs of Egyptians. Why the whole town is talking about the war already, and do you think that if Psamtik knew he'd got such splendid game in his net, he would let you loose? He would keep you as hostages, of course. No, no, my friends. Good-bye; may Auramazda send you his best blessings! and don't quite forget the jovial Zopyrus, who lived and died for love and war."

The captain of the band placed himself at the head of his men, gave the order to march, and in a few minutes Zopyrus was out of sight.

59. The man who concealed a murder was to be punished with the knout (ἔδει μαστιγοῦσθαι) and left three days and nights without food or drink. Diod. I. 77.

* See vol. 1. note 140.

CHAPTER XI.

ACCORDING to the law of Egypt, Zopyrus had deserved death.

As soon as his friends heard this, they resolved to go to Sais and try to rescue him by stratagem. Syloson, who had friends there and could speak the Egyptian language well, offered to help them.

Bartja and Darius disguised themselves so completely by dyeing their hair and eyebrows and wearing broad-brimmed felt-hats,[100] that they could scarcely recognize each other. Theopompus provided them with ordinary Greek dresses, and, an hour after Zopyrus' arrest, they met the splendidly-got-up Syloson on the shore of the Nile, entered a boat belonging to him and manned by his slaves, and, after a short sail, favored by the wind, reached Sais,—which lay above the waters of the inundation like an island,—before the burning midsummer sun had reached its noonday height.

They disembarked at a remote part of the town and walked across the quarter appropriated to the artisans. The workmen were busy at their calling, notwithstanding the intense noonday heat. The baker's men were at work in the open court of the bakehouse, kneading

100. These felt hats (πέτασος, petasus) were used as a protection from the rays of the sun, first among the Greeks, later by the Romans, and, as the sun-light in Egypt is especially dazzling, must certainly have been adopted by the Hellenic settlers on the Nile. Almost all the horsemen in the celebrated procession from the Parthenon (now in the British Museum) are represented with the Petasus. It was most generally used as a travelling-hat. A figure with a broad-brimmed hat on his back was meant to represent a traveller. Compare the way in which pilgrims are represented in the pictures of the middle ages.

bread—the coarser kind of dough with the feet, the finer with the hands. Loaves of various shapes were being drawn out of the ovens—round and oval cakes, and rolls in the form of sheep, snails and hearts. These were laid in baskets, and the nimble baker's boys would put three, four, or even five such baskets on their heads at once, and carry them off quickly and safely to the customers living in other quarters of the city.[101] A butcher was slaughtering an ox before his house, the creature's legs having been pinioned; and his men were busy sharpening their knives to cut up a wild goat.[102] Merry cobblers[103] were calling out to the passers-by from their stalls; carpenters, tailors, joiners and weavers[104] were all there, busy at their various callings. The wives of the work-people were going out marketing, leading their naked children by the hand, and some soldiers were loitering near a man who was offering beer and wine for sale.[105]

101. The life and manners of the working classes are often represented on the ancient monuments, and very vividly, especially in the tombs of Sakkara and the rock-sepulchres of Beni-hassan and Thebes. See Wilkinson, vols. 2. 3. Rosellini, *Mon. Civil.* T. 41. &c. Especially for the bakers see Genesis 40. 16. Herod. II. 36. Ebers, *Aegypten* I. p. 330 and following.

102. Butchers. Wilkinson II. 375. Dümichen, *Resultate*, T. VIII. and XI. Ebers, *Aegypten in Bild und Wort*. I. p. 155.

103. Shoemakers. Wilkinson III. 160.

104. Workers in wood. Wilkinson III. 144. 174. 183. Weavers II. 60. III. 134. 135. Rosellini, *Mon. Civil.* T. 41. and following. Lepsius, *Denkmäler* II. 126 from Benihassan. In the Berlin Museum there are some ancient Egyptian spindles, and in the Museum at Leyden is a beautiful thread-winder with red thread still wound round it, besides several specimens of ancient Egyptian stuffs.

105. The Egyptian beer, called by the Greeks (ξύθος) Zythos (Zythum), was well known among the ancients, but not much esteemed by them. It was said, like wine, to have been given to men by Osiris. Diod. I. 34. The best was brewed in Pelusium. Columella X. 116. Plin. *Hist. Nat.* XXII. 82. This beer is often mentioned in the ancient Egyptian writings and called "Hek." A special kind was

But our friends took very little notice of what was going on in the streets through which they passed; they followed Syloson in silence.

At the Greek guard-house he asked them to wait for him. Syloson, happening to know the Taxiarch who was on duty that day, went in and asked him if he had heard anything of a man accused of murder having been brought from Naukratis to Sais that morning.

"Of course," said the Greek. "It's not more than half an hour since he arrived. As they found a purse full of money in his girdle, they think he must be a Persian spy. I suppose you know that Cambyses is preparing for war with Egypt."

"Impossible!"

"No, no, it's a fact. The prince-regent has already received information. A caravan of Arabian merchants arrived yesterday at Pelusium, and brought the news."

"It will prove as false as their suspicions about this poor young Lydian. I know him well, and am very sorry for the poor fellow. He belongs to one of the richest families in Sardis, and only ran away for fear of the powerful satrap Oroetes, with whom he had had a quarrel. I'll tell you the particulars when you come to see me next in Naukratis. Of course you'll stay a few days and bring some friends. My brother has sent me some wine which beats everything I ever tasted. It's perfect nectar, and I confess I grudge offering it to any one who's not, like you, a perfect judge in such matters."

The Taxiarch's face brightened up at these words,

called Hek nezem, sweet beer. It may be interesting to notice that a connection has been found between Gambrinus and Egypt, the earliest beer-drinking country. It is said, namely, in the Aventinus *Annal. Boj.* I. 6. 11. that Gambrinus was the son of Isis. On intoxication, see Vol. I. note 132.

and grasping Syloson's hand, he exclaimed. "By the dog,* my friend, we shall not wait to be asked twice; we'll come soon enough and take a good pull at your wine-skins. How would it be if you were to ask Archidice,[106] the three flower-sisters, and a few flute-playing-girls to supper?"

"They shall all be there. By the bye, that reminds me that the flower-girls were the cause of that poor young Lydian's imprisonment. Some jealous idiot attacked him before their house with a number of comrades. The hot-brained young fellow defended himself . . . ."

"And knocked the other down?"

"Yes; and so that he'll never get up again."

"The boy must be a good boxer."

" He had a sword."

" So much the better for him."

" No, so much the worse; for his victim was an Egyptian."

"That's a bad job. I fear it can only have an unfortunate end. A foreigner, who kills an Egyptian, is as sure of death as if he had the rope already round his neck.[107] However, just now he'll get a few days' grace; the priests are all so busy praying for the dying king that they have no time to try criminals."

" I'd give a great deal to be able to save that poor fellow. I know his father."

" Yes, and then after all he only did his duty. A man must defend himself."

106. A celebrated Hetaira of Naukratis mentioned by Herod. II. 135. Flute-playing girls were seldom missing at the young Greeks' drinking-parties.

107. Criminals in Egypt were often hung. Genesis 40, 20-23. Rosellini, *Mon. Civ.* T. 124.

* See vol. I. note 186.

"Do you happen to know where he is imprisoned?"

"Of course I do. The great prison is under repair, and so he has been put for the present in the storehouse between the principal guard-house of the Egyptian body-guard and the sacred grove of the temple of Neith. I have only just come home from seeing them take him there."

"He is strong and has plenty of courage; do you think he could get away, if we helped him?"

"No, it would be quite impossible; he's in a room two stories high; the only window looks into the sacred grove, and that, you know, is surrounded by a ten-foot wall, and guarded like the treasury. There are double sentries at every gate. There's only one place where it is left unguarded during the inundation season, because, just here, the water washes the walls. These worshippers of animals are as cautious as water-wagtails."

"Well, it's a great pity, but I suppose we must leave the poor fellow to his fate. Good-bye, Dæmones; don't forget my invitation."

The Samian left the guard-room and went back directly to the two friends, who were waiting impatiently for him.

They listened eagerly to his tidings, and when he had finished his description of the prison, Darius exclaimed: "I believe a little courage will save him. He's as nimble as a cat, and as strong as a bear. I have thought of a plan."

"Let us hear it," said Syloson, "and let me give an opinion as to its practicability."

"We will buy some rope-ladders, some cord, and a good bow, put all these into our boat, and row to the unguarded part of the temple-wall at dusk. You must then help me to clamber over it. I shall take the things over with me and give the eagle's cry. Zopyrus will know at once, because, since we were children, we have been accustomed to use it when we were riding or hunting together. Then I shall shoot an arrow, with the cord fastened to it, up into his window, (I never miss), tell him to fasten a weight to it and let it down again to me. I shall then secure the rope-ladder to the cord, Zopyrus will draw the whole affair up again, and hang it on an iron nail,—which, by the bye, I must not forget to send up with the ladder, for who knows whether he may have such a thing in his cell. He will then come down on it, go quickly with me to the part of the wall where you will be waiting with the boat, and where there must be another rope-ladder, spring into the boat, and there he is—safe!"

"First-rate, first-rate!" cried Bartja.

"But very dangerous," added Syloson. "If we are caught in the sacred grove, we are certain to be severely punished. The priests hold strange nightly festivals there, at which every one but the initiated is strictly forbidden to appear. I believe, however, that these take place on the lake,* and that is at some distance from Zopyrus' prison."

"So much the better," cried Darius; "but now to the main point. We must send at once, and ask Theopompus to hire a fast trireme for us, and have it put in sailing order at once. The news of Cambyses' preparations have already reached Egypt; they take us for spies, and will be sure not to let either Zopyrus or his deliverers escape, if they can help it. It would be a

* See vol. I. note 150, and vol. II. note 162.

criminal rashness to expose ourselves uselessly to danger. Bartja, you must take this message yourself, and must marry Sappho this very day, for, come what may, we must leave Naukratis to-morrow. Don't contradict me, my friend, my brother! You know our plan, and you must see that as only one can act in it, your part would be that of a mere looker-on. As it was my own idea I am determined to carry it out myself. We shall meet again to-morrow, for Auramazda protects the friendship of the pure."

It was a long time before they could persuade Bartja to leave his friends in the lurch, but their entreaties and representations at last took effect, and he went down towards the river to take a boat for Naukratis, Darius and Syloson going at the same time to buy the necessary implements for their plan.

In order to reach the place where boats were to be hired, Bartja had to pass by the temple of Neith. This was not easy, as an immense crowd was assembled at the entrance-gates. He pushed his way as far as the obelisks near the great gate of the temple with its winged sun-disc and fluttering pennons, but there the temple-servants prevented him from going farther; they were keeping the avenue of sphinxes clear for a procession.* The gigantic doors of the Pylon opened, and Bartja, who, in spite of himself, had been pushed into the front row, saw a brilliant procession come out of the temple. The unexpected sight of many faces he had formerly known occupied his attention so much, that he scarcely noticed the loss of his broad-brimmed hat, which had been knocked off in the crowd. From the conversation of two Ionian mercenaries behind him he

* See vol. I. note 149.

learnt that the family of Amasis had been to the temple to pray for the dying king.

The procession was headed by richly-decorated priests, either wearing long white robes or pantherskins. They were followed by men holding office at the court, and carrying golden staves, on the ends of which peacocks' feathers and silver lotus-flowers were fastened, and these by Pastophori,[108] carrying on their shoulders a golden cow, the animal sacred to Isis. When the crowd had bowed down before this sacred symbol, the queen appeared. She was dressed in priestly robes and wore a costly head-dress with the winged disc and the Uræus. In her left hand she held a sacred golden sistrum,[109] the tones of which were to scare away

---

108. These were priests whose duty it was to carry the sacred animals and representations of the divinities at the religious processions. According to Clemens of Alexandria, *Strom.* VI. 663. and the bilingual stone of Rosetta, the priesthood was divided into high-priests, prophets, stolists,—to whom were entrusted the pictures and statues of the gods, the sacrifices and the office of teaching; those who had a right to wear the feather—writers of the sacred mystic cipher—hierogrammatists or sages (in Egyptian: "things having knowledge") to which order belonged the astronomers, astrologers. soothsayers and calendar-makers—the holy fathers, amongst whom the singers were reckoned and those who kept the precepts and rules of the royal life, and lastly the inferior priests, namely, the Pastophori, (bearers of the sacred pictures, statues and symbols in the processions), the Taricheuti or embalmers. the Neokori or temple-servants. &c. For details see Ebers, *Aegypten* p. 341. and following.

109. A musical instrument used in religious services, and often ornamented with much skill and art. It consisted of a bow with bars, and rings on the bars which could be sounded together. Plutarch describes it very exactly (Is. and Os. 63.), says it was used to scare away Typhon, and that on the rounded part of the metal was the likeness of a cat with human features. His description is confirmed by a bronze sistrum in the Berlin Museum, on the bend of which is a cat with the sun-disc over its head. On the handle of another is a double Isis-mask. See also Wilkinson I. 145. This instrument is said to have been used in the Egyptian war-music also. (Virgil. *Aen.* VIII. 696.) but the statement that it served instead of the trumpet is incorrect, as we see from the monuments that the trumpet was also in use. *Prop. III.* 11. 43.

Typhon, and in her right some lotus-flowers. The wife, daughter and sister of the high-priest followed her, in similar but less splendid ornaments.[110] Then came the heir to the throne, in rich robes of state, as priest and prince; and behind him four young priests in white carrying Tachot, (the daughter of Amasis and Ladice and the pretended sister of Nitetis,) in an open litter. The heat of the day, and the earnestness of her prayers, had given the sick girl a slight color. Her blue eyes, filled with tears, were fixed on the sistrum which her weak, emaciated hands had hardly strength to hold.

A murmur of compassion ran through the crowd; for they loved their dying king, and manifested openly and gladly the sympathy so usually felt for young lives from whom a brilliant future has been snatched by disease. Such was Amasis' young, fading daughter, who was now being carried past them, and many an eye grew dim as the beautiful invalid came in sight. Tachot seemed to notice this, for she raised her eyes from the sistrum and looked kindly and gratefully at the crowd. Suddenly the color left her face, she turned deadly pale, and the golden sistrum fell on to the stone pavement with a clang, close to Bartja's feet. He felt that he had been recognized and for one moment thought of hiding himself in the crowd; but only for one moment;—his chivalrous feeling gained the day, he darted forward, picked up the sistrum, and

---

110. Similar processions of women are to be found on the monuments, as, for example, at Thebes, where the wife of Rameses the Great and the mother, daughter and sister of a priest are going up to prayer. Wilkinson I. 260. The question whether these were priestesses or not has also been decided in the affirmative by the monuments, especially the bi-lingual tablet of Canopus.

forgetting the danger in which he was placing himself, held it out to the princess.

Tachot looked at him earnestly before taking the golden sistrum from his hands, and then said, in a low voice, which only he could understand: "Are you Bartja? Tell me,—in your mother's name—are you Bartja?"

"Yes, I am," was his answer, in a voice as low as her own, "your friend, Bartja."

He could not say more, for the priests pushed him back among the crowd. When he was in his old place, he noticed that Tachot, whose bearers had begun to move on again, was looking round at him. The color had come back into her cheeks, and her bright eyes were trying to meet his. He did not avoid them; she threw him a lotus-bud—he stooped to pick it up, and then broke his way through the crowd, for this hasty act had roused their attention.

A quarter of an hour later, he was seated in the boat which was to take him to Sappho and to his wedding. He was quite at ease now about Zopyrus. In Bartja's eyes his friend was already as good as saved, and in spite of the dangers which threatened himself, he felt strangely calm and happy, he could hardly say why.

Meanwhile the sick princess had been carried home, had had her oppressive ornaments taken off, and her couch carried on to one of the palace-balconies where she liked best to pass the hot summer days, sheltered by broad-leaved plants[111] and a kind of awning.

From this veranda, she could look down into the

---

111. Wilkinson II. 121. 129. From representations found in Thebes

great fore-court of the palace, which was planted with trees. To-day it was full of priests, courtiers, generals and governors of provinces. Anxiety and suspense were expressed in every face: Amasis' last hour was drawing very near.

Tachot could not be seen from below; but listening with feverish eagerness, she could hear much that was said. Now that they had to dread the loss of their king, every one, even the priests, were full of his praises. The wisdom and circumspection of his plans and modes of government, his unwearied industry, the moderation he had always shown, the keenness of his wit, were, each and all, subjects of admiration. "How Egypt has prospered under Amasis' government!" said a Nomarch. "And what glory he gained for our arms, by the conquest of Cyprus and the war with the Libyans!" cried one of the generals. "How magnificently he embellished our temples, and what great honors he paid to the goddess of Sais!" exclaimed one of the singers of Neith. "And then how gracious and condescending he was!" murmured a courtier. "How cleverly he managed to keep peace with the great powers!" said the secretary of state, and the treasurer, wiping away a tear, cried: "How thoroughly he understood the management of the revenue! Since the reign of Rameses III. the treasury has not been so well filled as now."[112] "Psamtik comes into a fine inheritance,"

---

112. Rhampsinit, of whose treasure-house Herodotus (II. 121. 122.) tells the amusing story which has been dramatized by Count Platen. We can hardly believe Appian when he says that the treasury of Ptolemy Philadelphus contained 740,000 Egyptian talents, for this, even if we reckon the Egyptian talent at half the value of the Aeginetan, would give the sum of £83,250,000. Perhaps Böckh (Staatshaushalt d. Ath. I. p. 14.) is right in his conjecture, that this sum represented the total receipts of his reign of 38 years. There is said, however, to

lisped the courtier, and the soldier exclaimed, " Yes, but it's to be feared that he'll not spend it in a glorious war; he's too much under the influence of the priests." " No, you are wrong there," answered the temple-singer. " For some time past, our lord and master has seemed to disdain the advice of his most faithful servants." " The successor of such a father will find it difficult to secure universal approbation," said the Nomarch. " It is not every one who has the intellect, the good fortune and the wisdom of Amasis." " The gods know that!" murmured the warrior with a sigh.

Tachot's tears flowed fast. These words were a confirmation of what they had been trying to hide from her: she was to lose her dear father soon.

After she had made this dreadful certainty clear to her own mind, and discovered that it was in vain to beg her attendants to carry her to her dying father, she left off listening to the courtiers below, and began looking at the sistrum which Bartja himself had put into her hand, and which she had brought on to the balcony with her, as if seeking comfort there. And she found what she sought; for it seemed to her as if the sound of its sacred rings bore her away into a smiling, sunny landscape.

have been an inscription on the treasury of Rameses the Great (Osymandyas) to the effect that the gold and silver mines of Egypt yielded a yearly revenue of 32 million minæ or £90,000,000. Diod. I. 49. According to the same historian (I. 62.) the treasury of Rhampsinit contained four million talents, which, reckoning as before in Egyptian talents, would give £450,000,000. By a fortunate chance a representation of this rich king's treasure-house, so celebrated through the before-mentioned tale, has come down to us. It is in the temple of Medinet Haboo and has been published by Dümichen in his *Historischen Inschriften Altägyptischer Denkmäler*, Taff. XXX. and following. The mass of treasure represented is really enormous, in gold, silver, copper, and even Arabian spices. The precious metals are stored in sacks, vases, and heaps; the baser in bars.

That faintness which so often comes over people in decline, had seized her and was sweetening her last hours with pleasant dreams.

The female slaves, who stood round to fan away the flies, said afterwards that Tachot had never looked so lovely.

She had lain about an hour in this state, when her breathing became more difficult, a slight cough made her breast heave, and the bright red blood trickled down from her lips on to her white robe. She awoke, and looked surprised and disappointed on seeing the faces round her. The sight of her mother, however, who came on to the veranda at that moment, brought a smile to her face, and she said, " O mother, I have had such a beautiful dream."

"Then our visit to the temple has done my dear child good ?" asked the queen, trembling at the sight of the blood on the sick girl's lips.

" Oh, yes, mother, so much! for I saw him again."

Ladice's glance at the attendants seemed to ask: " Has your poor mistress lost her senses ?" Tachot understood the look and said, evidently speaking with great difficulty: "You think I am wandering, mother. No, indeed, I really saw and spoke to him. He gave me my sistrum again, and said he was my friend, and then he took my lotus-bud and vanished. Don't look so distressed and surprised, mother. What I say is really true; it is no dream.—There, you hear, Tentrut saw him too. He must have come to Sais for my sake, and so the child-oracle in the temple-court did not deceive me, after all. And now I don't feel anything more of my illness; I dreamt I was lying in a field of blooming poppies, as red as the blood of the young lambs that are offered in sacrifice; Bartja was sitting by my side, and Nitetis was kneeling close to us and playing wonderful songs on a Nabla* made of ivory. And there was such a lovely sound in the air that I felt as if Horus, the beautiful god of morning, spring, and the resurrection, was kissing me. Yes, mother, I tell you he is coming soon, and when I am well, then—then—ah, mother what is this? . . . I am dying!"

Ladice knelt down by her child's bed and pressed her lips in burning kisses on the girl's eyes as they grew dim in death.

An hour later she was standing by another bedside—her dying husband's.

Severe suffering had disfigured the king's features, the cold perspiration was standing on his forehead, and his hands grasped the golden lions[113] on the arms of the deep-seated invalid chair in which he was resting, almost convulsively.

When Ladice came in he opened his eyes; they were as keen and intelligent as if he had never lost his sight.

"Why do not you bring Tachot to me?" he asked in a dry voice.

"She is too ill, and suffers so much, that . . ."

"She is dead! Then it is well with her, for death is not punishment; it is the end and aim of life,—the only end that we can attain without effort, but through sufferings!—the gods alone know how great. Osiris has taken her to himself, for she was innocent. And Nitetis is dead too. Where is Nebenchari's letter?—

---

113. From Wilkinson and Rosellini. See also, Vol. I. note 133.

* An ancient Egyptian stringed instrument.

Here is the place: 'She took her own life, and died calling down a heavy curse on thee and thine. The poor, exiled, scorned and plundered oculist Nebenchari in Babylon sends thee this intelligence to Egypt. It is as true as his own hatred of thee.' Listen to these words, Psamtik, and remember how on his dying bed thy father told thee that, for every drachm of pleasure purchased on earth by wrong-doing, the dying bed will be burdened by a talent's weight of remorse. Fearful misery is coming on Egypt for Nitetis' sake. Cambyses is preparing to make war on us. He will sweep down on Egypt like a scorching wind from the desert. Much, which I have staked my nightly sleep and the very marrow of my existence to bring into existence, will be annihilated. Still I have not lived in vain. For forty years I have been the careful father and benefactor of a great nation. Children and children's children will speak of Amasis as a great, wise and humane king; they will read my name on the great works which I have built in Sais and Thebes, and will praise the greatness of my power. Neither shall I be condemned by Osiris and the forty-two judges of the nether world; the goddess of truth, who holds the balances,"[114] will find that my good deeds outweigh my bad."—Here the king sighed deeply and remained silent for some time. Then, looking tenderly at his wife, he said: " Ladice, thou hast been a faithful, virtuous wife to me. For this I thank thee, and ask thy forgiveness for much. We have often misunderstood

[114]. The goddess of truth was called the "mistress of the balances," because she weighed the souls of the dead in the lower world. This can be seen in the books of the dead, in nearly all of which the weighing of the soul is represented in the largest vignette (to Chap. 125.).

one another. Indeed it was easier for me to accustom myself to the Greek modes of thought, than for a Greek to understand our Egyptian ideas. Thou know'st my love of Greek art,—thou know'st how I enjoyed the society of thy friend Pythagoras, who was thoroughly initiated in all that we believe and know, and adopted much from us. He comprehended the deep wisdom which lies in the doctrines that I reverence most, and he took care not to speak lightly of truths which our priests are perhaps too careful to hide from the people; for though the many bow down before that which they cannot understand, they would be raised and upheld by those very truths, if explained to them. To a Greek mind our worship of animals presents the greatest difficulty, but to my own the worship of the Creator in his creatures seems more just and more worthy of a human being, than the worship of his likeness in stone. The Greek deities are moreover subject to every human infirmity; indeed I should have made my queen very unhappy by living in the same manner as her great god Zeus."

At these words the king smiled, and then went on: "And what has given rise to this? The Hellenic love of beauty in form, which, in the eye of a Greek, is superior to every thing else. He cannot separate the body from the soul, because he holds it to be the most glorious of formed things, and indeed, believes that a beautiful spirit must necessarily inhabit a beautiful body. Their gods, therefore, are only elevated human beings, but we adore an unseen power working in nature and in ourselves. The animal takes its place between ourselves and nature; its actions are guided, not, like our own, by the letter, but by the eternal laws of nature,"[115] which owe their origin to the Deity, while the letter is a device of man's own mind. And then, too, where amongst ourselves do we find so earnest a longing and endeavor to gain freedom, the highest good, as among the animals? Where such a regular and well-balanced life from generation to generation, without instruction or precept?"

Here the king's voice failed. He was obliged to pause for a few moments, and then continued: " I know that my end is near; therefore enough of these matters. My son and successor, hear my last wishes and act upon them; they are the result of experience. But alas! how often have I seen, that rules of life given by one man to another are useless. Every man must earn his own experience. His own losses make him prudent, his own learning wise. Thou, my son, art coming to the throne at a mature age; thou hast had time and opportunity to judge between right and wrong, to note what is beneficial and what hurtful, to see and compare many things. I give thee, therefore, only a few wholesome counsels, and only fear that though I offer them with my right hand, thou wilt accept them with the left.

" First, however, I must say that, notwithstanding my blindness, my indifference to what has been going on during the past months has been only apparent. I left you to your own devices with a good intention. Rhodopis told me once one of her teacher Æsop's fables: 'A traveller, meeting a man on his road, asked him how long it would be before he reached the nearest town.' 'Go on, go on,' cried the other. 'But I want to know first when I shall get to the town.' 'Go on,

115. From Anacharsis in Diodorus.

only go on,' was the answer. The traveller left him with angry words and abuse; but he had not gone many steps when the man called after him: 'You will be there in an hour. I could not answer your question until I had seen your pace.'

"I bore this fable in my mind for my son's sake, and watched in silence at what pace he was ruling his people. Now I have discovered what I wish to know, and this is my advice: Examine into everything yourself. It is the duty of every man, but especially of a king, to acquaint himself intimately with all that concerns the weal or woe of his people. You, my son, are in the habit of using the eyes and ears of other men instead of going to the fountain-head yourself. I am sure that your advisers, the priests, only desire what is good; but . . . Neithotep, I must beg you to leave us alone for a few moments."

When the priest was gone the king exclaimed: "They wish for what is good, but good only for themselves. But we are not kings of priests and aristocrats only, we are kings of a nation! Do not listen to the advice of this proud caste alone, but read every petition yourself, and, by appointing Nomarchs devoted to the king and beloved by the people, make yourself acquainted with the needs and wishes of the Egyptian nation. It is not difficult to govern well, if you are aware of the state of feeling in your land. Choose fit men to fill the offices of state. I have taken care that the kingdom shall be properly divided. The laws are good, and have proved themselves so; hold fast by these laws, and trust no one who sets himself above them; for law is invariably wiser than the individual man, and its transgressor deserves his punishment. The people understand this well, and are ready to sacrifice themselves for us, when they see that we are ready to give up our own will to the law. You do not care for the people. I know their voice is often rude and rough, but it utters wholesome truths, and no one needs to hear truth more than a king. The Pharaoh who chooses priests and courtiers for his advisers, will hear plenty of flattering words, while he who tries to fulfil the wishes of the nation will have much to suffer from those around him; but the latter will feel peace in his own heart, and be praised in the ages to come. I have often erred, yet the Egyptians will weep for me, as one who knew their needs and considered their welfare like a father. A king who really knows his duties, finds it an easy and beautiful task to win the love of the people—an unthankful one to gain the applause of the great—almost an impossibility to content both.

"Do not forget,—I say it again,—that kings and priests exist for the people, and not the people for their kings and priests. Honor religion for its own sake and as the most important means of securing the obedience of the governed to their governors; but at the same time show its promulgators that you look on them, not as receptacles, but as servants, of the Deity. Hold fast, as the law commands, by what is old; but never shut the gates of your kingdom against what is new, if better. Bad men break at once with the old traditions; fools only care for what is new and fresh; the narrow-minded and the selfish privileged class cling indiscriminately to all that is old, and pronounce progress to be a sin; but the wise endeavor to retain all that has approved itself in the past, to remove all that has become defective, and to adopt whatever is good, from whatever source it may have sprung. Act thus, my son. The priests will try to keep you back—the Greeks to urge you forward. Choose one party or the other, but beware of indecision—of yielding to the one to-day, to the other to-morrow. Between two stools a man falls to the ground. Let the one party be your friends, the other your enemies; by trying to please both, you will have both opposed to you. Human beings hate the man who shows kindness to their enemies. In the last few months, during which you have ruled independently, both parties have been offended by your miserable indecision. The man who runs backwards and forwards like a child, makes no progress, and is soon weary. I have till now—till I felt that death was near—always encouraged the Greeks and opposed the priests. In the active business of life, the clever, brave Greeks seemed to me especially serviceable;—at death, I want men who can make me out a pass into the nether regions. The gods forgive me for not being able to resist words that sound so like a joke, even in my last hour! They created me and must take me as I am. I rubbed my hands for joy when I became king; with thee, my son, coming to the throne is a graver matter.—Now call Neithotep back; I have still something to say to you both."

The king gave his hand to the high-priest as he entered, saying: "I leave you, Neithotep, without ill-will, though my opinion that you have been a better priest than a servant to your king, remains unaltered. Psamtik will probably prove a more obedient follower than I have been, but one thing I wish to impress earnestly on you both: Do not dismiss the Geeek mercenaries until the war with the Persians is over, and has ended—

we will hope—in victory for Egypt. My former predictions are not worth anything now; when death draws near, we get depressed, and things begin to look a little black. Without the auxiliary troops we shall be hopelessly lost, but with them victory is not impossible. Be clever; show the Ionians that they are fighting on the Nile for the freedom of their own country—that Cambyses, if victorious, will not be contented with Egypt alone, while his defeat may bring freedom to their own enslaved countrymen in Ionia. I know you agree with me, Neithotep, for in your heart you mean well to Egypt.—Now read me the prayers. I feel exhausted; my end must be very near. If I could only forget that poor Nitetis! had she the right to curse us? May the judges of the dead—may Osiris—have mercy on our souls! Sit down by me, Ladice; lay thy hand on my burning forehead. And Psamtik, in presence of these witnesses, swear to honor and respect thy step-mother, as if thou wert her own child. My poor wife! Come and seek me soon before the throne of Osiris. A widow and childless, what hast thou to do with this world? We brought up Nitetis as our own daughter, and yet we are so heavily punished for her sake. But her curse rests on us—and only on us;—not on thee, Psamtik, nor on thy children. Bring my grandson. Was that a tear? Perhaps; well, the little things to which one has accustomed one's self are generally the hardest to give up."

Rhodopis entertained a fresh guest that evening; Kallias, the son of Phœnippus,* the same who first

* See vol. I. notes 63 and 69.

appeared in our tale as the bearer of news from the Olympic games.

The lively, cheerful Athenian had just come back from his native country, and, as an old and tried friend, was not only received by Rhodopis, but made acquainted with the secret of Sappho's marriage.

Knakias, her old slave, had, it is true, taken in the flag which was the sign of reception, two days ago; but he knew that Kallias was always welcome to his mistress, and therefore admitted him just as readily as he refused every one else.

The Athenian had plenty to tell, and when Rhodopis was called away on business, he took his favorite Sappho into the garden, joking and teasing her gaily as they looked out for her lover's coming. But Bartja did not come, and Sappho began to be so anxious that Kallias called old Melitta, whose longing looks in the direction of Naukratis were, if possible, more anxious even than those of her mistress, and told her to fetch a musical instrument which he had brought with him.

It was a rather large lute, made of gold and ivory, and as he handed it to Sappho, he said, with a smile: "The inventor of this glorious instrument, the divine Anakreon, had it made expressly for me, at my own wish. He calls it a Barbiton,[116] and brings wonderful tones from its chords—tones that must echo on even into the land of shadows.[117] I have told this poet,

---

116. Barbitos and Barbiton (βάρβιτος and βάρβιτον). A stringed instrument in use among the Greeks, larger than the ordinary lyre (*Jul. Poll.* IV. 59.) and which seems, as Anthony Rich appropriately says, to have borne the same relation to the usual lute that the violoncello does to the violin. Anakreon accompanied his songs on this instrument, and is said to have invented it. (?)

117. See Vol. I. note 36. and Athen. IV. p. 175. *Griech Blumenlese*, III. 47. (Simonides) 50. 51. (Antipater of Sidon) and others.

who offers his life as one great sacrifice to the Muses, Eros and Dionysus,[118] a great deal about you, and he made me promise to bring you this song, which he wrote on purpose for you, as a gift from himself. Now, listen:

> "The Phrygian rock, that braves the storm,
> Was once a weeping matron's form;
> And Prokne, hapless, frantic maid,
> Is now a swallow in the shade.
>
> "Oh! that a mirror's form were mine
> To sparkle with that smile divine;
> And like my heart I then should be
> Reflecting thee, and only thee!
>
> "Or were I, love, the robe which flows
> O'er every charm that secret glows,
> In many a lucid fold to swim,
> And cling and grow to every limb!
>
> "Oh! could I, as the streamlet's wave,
> Thy warmly-mellowing beauties lave,
> Or float as perfume on thine hair,
> And breathe my soul in fragrance there!
>
> "I wish I were the zone that lies,
> Warm to thy breast, and feels its sighs!
> Or like those envious pearls that show
> So faintly round that neck of snow;
> Yes I would be a happy gem,
> Like them to hang, to fade like them.
>
> "What more would thy Anacreon be?
> Oh! anything that touches thee.
> Nay, sandals for those airy feet—
> Thus to be pressed by thee were sweet!" *

---

118. See Antipater of Sidon. *Epigram on Anakreon*. *Griech. Blumenlese* III. 52. and also the following translation by Moore.
> "To beauty's smile and wine's delight,
>   To joys he loved on earth so well,
> Still shall his spirit all the night
>   Attune the wild aërial shell."

* Translated by Moore.

"Are you angry with the poet for his presumption?"

"How could I be? Poets must always be allowed a certain freedom."

"And especially such a poet!"

"Who chooses such a master in the art of song as bearer of his verses."

"You little flatterer! Well, when I was twenty years younger, they had some right to praise my voice and style of singing; but now . . ."

"Now you're trying to get some more praise; you shall not succeed in extorting another word. But I should like to know whether this Barbiton, as you say it is called, with its soft tones, would do as accompaniment for other songs beside Anakreon's?"

"Of course. Take the Plectrum [119] and try its chords yourself; though I fear your delicate fingers will find them a little unmanageable."

"I cannot sing. I feel too anxious at Bartja's remaining so long away."

"Or, in other words, longing for him has taken away your voice. There is a song by your Lesbian aunt, the great Sappho, which just describes the state of mind you are probably in at this moment. Do you know it?"

"No, I think not."

"Then listen. It used to be the song I liked best to show off in. One would think Eros himself and not a woman, had written it.

> "Blest as th'immortal gods is he,
> The youth who fondly sits by thee,
> And hears and sees thee all the while
> Softly speak and sweetly smile.

119. A little ivory stick, which was used in playing on the stringed instruments.

"'Twas that deprived my soul of rest,
And raised such tumults in my breast;
For while I gazed, in transport toss'd,
My breath was gone, my voice was lost,"

"My bosom glow'd; the subtle flame
Ran quick through all my vital frame:
On my dim eyes a darkness hung,
My ears with hollow murmurs rung:

"With dewy damp my limbs were chill'd;
My blood with gentle horrors thrilled;
My feeble pulse forgot to play;
I fainted, sank, and died away." [120]

"Now, what do you say to this song? But by Hercules, child, how pale you are! Have the verses affected you so much, or are you frightened at this likeness of your own longing heart? Calm yourself, girl. Who knows what may have happened to keep your lover?"

"Nothing has happened,—nothing," cried a gay, manly voice, and in a few seconds Sappho was in the arms of him she loved.

Kallias looked on quietly, smiling at the wonderful beauty of these two young lovers.

"But now," said the prince, after Sappho had made him acquainted with Kallias, "I must go at once to your grandmother. We dare not wait four days for our wedding. It must be to-day! There is danger in every hour of delay. Is Theopompus here?"

---

[120]. This song is the second of the only two odes of Sappho, which have reached us entire. It was preserved by Longinus, and imitated in Latin by Catullus. The English version is by Ambrose Phillips. Köchly, *Academische Vorträge und Reden*, p. 191 believed that the fiery words of the ode were composed to congratulate a young friend of the poetess (Attis) on her approaching nuptials with the man she loved. But the passionate fervor of the song seems to justify our opinion, though we too should expect of Sappho something different from our ordinary congratulatory verses.

"I think he must be," said Sappho. "I know of nothing else, that could keep my grandmother so long in the house. But tell me, what is this about our marriage? It seems to me..."

"Let us go in first, love. I fancy a thunder-storm must be coming on. The sky is so dark, and it's so intolerably sultry."

"As you like, only make haste, unless you mean me to die of impatience. There is not the slightest reason to be afraid of a storm. Since I was a child there has not been either lightning or thunder in Egypt at this time of year." [121]

"Then you will see something new to-day," said Kallias, laughing; "for a large drop of rain has just fallen on my bald head,—the Nile-swallows were flying close to the water as I came here, and you see there is a cloud coming over the moon already. Come in quickly, or you will get wet. Ho, slave, see that a black lamb is offered to the gods of the lower world." [122]

They found Theopompus sitting in Rhodopis' own apartment, as Sappho had supposed. He had finished telling her the story of Zopyrus' arrest, and of the

121. Thunder-storms do occur in Egypt, though very rarely. One happened when Lepsius was there, *Briefe aus Aegypten*, p. 26. That rain had fallen in Upper Egypt at the date of our tale, is related by Herodotus (III. 10.) as a miracle. We encountered one in January, 1870, near Antinoe in Upper Egypt. It was so violent that Arabian boats were upset on the Nile, and streams rushed down from the arid Arabian mountains. Several fellah huts were washed away, and palm-trees were uprooted. The old governor of the place assured us that he had never witnessed such a storm in his life.

122. When a thunder-storm threatened, the Greeks were accustomed to offer a black lamb to the storms, who were reckoned among the divinities of the lower regions. In the Frogs of Aristophanes, when Aeschylus is beginning a frightfully violent attack on Euripides, Dionysus calls out: "Slaves, bring a lamb, a black lamb, a fearful storm is coming on!" *Frogs* of Aristophanes 853.

journey which Bartja and his friends had taken on his behalf.

Their anxiety on the matter was beginning to be so serious, that Bartja's unexpected appearance was a great relief. His words flew as he repeated the events of the last few hours, and begged Theopompus to look out at once for a ship in sailing order, to convey himself and his friends from Egypt.

"That suits famously," exclaimed Kallias. "My own trireme brought me from Naukratis to-day; it is lying now, fully equipped for sea, in the port, and is quite at your service. I have only to send orders to the steersman to keep the crew together and everything in sailing order.—You are under no obligations to me; on the contrary it is I who have to thank you for the honor you will confer on me. Ho, Knakias!—tell my slave Philomelus,—he's waiting in the hall,—to take a boat to the port, and order my steersman Nausarchus to keep the ship in readiness for starting. Give him this seal; it empowers him to do all that is necessary."

"And my slaves?" said Bartja.

"Knakias can tell my old steward to take them to Kallias' ship," answered Theopompus.

"And when they see this," said Bartja, giving the old servant his ring, "they will obey without a question."

Knakias went away with many a deep obeisance, and the prince went on: "Now, my mother, I have a great petition to ask of you."

"I guess what it is," said Rhodopis, with a smile. "You wish your marriage to be hastened, and I see that I dare not oppose your wish."

"If I'm not mistaken," said Kallias, "we have a

remarkable case here. Two people are in great peril, and find that very peril a matter of rejoicing."

"Perhaps you are right there," said Bartja, pressing Sappho's hand unperceived. And then, turning to Rhodopis again, he begged her to delay no longer in trusting her dearest treasure to his care,—a treasure whose worth he knew so well.

Rhodopis rose, she laid her right hand on Sappho's head and her left on Bartja's, and said: "There is a myth which tells of a blue lake in the land of roses; its waves are sometimes calm and gentle, but at others they rise into a stormy flood; the taste of its waters is partly sweet as honey, partly bitter as gall. Ye will learn the meaning of this legend in the marriage-land of roses. Ye will pass calm and stormy—sweet and bitter hours there. So long as thou wert a child, Sappho, thy life passed on like a cloudless spring morning, but when thou becam'st a maiden, and hadst learnt to love, thine heart was opened to admit pain; and during the long months of separation pain was a frequent guest there. This guest will seek admission as long as life lasts. Bartja, it will be your duty to keep this intruder away from Sappho, as far as it lies in your power. I know the world. I could perceive, —even before Crœsus told me of your generous nature, —that you were worthy of my Sappho. This justified me in allowing you to eat the quince* with her; this induces me now to entrust to you, without fear, what I have always looked upon as a sacred pledge committed to my keeping. Look upon her too only as a loan. Nothing is more dangerous to love, than a comfortable assurance of exclusive possession.—I have

* See note 97.

been blamed for allowing such an inexperienced child to go forth into your distant country, where custom is so unfavorable to women; but I know what love is;— I know that a girl who loves, knows no home but the heart of her husband;—the woman whose heart has been touched by Eros no misfortune but that of separation from him whom she has chosen. And besides, I would ask you, Kallias and Theopompus, is the position of your own wives so superior to that of the Persian women? Are not the women of Ionia and Attica forced to pass their lives in their own apartments, thankful if they are allowed to cross the street accompanied by suspicious and distrustful slaves? As to the custom which prevails in Persia of taking many wives, I have no fear either for Bartja or Sappho. He will be more faithful to his wife than are many Greeks, for he will find in her what you are obliged to seek, on the one hand in marriage, on the other in the houses of the cultivated Hetaere:*—in the former, housewives and mothers, in the latter, animated and enlivening intellectual society. Take her, my son. I give her to you as an old warrior gives his sword, his best possession, to his stalwart son:—he gives it gladly and with confidence. Whithersoever she may go she will always remain a Greek, and it comforts me to think that in her new home she will bring honor to the Greek name and friends to our nation. Child, I thank thee for those tears. I can command my own, but fate has made me pay an immeasurable price for the power of doing so. The gods have heard your oath, my noble Bartja. Never forget it, but take her as your own,— your friend,—your wife. Take her away as soon as

* See vol. I. note 10.

your friends return; it is not the will of the gods that the Hymenæus should be sung at Sappho's nuptial rites."[123]

As she said these words she laid Sappho's hand in Bartja's, embraced her with passionate tenderness, and breathed a light kiss on the forehead of the young Persian. Then turning to her Greek friends, who stood by, much affected:

"That was a quiet nuptial ceremony," she said; "no songs, no torch-light! May their union be so much the happier. Melitta, bring the bride's marriage-ornaments, the bracelets and necklaces which lie in the bronze casket on my dressing-table, that our darling may give her hand to her lord attired as beseems a future princess."[124]

"Yes, and do not linger on the way," cried Kallias, whose old cheerfulness had now returned. "Neither can we allow the niece of the greatest of Hymen's poets* to be married without the sound of song and music. The young husband's house is, to be sure, too far off for our purpose, so we will suppose that the

---

123. The Hymenæus was the wedding-song, so called because of its *refrain* "Hymen O! Hymenae' O!" The god of marriage, Hymen, took his origin and name from the hymn, was afterwards decked out richly with myths, and finally, according to Catullus, received a seat on Mount Helikon with the Muses. Köchly (Sappho, p. 195.) thinks that these Hymenæi may be called a kind of lyric drama, as they were composed of different portions like the acts of a play, in which the characteristic parts of the marriage-ceremony were described in song and accompanied by appropriate action.

124. A Greek bride was beautifully adorned for her marriage, and her bridesmaids received holiday garments. Homer, *Odyss*. VI. 27. Besides which, after the bath, which both bride and bridegroom were obliged to take, she was anointed with sweet-smelling essences. Thucyd. II. 15. Xenoph. *Symp.* II. 3. Böttiger, *Aldobr. Hochzeit.* p. 41.

* The Lesbian Sappho.

andronitis is his dwelling. We will conduct the maiden thither by the centre door, and there we will enjoy a merry wedding-feast by the family hearth. Here, slave-girls, come and form yourselves into two choruses. Half of your number take the part of the youths; the other half that of the maidens, and sing us Sappho's Hymenæus. I will be the torch-bearer;"[125] that dignity is mine by right. You must know, Bartja, that my family has an hereditary right to carry the torches at the Eleusinian mysteries and we are therefore called Daduchi or torch-bearers.* Ho, slave! see that the door of the *andronitis* is hung with flowers, and tell your comrades to meet us with a shower of sweetmeats as we enter.[126] That's right, Melitta; why, how did you manage to get those lovely violet and myrtle marriage-crowns made so quickly?** The rain is streaming through the opening above. You see, Hymen has persuaded Zeus to help him; so that not a single marriage-rite shall be omitted. You could not take the bath, which ancient custom prescribes for the bride and bridegroom on the morning of their wedding-day, so you have only to stand here a moment and take the rain of Zeus as an equivalent for the waters of the sacred spring. Now, girls, begin your song. Let the maidens bewail the rosy days of childhood, and the youths praise the lot of those who marry young."

Five well-practised treble voices now began to sing the chorus of virgins in a sad and plaintive tone.

---
125. The mother of the bride lighted the torch. *Iphig. a. Aulis.* 722. The torch-bearer was probably intended to represent Hymen, *Aldobr. Hochzeit,* p. 142. Becker, *Charikles,* III. p. 306.

126. A custom also in vogue at Rome. *Schol.* Aristoph. Plutarch 768. Becker, *Charikles,* III. p. 306.

* See vol. 1. note 69.   ** See vol. 1. note 213.

"When in the garden's fenced and cultured ground,
Where browse no flocks, where ploughshares never wound,
By sunbeams strengthen'd, nourish'd by the shower,
And sooth'd by zephyr, blooms the lovely flower;
Maids long to place it in their modest zone,
And youths enraptur'd wish it for their own.
But from the stem once plucked, in dust it lies,
Nor youth nor maid will then desire or prize.
The virgin thus her blushing beauty rears,
Loved by her kindred, and her young compeers;
But if her simple charm, her maiden grace,
Is sullied by one spoiler's rude embrace,
Adoring youths no more her steps attend,
Nor loving maidens greet the maiden friend,
O Hymen, hear! O sacred Hymen haste;
Come, god and guardian of the fond and chaste!"

And the second chorus returned answer in deeper voices and cheerful tones:

"As in the naked field the vine's weak shoot
Nor lifts its languid stem, nor glows with fruit;
But, by itself weighed down, it lonely strays
And on its root its highest tendril lays.
The herdsmen then, the passing hinds, neglect
The lonely vine, nor cherish nor protect.
If by some happy chance its feeble boughs
Twined round the trunk shall make the elm a spouse;
No herdsmen then, nor passing hinds, neglect
The wedded vine, but cherish and protect.
So is the fair beloved who binds her fate
In wedlock chaste to some accordant mate
She gives the joys that warm her husband's breast,
And doting parents by her bliss are blest.
O Hymen, hear! O sacred Hymen, haste;
Come, god and guardian of the fond and chaste!" [127]

Then the two choruses joined in repeating the call

---

[127]. Only the first two verses of this song have come down to us as Sappho wrote them; for the latter part we are obliged to make use of the imitation, by Catullus, which, however, judging by the original verses which we do possess, may almost be called a translation. The English version is by Lamb.

on Hymen, again and again, in tones of mingled desire and exultation.

Suddenly the song was hushed, for a flash of lightning had shone down through the aperture beneath which Kallias had stationed the bride and bridegroom, followed by a loud peal of thunder. "See!" cried the Daduchus, raising his hand to heaven, "Zeus himself has taken the nuptial-torch, and sings the Hymenæus for his favorites."

At dawn the next morning, Sappho and Bartja left the house and went into the garden. After the violent storm which had raged all night, the garden was looking as fresh and cheerful in the morning light as the faces of the newly-married pair.

Bartja's anxiety for his friends, whom he had almost forgotten in the excitement of his marriage, had roused them so early.

The garden had been laid out on an artificial hill, which overlooked the inundated plain. Blue and white lotus-blossoms floated on the smooth surface of the water, and vast numbers of water-birds hovered along the shores or over the flood. Flocks of white herons appeared on the banks, their plumage gleaming like glaciers on distant mountain peaks; a solitary eagle circled upward on its broad pinions through the pure morning air, turtle-doves nestled in the tops of the palm-trees; pelicans and ducks fluttered screaming away, whenever a gay sail appeared. The air had been cooled by the storm, a fresh north-wind was blowing, and, notwithstanding the early hour, there were a number of boats sailing over the deluged fields before the breeze. The songs of the rowers, the plashing strokes of their oars and the cries of the birds, all contributed to enliven the watery landscape of the Nile valley, which, though varied in color, was somewhat monotonous.

Bartja and Sappho stood leaning on each other by the low wall which ran round Rhodopis' garden, exchanging tender words and watching the scene below, till at last Bartja's quick eye caught sight of a boat making straight for the house and coming on fast by the help of the breeze and powerful rowers.

A few minutes later the boat put in to shore and Zopyrus with his deliverers stood before them.

Darius's plan had succeeded perfectly, thanks to the storm, which, by its violence and the unusual time of its appearance, had scared the Egyptians; but still there was no time to be lost, as it might reasonably be supposed that the men of Sais would pursue their fugitive with all the means at their command.

Sappho, therefore, had to take a short farewell of her grandmother,—all the more tender, however, for its shortness,—and then, led by Bartja and followed by old Melitta, who was to accompany her to Persia, she went on board Syloson's boat. After an hour's sail they reached a beautifully-built and fast-sailing vessel, the Hygieia, which belonged to Kallias.

He was waiting for them on board his trireme. The leave-taking between himself and his young friends was especially affectionate. Bartja hung a heavy and costly gold chain round the neck of the old man in token of his gratitude, while Syloson, in remembrance of the dangers they had shared together, threw his purple cloak over Darius' shoulders. It was a masterspecimen of Tyrian dye, and had taken the latter's fancy. Darius accepted the gift with pleasure, and said, as he took leave: "You must never forget that I am indebted to you, my Greek friend, and as soon as possible give me an opportunity of doing you service in return."

"You ought to come to me first, though," exclaimed Zopyrus, embracing his deliverer. "I am perfectly ready to share my last gold piece with you; or what is more, if it would do you a service, to sit a whole week in that infernal hole from which you saved me.—Ah! they're weighing anchor. Farewell, you brave Greek! Remember me to the flower-sisters, especially to the pretty, little Stephanion, and tell her her long-legged lover won't be able to plague her again for some time to come at least. And then, one more thing;—take this purse of gold for the wife and children of that impertinent fellow, whom I struck too hard in the heat of the fray."

The anchors fell rattling on to the deck, the wind filled the sails, the Trieraules* took his flute and set the measure of the monotonous Keleusma or rowing-song, which echoed again from the hold of the vessel.** The beak of the ship bearing the statue of Hygieia,*** carved in wood, began to move. Bartja and Sappho stood at the helm and gazed towards Naukratis, until the shores of the Nile vanished and the green waves of the Hellenic sea splashed their foam over the deck of the trireme.

---

* Flute-player to a trireme. ** See vol. 1. note 214.
*** The goddess of health.

CHAPTER XII.

Our young bride and bridegroom had not travelled farther than Ephesus, when the news reached them that Amasis was dead. From Ephesus they went to Babylon, and thence to Pasargadæ, which Kassandane, Atossa and Crœsus had made their temporary residence. Kassandane was to accompany the army to Egypt, and wished, now that Nebenchari had restored her sight, to see the monument which had lately been built to her great husband's memory after Crœsus' design, before leaving for so long a journey. She rejoiced in finding it worthy of the great Cyrus, and spent hours every day in the beautiful gardens which had been laid out round the mausoleum.

It consisted of a gigantic sarcophagus made of solid marble blocks, and resting like a house on a substructure composed of six high marble steps. The interior was fitted up like a room, and contained, beside the golden coffin in which were preserved such few remains of Cyrus as had been spared by the dogs, vultures, and elements, a silver bed and a table of the same metal, on which were golden drinking-cups and numerous garments ornamented with the rarest and most costly jewels.

The building was forty feet high. The shady paradises* and colonnades by which it was surrounded had been planned by Crœsus, and in the midst of the

* Persian pleasure-gardens.

sacred grove was a dwelling-house for the Magi appointed to watch over the tomb.

The palace of Cyrus could be seen in the distance —a palace in which he had appointed that the future kings of Persia should pass at least some months of every year. It was a splendid building in the style of a fortress, and so inaccessibly placed that it had been fixed on as the royal treasure-house.[128]

Here, in the fresh mountain air of a place dedicated to the memory of the husband she had loved so much, Kassandane felt well and at peace; she was glad too to see that Atossa was recovering the old cheerfulness, which she had so sadly lost since the death of Nitetis and the departure of Darius. Sappho soon became the friend of her new mother and sister, and all three felt very loath to leave the lovely Pasargadæ.

Darius and Zopyrus had remained with the army which was assembling in the plains of the Euphrates, and Bartja too had to return thither before the march began.

Cambyses went out to meet his family on their return; he was much impressed with Sappho's great beauty, but she confessed to her husband that his brother only inspired her with fear.

The king had altered very much in the last few months. His formerly pale and almost noble features

---

128. Strabo 730. according to Aristobulus, Arrian, *Anab.* VI. Curtius X. 1. Pliny. VI. 29. Kugler, *Geschichte der Baukunst* I. p. 99. Schnaase, *Kunstgeschichte* I. 213. Rich. Narrative of a Journey to the Site of Babylon. Ritter, *Erdkunde* VIII. p. 492. Niebuhr, *Reisen* etc. This building, without question, suggests a connection with the rules of architecture held by the Greeks. Herder and Anquetil are also of opinion, that in the matter of architecture, the Persians borrowed more from the Greeks than from the Egyptians.

were reddened and disfigured by the quantities of wine he was in the habit of drinking. In his dark eyes there was the old fire still, but dimmed and polluted. His hair and beard, formerly so luxuriant, and black as the raven's wing, hung down grey and disordered over his face and chin, and the proud smile which used so to improve his features had given way to an expression of contemptuous annoyance and harsh severity.

Sometimes he laughed,—loudly, immoderately and coarsely; but this was only when intoxicated, a condition which had long ceased to be unusual with him.

He continued to retain an aversion to his wives; so much so that the royal harem was to be left behind in Susa, though all his court took their favorite wives and concubines with them on the campaign. Still no one could complain that the king was ever guilty of injustice; indeed he insisted more eagerly now than before on the rigid execution of the law; and wherever he detected an abuse his punishments were cruel and inexorable. Hearing that a judge, named Sisamnes, had been bribed to pronounce an unjust sentence, he condemned the wretched man to be flayed, ordered the seat of justice to be covered with his skin, appointed the son to the father's vacant place and compelled him to occupy this fearful seat.[129] Cambyses was untiring as commander of the forces, and superintended the drilling of the troops assembled near Babylon with the greatest rigor and circumspection.

The hosts were to march after the festival of the New Year,* which Cambyses celebrated this time with immense expense and profusion. The ceremony over,

---

129. Herodot. V. 25.

* In our month of March.

he betook himself to the army. Bartja was there. He came up to his brother, beaming with joy, kissed the hem of his robe, and told him in a tone of triumph that he hoped to become a father. The king trembled as he heard the words, vouchsafed his brother no answer, drank himself into unconsciousness that evening, and the next morning called the soothsayers, Magi and Chaldæans together, in order to submit a question to them. "Shall I be committing a sin against the gods, if I take my sister to wife and thus verify the promise of the dream, which ye formerly interpreted to mean that Atossa should bear a future king to this realm?"

The Magi consulted a short time together. Then Oropastes cast himself at the king's feet and said, "We do not believe, O King, that this marriage would be a sin against the gods; inasmuch as, first: it is a custom among the Persians to marry with their own kin;[130]— and secondly, though it be not written in the law that the pure man may marry his sister, it is written that the king may do what seemeth good in his own eyes.[131] That which pleaseth thee is therefore always lawful."

Cambyses sent the Magi away with rich gifts, gave Oropastes full powers as regent of the kingdom in his absence, and soon after told his horrified mother that, as soon as the conquest of Egypt and the punishment of the son of Amasis should have been achieved, he intended to marry his sister Atossa.

At length the immense host, numbering more than

---

130. Anquetil tells us that the modern Parsees still consider a marriage between very near relations as especially advisable. See note 154. to this volume.

131. According to Herod. III. 31.

800,000 fighting men, departed in separate divisions, and reached the Syrian desert in two months. Here they were met by the Arabian tribes whom Phanes had propitiated—the Amalekites and Geshurites—bringing camels and horses laden with water for the host.

At Accho, in the land of the Canaanites, the fleets of the Syrians, Phœnicians and Ionians belonging to Persia, and the auxiliary ships from Cyprus and Samos, won by the efforts of Phanes, were assembled. The case of the Samian fleet was a remarkable one. Polykrates saw in Cambyses' proposal a favorable opportunity of getting rid of all the citizens who were discontented with his government, manned forty triremes with eight thousand malcontent Samians, and sent them to the Persians with the request that not one might be allowed to return home.[132]

As soon as Phanes heard this he warned the doomed men, who at once, instead of sailing to join the Persian forces, returned to Samos and attempted to overthrow Polykrates. They were defeated, however, on land, and escaped to Sparta to ask help against the tyrant.

A full month before the time of the inundation, the Persian and Egyptian armies were standing face to face near Pelusium on the north-east coast of the Delta.

Phanes' arrangements had proved excellent. The Arabian tribes had kept faith so well that the journey through the desert, which would usually have cost thousands of lives, had been attended with very little loss, and the time of year had been so well chosen that the Persian troops reached Egypt by dry roads and without inconvenience.

The king met his Greek friend with every mark of

132. Herod. III. 44.

distinction, and returned a friendly nod when Phanes said: "I hear that you have been less cheerful than usual since the death of your beautiful bride. A woman's grief passes in stormy and violent complaint, but the sterner character of a man cannot so soon be comforted. I know what you feel, for I have lost my dearest too. Let us both praise the gods for granting us the best remedy for our grief—war and revenge."

Phanes accompanied the king to an inspection of the troops and to the evening revel. It was marvellous to see the influence he exercised over this fierce spirit, and how calm—nay even cheerful—Cambyses became, when the Athenian was near.

The Egyptian army was by no means contemptible, even when compared with the immense Persian hosts. Its position was covered on the right by the walls of Pelusium, a frontier fortress designed by the Egyptian kings as a defence against incursions from the east. The Persians were assured by deserters that the Egyptian army numbered altogether nearly six hundred thousand men. Beside a great number of chariots of war, thirty thousand Karian and Ionian mercenaries, and the corps of the Mazai,* two hundred and fifty thousand Kalasirians, one hundred and sixty thousand Hermotybians, twenty thousand horsemen,[133] and auxil-

133. Herodotus informs us (II. 64.) that the entire Egyptian army consisted of two divisions: Hermotybians and Kalasirians. A great many conjectures have been made as to the signification of these two words, some even by Herodotus himself. See S. Birch, *Lettre à M. Letronne sur l'expression hieroglyphique du mot égyptien calasiris. Revue Archéol.* 1847. p. 149. In Egyptian the Kalasirians are called Klaschr, and are bowmen. The Hermotybians probably took their name from the apron which they wore; Hemitybion (ἡμιτύβιον), Aristotle, Plut. 729. This was Egyptian, according to Pollux. VII. 71.—We find

* A kind of police force partly composed of foreigners, who had to guard prisoners of war, and perform other similar duties.

iary troops, amounting to more than fifty thousand, were assembled under Psamtik's banner; amongst these last the Libyan Maschawascha* were remarkable for their military deeds, and the Ethiopians for their numerical superiority.

The infantry were divided into regiments and companies, under different standards,[134] and variously equipped. The heavy-armed soldiers carried large shields, lances, and daggers; the swordsmen[135] and those who fought with battle-axes had smaller shields and light clubs; beside these, there were slingers, but the main body of the army was composed of archers,

chariot-soldiers on almost all the ancient monuments, sometimes wonderfully true to nature. See Rosellini, *Mon. Stor.* II. Pl. 103. I. Pl. 78. Lepsius, *Denkmäler* especially in Abth. III.—The number of the Egyptian chariot-soldiers was known and praised even by Homer. *Il.* IX. 383. and though only representations of five warriors on horseback have been discovered on the Egyptian monuments, (the finest on a relief in the Ethnographical Museum at Bologna, which is far too little known), their inscriptions and numerous statements made by other nations prove that they made use of horse-soldiers also. Diodorus reports that King Rameses led 24,000 horsemen to war and Sesonchis (Sheshenk or Shishak) came up against Jerusalem with threescore thousand. Chron. II. 12. 3. Isaiah 36. 9. According to Herodotus King Amasis was on horseback, when the messenger from Hophra came to him.

134. A number of drawings of such standards or military signs are to be found in Wilkinson I. 294. and Rosellini, *Mon. Civ.* 121. Each Nomos had its own coat of arms. The lists of districts in the temples, especially those belonging to the reigns of the Ptolemies, whose meaning was first discovered by Mr. Harris, English Consul at Alexandria, are particularly instructive.

135. In these and the descriptions immediately following, we have drawn our information, either from the drawings made from Egyptian monuments in Champollion, Wilkinson, Rosellini and Lepsius, or from the monuments themselves. There is a dagger in the Berlin Museum, the blade of which is of bronze, the hilt of ivory and the sheath of leather. Large swords are only to be seen in the hands of the foreign auxiliaries, but the native Egyptians are armed with small ones, like daggers. The largest one of which we have any knowledge is in the possession of Herr E. Brugsch at Cairo. It is more than two feet long.

* Probably the Maxyer of North Africa, spoken of by Herodotus.

whose bows unbent were nearly the height of a man. The only clothing of the horse-soldiers was the apron, and their weapon a light club in the form of a mace or battle-axe. Those warriors, on the contrary, who fought in chariots belonged to the highest rank of the military caste, spent large sums on the decoration of their two-wheeled chariots[136] and the harness of their magnificent horses,* and went to battle in their most costly ornaments. They were armed with bows and lances, and a charioteer stood beside each, so that their undivided attention could be bestowed upon the battle.

The Persian foot was not much more numerous than the Egyptian, but they had six times the number of horse-soldiers.

As soon as the armies stood face to face, Cambyses caused the great Pelusian plain to be cleared of trees and brushwood, and had the sand-hills removed which were to be found here and there, in order to give his cavalry and scythe-chariots a fair field of action.[137] Phanes' knowledge of the country was of great use. He had drawn up a plan of action with great military skill, and succeeded in gaining not only Cambyses' approval, but that of the old general Megabyzus and the best tacticians among the Achæmenidæ. His local knowledge was especially valuable on account of the marshes which intersected the Pelusian plain, and might, unless carefully avoided, have proved fatal to the Persian enterprise. At the close of the council of war Phanes begged to be heard once more: "Now, at length," he said, "I am at

---
136. Rosellini gives drawings of especially-beautiful war-chariots. *Mon. Stor.* I. Pl. 78. *Mon Civ.* Pl. 122. Wilkinson I. p. 346.

137. See the battle of Gaugamela. Curtius IV. Arrian III. 11.

* See vol. 1 note 30.

liberty to satisfy your curiosity in reference to the closed waggons full of animals, which I have had transported hither. They contain five thousand cats! Yes, you may laugh, but I tell you these creatures will be more serviceable to us than a hundred thousand of our best soldiers. Many of you are aware that the Egyptians have a superstition which leads them rather to die than kill a cat. I, myself, nearly paid for such a murder once with my life. Remembering this, I have been making a diligent search for cats during my late journey; in Cyprus. where there are splendid specimens, in Samos and in Crete. All I could get I ordered to be caught, and now propose that they be distributed among those troops who will be opposed to the native Egyptian soldiers. Every man must be told to fasten one firmly to his shield and hold it out as he advances towards the enemy. I will wager that there's not one real Egyptian, who would not rather fly from the battle-field than take aim at one of these sacred animals."*

This speech was met by a loud burst of laughter; on being discussed. however, it was approved of, and ordered to be carried out at once. The ingenious Greek was honored by receiving the king's hand to kiss, his expenses were reimbursed by a magnificent present, and he was urged to take a daughter of some noble Persian family in marriage.[138] The king concluded by inviting him to supper, but this the Athenian declined, on the plea that he must review the Ionian troops, with whom he was as yet but little acquainted, and withdrew.

---

138. Themistocles too, on coming to the Persian court, received a high-born Persian wife in marriage. Diod. XI. 57.

* See vol. I. note 51.

At the door of his tent he found his slaves disputing with a ragged, dirty and unshaven old man, who insisted on speaking with their master. Fancying he must be a beggar, Phanes threw him a piece of gold; the old man did not even stoop to pick it up, but, holding the Athenian fast by his cloak, cried, " I am Aristomachus the Spartan!"

Cruelly as he was altered, Phanes recognized his old friend at once, ordered his feet to be washed and his head anointed, gave him wine and meat to revive his strength, took his rags off and laid a new *chiton* over his emaciated, but still sinewy, frame.

Aristomachus received all in silence; and when the food and wine had given him strength to speak, began the following answer to Phanes' eager questions.

On the murder of Phanes' son by Psamtik, he had declared his intention of leaving Egypt and inducing the troops under his command to do the same, unless his friend's little daughter were at once set free, and a satisfactory explanation given for the sudden disappearance of the boy. Psamtik promised to consider the matter. Two days later, as Aristomachus was going up the Nile by night to Memphis, he was seized by Egyptian soldiers, bound and thrown into the dark hold of a boat, which, after a voyage of many days and nights, cast anchor on a totally unknown shore. The prisoners were taken out of their dungeon and led across a desert under the burning sun, and past rocks of strange forms, until they reached a range of mountains with a colony of huts at its base. These huts were inhabited by human beings, who, with chains on their feet, were driven every morning into the shaft of a mine and there compelled to hew grains of gold out of the stony rock."[139] Many of these miserable men had passed forty years in this place, but most died soon, overcome by the hard work and the fearful extremes of heat and cold to which they were exposed on entering and leaving the mine.

"My companions," continued Aristomachus, "were either condemned murderers to whom mercy had been granted, or men guilty of high treason whose tongues had been cut out, and others such as myself whom the king had reason to fear. Three months I worked among this set, submitting to the strokes of the overseer, fainting under the fearful heat, and stiffening under the cold dews of night. I felt as if picked out for death and only kept alive by the hope of vengeance. It happened, however, by the mercy of the gods, that at the feast of Pacht,* our guards, as is the custom of the

---

139. Diodorus (III. 12.) describes the compulsory work in the gold mines with great minuteness. The convicts were either prisoners taken in war, or people whom despotism in its blind fury found it expedient to put out of the way. The mines lay in the plain of Koptos, not far from the Red Sea. Traces of them have been discovered in modern times. Interesting inscriptions of the time of Rameses the Great, (14 centuries B. C.) referring to the gold-mines, have been found, one at Radesieh, the other at Kuban, and have been published and deciphered in Europe. (Lepsius, *Denkm.* Abth. III. 139-141.) The Stela of Kuban, first edited by Prisse d'Avennes, *Mon. Égypte.* Pl. 21. and treated by Birch, *Archaeologia.* Part. 34. Also, by Chabas in his publication: *Les inscriptions des mines d'or.* Paris 1862. accompanied by an exact photograph. The subject of both inscriptions is the improvement of the road to the gold-mines in the desert between Kuban and the Red Sea, by the introduction of drinking-water. There is a very interesting papyrus in the Turin Museum connected with this subject, which has a map giving a most remarkable outline of the mineral region spoken of in the two Stelæ. Chabas has a first-rate colored fac-simile of this. (It was published in Lepsius' *Auswahl von Urkunden des Aegyptischen Alterthums,* 1842. Taf. 22. Rightly estimated by Birch and in Chabas' publication.) The mountains containing gold are colored red, and the words "*tu en nub*" (gold-mountain) written over them in the hieratic character. See Ebers, *Aegypten* p. 269. and following. Also Ebers, *Durch Gosen zum Sinai,* p. 144. and following.

* See vol. 1, notes 53 and 288.

Egyptians, drank so freely as to fall into a deep sleep, during which I and a young Jew who had been deprived of his right hand for having used false weights in trade, managed to escape unperceived. Zeus Lacedæmonius and the great God whom this young man worshipped helped us in our need, and, though we often heard the voices of our pursuers, they never succeeded in capturing us. I had taken a bow from one of our guards; with this we obtained food, and when no game was to be found we lived on roots, fruits and birds' eggs. The sun and stars showed us our road. We knew that the gold-mines were not far from the Red Sea and lay to the south of Memphis. It was not long before we reached the coast; and then, pressing onwards in a northerly direction, we fell in with some friendly mariners, who took care of us until we were taken up by an Arabian boat. The young Jew understood the language spoken by the crew, and in their care we came to Eziongeber in the land of Edom. There we heard that Cambyses was coming with an immense army against Egypt, and travelled as far as Harma under the protection of an Amalekite caravan bringing water to the Persian army. From thence I went on to Pelusium in the company of some stragglers from the Asiatic army, who now and then allowed me a seat on their horses, and here I heard that you had accepted a high command in Cambyses' army. I have kept my vow, I have been true to my nation in Egypt; now it is your turn to help old Aristomachus in gaining the only thing he still cares for—revenge on his persecutors."

"And that you shall have!" cried Phanes, grasping the old man's hand. "You shall have the command of the heavy-armed Milesian troops, and liberty to commit what carnage you like among the ranks of our enemies. This, however, is only paying half the debt I owe you. Praised be the gods, who have put it in my power to make you happy by one single sentence. Know then, Aristomachus, that, only a few days after your disappearance, a ship arrived in the harbor of Naukratis from Sparta. It was guided by your own noble son and expressly sent by the Ephori[*] in your honor—to bring the father of two Olympic victors back to his native land."

The old man's limbs trembled visibly at these words, his eyes filled with tears and he murmured a prayer. Then smiting his forehead, he cried in a voice trembling with feeling: "Now it is fulfilled! now it has become a fact! If I doubted the words of thy priestess, O Phœbus Apollo! pardon my sin! What was the promise of the oracle?

"If once the warrior hosts from the snow-topped mountains descending,
Come to the fields of the stream watering richly the plain,
Then shall the lingering boat to the beckoning meadows convey thee,
Which to the wandering foot peace and a home can afford.
When those warriors come, from the snow-topped mountains descending,
Then will the powerful Five grant thee what long they refused."

"The promise of the god is fulfilled. Now I may return home, and I will; but first I raise my hands to Dice, the unchanging goddess of justice, and implore her not to deny me the pleasure of revenge."

"The day of vengeance will dawn to-morrow," said Phanes, joining in the old man's prayer. "To-

[* See vol. 1. note 83.]

morrow I shall slaughter the victims for the dead—for my son—and will take no rest until Cambyses has pierced the heart of Egypt with the arrows which I have cut for him. Come, my friend, let me take you to the king. One man like you can put a whole troop of Egyptians to flight."

It was night. The Persian soldiers, their position being unfortified, were in order of battle, ready to meet any unexpected attack. The foot-soldiers stood leaning on their shields, the horsemen held their horses saddled and bridled near the camp-fires. Cambyses was riding through the ranks, encouraging his troops by words and looks.[140] Only one part of the army was not yet ranged in order of battle—the centre. It was composed of the Persian body-guard, the apple-bearers,* Immortals, and the king's own relatives, who were always led into battle by the king in person.

The Ionian Greeks too had gone to rest, at Phanes' command. He wanted to keep his men fresh, and allowed them to sleep in their armor, while he kept watch. Aristomachus was welcomed with shouts of joy by the Greeks, and kindly by Cambyses, who assigned him, at the head of one half the Greek troops, a place to the left of the centre attack, while Phanes, with the other half, had his place at the right. The king himself was to take the lead at the head of the ten thousand Immortals, preceded by the blue, red

---

140. Battle of Gaugamela or Arbela. Curtius IV. 14. 12.

* See vol. I. p. 272.

and gold imperial banner[141] and the standard of Kawe. Bartja was to lead the regiment of mounted guards numbering a thousand men, and that division of the cavalry which was entirely clothed in mail.

Crœsus commanded a body of troops whose duty it was to guard the camp with its immense treasures, the wives of Cambyses' nobles, and his own mother and sister.

At last Mithras appeared and shed his light upon the earth; the spirits of the night retired to their dens, and the Magi stirred up the sacred fire which had been carried before the army the whole way from Babylon, until it became a gigantic flame. They and the king united in feeding it with costly perfumes, Cambyses offered the sacrifice, and, holding the while a golden bowl high in the air, besought the gods to grant him victory and glory. He then gave the password, "Auramazda, the helper and guide," and placed himself at the head of his guards, who went into the battle with wreaths on their tiaras. The Greeks offered their own sacrifices, and shouted with delight on hearing that the omens were auspicious. Their war-cry was "Hebe."[142]

Meanwhile the Egyptian priests had begun their day also with prayer and sacrifice, and had then placed their army in order of battle.

Psamtik, now King of Egypt, led the centre. He was mounted on a golden chariot; the trappings of his

---

141. These are the colors of the imperial banner, according to Firdusi. The standard of Kawe consisted of the leather apron of the bold smith, who, according to the Persian myth, caused rebellion against the wicked Zohak and helped Feridun overthrow the cruel destroyer of the empire.

142. Taken from various descriptions by the ancient writers of battles in which Greeks and Persians fought together. "Hebe" was the Greek pass-word at the battle of Mykale. Herod. IX. 98.

horses were of gold and purple, and plumes of ostrich-feathers nodded on their proud heads. He wore the double crown of Upper and Lower Egypt, and the charioteer who stood at his left hand holding the reins and whip, was descended from one of the noblest Egyptian families.[143]

The Hellenic and Karian mercenaries were to fight at the left of the centre, the horse at the extreme of each wing, and the Egyptian and Ethiopian foot were stationed, six ranks deep, on the right and left of the armed chariots, and Greek mercenaries.

Psamtik drove through the ranks of his army, giving encouraging and friendly words to all the men. He drew up before the Greek division, and addressed them thus: "Heroes of Cyprus and Libya! your deeds in arms are well known to me, and I rejoice in the thought of sharing your glory to-day and crowning you with fresh laurels. Ye have no need to fear, that in the day of victory I shall curtail your liberties. Malicious tongues have whispered that this is all ye have to expect from me; but I tell you, that if we conquer, fresh favors will be shown to you and your descendants; I shall call you the supporters of my throne. Ye are fighting to-day, not for me alone, but for the freedom of your own distant homes. It is

---

143. The manner in which the kings behaved to their charioteers proves that the latter must have belonged to the aristocracy. See the picture of Rameses and his charioteer at Thebes. Wilkinson I. 338. The poem of Pentaur, the national epic poem of Egypt, several copies of which have been preserved, represents Pharaoh as having been nearly related to his charioteer. We possess, in addition to this, a papyrus containing a description of the trials which a young Egyptian chariot-soldier had to go through. We see him at the military academy, and, when that period of his life is over, he receives his horses out of the royal stable from the hands of the Pharaoh himself. This favor could only have been shown to the chosen few.

easy to perceive that Cambyses, once lord of Egypt, will stretch out his rapacious hand over your beautiful Hellas and its islands. I need only remind you, that they lie between Egypt and your Asiatic brethren who are already groaning under the Persian yoke. Your acclamations prove that ye agree with me already, but I must ask for a still longer hearing. It is my duty to tell you *who* has sold, not only Egypt, but his own country to the King of Persia, in return for immense treasures. The man's name is Phanes! You are angry and inclined to doubt? I swear to you, that this very Phanes has accepted Cambyses' gold and promised not only to be his guide to Egypt, but to open the gates of your own Greek cities to him. He knows the country and the people, and can be bribed to every perfidy. Look at him! there he is, walking by the side of the king. See how he bows before him! I thought I had heard once, that the Greeks only prostrated themselves before their gods. But of course, when a man sells his country, he ceases to be its citizen. Am I not right? Ye scorn to call so base a creature by the name of countryman? Yes? then I will deliver the wretch's daughter into your hands. Do what ye will with the child of such a villain. Crown her with wreaths of roses, fall down before her, if it please you, but do not forget that she belongs to a man who has disgraced the name of Hellene, and has betrayed his countrymen and country!"

As he finished speaking the men raised a wild cry of rage and took possession of the trembling child. A soldier held her up, so that her father—the troops not being more than a bow-shot apart—could see all that happened. At the same moment an Egyptian, who afterwards earned celebrity through the loudness of his voice,[144] cried: "Look here, Athenian! see how treachery and corruption are rewarded in this country!" A bowl of wine stood near, provided by the king, from which the soldiers had just been drinking themselves into intoxication. A Karian seized it, plunged his sword into the innocent child's breast, and let the blood flow into the bowl; filled a goblet with the awful mixture, and drained it, as if drinking to the health of the wretched father. Phanes stood watching the scene, as if struck into a statue of cold stone. The rest of the soldiers then fell upon the bowl like madmen, and wild beasts could not have lapped up the foul drink with greater eagerness.[145]

In the same moment Psamtik triumphantly shot off his first arrow into the Persian ranks.

The mercenaries flung the child's dead body on to the ground; drunk with her blood, they raised their battle-song, and rushed into the strife far ahead of their Egyptian comrades.

But now the Persian ranks began to move. Phanes, furious with pain and rage, led on his heavy-armed troops, indignant too at the brutal barbarity of their countrymen, and dashed into the ranks of those very soldiers, whose love he had tried to deserve during ten years of faithful leadership.

At noon, fortune seemed to be favoring the Egyptians; but at sunset the Persians had the advantage, and when the full-moon rose, the Egyptians were flying wildly from the battle-field, perishing in the marshes and in the arm of the Nile which flowed

144. Herod. IV. 141.
145. Herodotus tells this fearful tale (III. 11.)

behind their position, or being cut to pieces by the swords of their enemies.

Twenty thousand Persians and fifty thousand Egyptians lay dead on the blood-stained sea-sand. The wounded, drowned, and prisoners could scarcely be numbered.[146] Psamtik had been one of the last to fly. He was well mounted, and, with a few thousand faithful followers, reached the opposite bank of the Nile and made for Memphis, the well-fortified city of the Pyramids.

Of the Greek mercenaries very few survived, so furious had been Phanes' revenge, and so well had he been supported by his Ionians. Ten thousand Karians were taken captive and the murderer of his little child was killed by Phanes' own hand.

Aristomachus too, in spite of his wooden leg, had performed miracles of bravery; but, notwithstanding all their efforts, neither he, nor any of his confederates in revenge, had succeeded in taking Psamtik prisoner.

When the battle was over, the Persians returned in triumph to their tents, to be warmly welcomed by Crœsus and the warriors and priests who had remained behind, and to celebrate their victory by prayers and sacrifices.

The next morning Cambyses assembled his generals and rewarded them with different tokens of distinction, such as costly robes, gold chains, rings, swords, and stars formed of precious stones.[147] Gold and silver coins were distributed among the common soldiers.

146. Herod. III. 12. Ktesias, *Persica* 9. In ancient history the loss of the conquered is always far greater than that of the conquerors. To a certain extent this holds good in the present day, but the proportion is decidedly not so unfavorable for the vanquished. We would remind our readers of the campaign of 1866.

147. Herod. III. 130. VIII. 118. Xenoph. *Cyrop.* VIII. 3.

The principal attack of the Egyptians had been directed against the centre of the Persian army, where Cambyses commanded in person; and with such effect that the guards had already begun to give way. At that moment Bartja, arriving with his troop of horsemen, had put fresh courage into the wavering, had fought like a lion himself, and by his bravery and promptitude decided the day in favor of the Persians.

The troops were exultant in their joy: they shouted his praises, as "the conqueror of Pelusium" and the "best of the Achæmenidæ."

Their cries reached the king's ears and made him very angry. He knew he had been fighting at the risk of life, with real courage and the strength of a giant, and yet the day would have been lost if this boy had not presented him with the victory. The brother who had embittered his days of happy love, was now to rob him of half his military glory. Cambyses felt that he hated Bartja, and his fist clenched involuntarily as he saw the young hero looking so happy in the consciousness of his own well-earned success.

Phanes had been wounded and went to his tent; Aristomachus lay near him, dying.

"The oracle has deceived me, after all," he murmured. "I shall die without seeing my country again."

"The oracle spoke the truth," answered Phanes. "Were not the last words of the Pythia?

' Then shall the lingering boat to the beckoning meadows convey thee, Which to the wandering foot peace and a home will afford?'

"Can you misunderstand their meaning? They

speak of Charon's lingering boat, which will convey you to your last home, to the one great resting-place for all wanderers—the kingdom of Hades."

"Yes, my friend, you are right there. I am going to Hades."

"And the Five have granted you, before death, what they so long refused,—the return to Lacedæmon. You ought to be thankful to the gods for granting you such sons and such vengeance on your enemies. When my wound is healed, I shall go to Greece and tell your son that his father died a glorious death, and was carried to the grave on his shield, as beseems a hero."

"Yes, do so, and give him my shield as a remembrance of his old father. There is no need to exhort him to virtue."

"When Psamtik is in our power, shall I tell him what share you had in his overthrow?"

"No; he saw me before he took to flight, and at the unexpected vision his bow fell from his hand. This was taken by his friends as a signal for flight, and they turned their horses from the battle."

"The gods ordain, that bad men shall be ruined by their own deeds. Psamtik lost courage, for he must have believed that the very spirits of the lower world were fighting against him."

"We mortals gave him quite enough to do. The Persians fought well. But the battle would have been lost without the guards and our troops."

"Without doubt."

"I thank thee, O Zeus Lacedæmonius."

"You are praying?"

"I am praising the gods for allowing me to die at ease as to my country. These heterogeneous masses can never be dangerous to Greece. Ho, physician, when am I likely to die?"

The Milesian physician, who had accompanied the Greek troops to Egypt, pointed to the arrow-head sticking fast in his breast, and said with a sad smile, "You have only a few hours more to live. If I were to draw the arrow from your wound, you would die at once."

The Spartan thanked him, said farewell to Phanes, sent a greeting to Rhodopis, and then, before they could prevent him, drew the arrow from his wound with an unflinching hand. A few moments later Aristomachus was dead.

The same day a Persian embassy set out for Memphis on board one of the Lesbian vessels. It was commissioned to demand from Psamtik the surrender of his own person and of the city at discretion. Cambyses followed, having first sent off a division of his army under Megabyzus to invest Sais.

At Heliopolis he was met by deputations from the Greek inhabitants of Naukratis and the Libyans, praying for peace and his protection, and bringing a golden wreath and other rich presents. Cambyses received them graciously and assured them of his friendship; but repulsed the messengers from Cyrene and Barka indignantly, and flung, with his own hand, their tribute of five hundred silver minæ* among his soldiers, disdaining to accept so contemptible an offering.

In Heliopolis he also heard that, at the approach of his embassy, the inhabitants of Memphis had flocked to

*£1,875. Herod. III. 3.

the shore, bored a hole in the bottom of the ship, torn his messengers in pieces without distinction, as wild beasts would tear raw flesh, and dragged them into the fortress.[148] On hearing this he cried angrily: "I swear, by Mithras, that these murdered men shall be paid for; ten lives for one."

Two days later and Cambyses with his army stood before the gates of Memphis. The siege was short, as the garrison was far too small for the city, and the citizens were discouraged by the fearful defeat at Pelusium.

King Psamtik himself came out to Cambyses, accompanied by his principal nobles, in rent garments, and with every token of mourning. Cambyses received him coldly and silently, ordering him and his followers to be guarded and removed. He treated Ladice, the widow of Amasis, who appeared at the same time as her step-son, with consideration, and, at the intercession of Phanes, to whom she had always shown favor, allowed her to return to her native town of Cyrene under safe conduct. She remained there until the fall of her nephew, Arcesilaus III. and the flight of her sister Pheretime, when she betook herself to Anthylla, the town in Egypt which belonged to her, and where she passed a quiet, solitary existence, dying at a great age.[149]

Cambyses not only scorned to revenge the imposture which had been practised on him on a woman, but, as a Persian, had far too much respect for a mother, and

---

148. Herod. III. 13.

149. According to Athenæus I. 25. Anthylla belonged to the queen for the time being. For Cyrene and Arcesilaus see Herod. IV. 163-165.

especially for the mother of a king, to injure Ladice in any way.

While he was engaged in the siege of Sais, Psamtik passed his imprisonment in the palace of the Pharaohs, treated in every respect as a king, but strictly guarded.

Among those members of the upper class who had incited the people to resistance, Neithotep, the high-priest of Neith, had taken the foremost place. He was therefore sent to Memphis and put in close confinement, with one hundred of his unhappy confederates. The larger number of the Pharaoh's court, on the other hand, did homage voluntarily to Cambyses at Sais, entitled him Ramestu, "child of the sun," and suggested that he should cause himself to be crowned King of Upper and Lower Egypt, with all the necessary formalities, and admitted into the priestly caste according to ancient custom. By the advice of Crœsus and Phanes, Cambyses gave in to these proposals, though much against his own will: he went so far, indeed, as to offer sacrifice in the temple of Neith, and allowed the newly-created high-priest of the goddess to give him a superficial insight into the nature of the mysteries. Some of the courtiers he retained near himself, and promoted different administrative functionaries to high posts; the commander of Amasis' Nile fleet succeeded so well in gaining the king's favor, as to be appointed one of those who ate at the royal table.[150] On leaving Sais, Cam-

[150]. On a statue in the Gregorian Museum in the Vatican, there is an inscription giving an account of Cambyses' sojourn at Sais, which agrees with the facts related in our text. He was lenient to his conquered subjects, and, probably in order to secure his position as the lawful Pharaoh, yielded to the wishes of the priests, was even initiated into the mysteries and did much for the temple of Neith. His adoption of the name Ramestu is also confirmed by this statue. E. de Rougé, *Mémoire sur la statuette naophore du musée Grégorien, au Vatican. Revue Archéol.* 1851. Brugsch, *Geograph. Inschr.* I. p. 247.

byses placed Megabyzus in command of the city; but scarcely had the king quitted their walls than the smothered rage of the people broke forth; they murdered the Persian sentinels, poisoned the wells, and set the stables of the cavalry on fire. Megabyzus at once applied to the king, representing that such hostile acts, if not repressed by fear, might soon be followed by open rebellion. "The two thousand noble youths from Memphis whom you have destined to death as an indemnification for our murdered ambassadors," said he, "ought to be executed at once; and it would do no harm if the son of Psamtik were added to the number, as he can some day become a rallying centre for the rebels. I hear that the daughters of the dethroned king and of the high-priest Neithotep have to carry water for the baths of the noble Phanes."

The Athenian answered with a smile: "Cambyses has allowed me to employ these aristocratic female attendants, my lord, at my own request."

"But has forbidden you to touch the life of one member of the royal house," added Cambyses. "None but a king has the right to punish kings."

Phanes bowed. The king turned to Megabyzus and ordered him to have the prisoners executed the very next day, as an example. He would decide the fate of the young prince later; but at all events he was to be taken to the place of execution with the rest. "We must show them," he concluded, "that we know how to meet all their hostile manifestations with sufficient rigor."

Crœsus ventured to plead for the innocent boy. "Calm yourself, old friend," said Cambyses with a smile;

"the child is not dead yet, and perhaps will be as well off with us as your own son, who fought so well at Pelusium. I confess I should like to know, whether Psamtik bears his fate as calmly and bravely as you did twenty-five years ago."

"That we can easily discover, by putting him on trial," said Phanes. "Let him be brought into the palace-court to-morrow, and let the captives and the condemned be led past him. Then we shall see whether he is a man or a coward."

"Be it so," answered Cambyses. "I will conceal myself and watch him unobserved. You, Phanes, will accompany me, to tell me the name and rank of each of the captives."

The next morning Phanes accompanied the king on to a balcony which ran round the great court of the palace—the court we have already described as being planted with trees. The listeners were hidden by a grove of flowering shrubs, but they could see every movement that took place, and hear every word that was spoken beneath them. They saw Psamtik, surrounded by a few of his former companions. He was leaning against a palm-tree, his eyes fixed gloomily on the ground, as his daughters entered the court. The daughter of Neithotep was with them, and some more young girls, all dressed as slaves; they were carrying pitchers of water. At sight of the king, they uttered such a loud cry of anguish as to wake him from his reverie. He looked up, recognized the miserable girls, and bowed his head lower than before; but only for a moment. Drawing himself up quickly, he asked his eldest daughter for whom she was carrying water. On hearing that she was forced to do the work of a slave for Phanes, he turned deadly pale, nodded his head, and cried to the girls, "Go on."

A few minutes later the captives were led into the court, with ropes round their necks, and bridles in their mouths.[151] At the head of the train was the little prince Necho. He stretched his hands out to his father, begging him to punish the bad foreigners who wanted to kill him. At this sight the Egyptians wept in their exceeding great misery; but Psamtik's eyes were dry. He bowed his tearless face nearly to the earth, and waved his child a last farewell.

After a short interval, the captives taken in Sais entered. Among them was Neithotep, the once powerful high-priest, clothed in rags and moving with difficulty by the help of a staff. At the entrance-gate he raised his eyes and caught sight of his former pupil Darius. Reckless of all the spectators around him, he went straight up to the young man, poured out the story of his need, besought his help, and ended by begging an alms. Darius complied at once, and by so doing, induced others of the Achæmenidæ, who were standing by, to hail the old man jokingly and throw him little pieces of money, which he picked up laboriously and thankfully from the ground.

At this sight Psamtik wept aloud, and smote upon his forehead, calling on the name of his friend in a voice full of woe.

Cambyses was so astonished at this, that he came forward to the balustrade of the veranda, and pushing the flowers aside, exclaimed: "Explain thyself, thou

---

151. This statement of Herodotus (III. 14.) is confirmed by the monuments, on which we often see representations of captives being led along with ropes round their necks. What follows is taken entirely from the same passage in Herodotus.

strange man; the misfortunes of a beggar, not even akin to thee, move thy compassion, but thou canst behold thy son on the way to execution and thy daughters in hopeless misery without shedding a tear, or uttering a lament!"

Psamtik looked up at his conqueror, and answered: "The misfortunes of my own house, O son of Cyrus, are too great for tears; but I may be permitted to weep over the afflictions of a friend, fallen, in his old age, from the height of happiness and influence into the most miserable beggary."

Cambyses' face expresseed his approval, and on looking round he saw that his was not the only eye which was filled with tears. Crœsus, Bartja, and all the Persians—nay, even Phanes himself, who had served as interpreter to the kings—were weeping aloud.

The proud conqueror was not displeased at these signs of sympathy, and turning to the Athenian: "I think, my Greek friend" he said, "we may consider our wrongs as avenged. Rise, Psamtik, and endeavor to imitate yonder noble old man, (pointing to Crœsus) by accustoming yourself to your fate. Your father's fraud has been visited on you and your family. The crown, which I have wrested from you is the crown of which Amasis deprived my wife,—my never-to-be-forgotten Nitetis. For her sake I began this war, and for her sake I grant you now the life of your son—she loved him. From this time forward you can live undisturbed at our court, eat at our table and share the privileges of our nobles. Gyges, fetch the boy hither. He shall be brought up as you were, years ago, among the sons of the Achæmenidæ."

The Lydian was hastening to execute this delightful commission, but Phanes stopped him before he could reach the door, and placing himself proudly between the king and the trembling, thankful Psamtik, said: "You would be going on a useless errand, noble Lydian. In defiance of your command, my Sovereign, but in virtue of the full powers you once gave me, I have ordered the grandson of Amasis to be the executioner's first victim. You have just heard the sound of a horn; that was the sign that the last heir to the Egyptian throne born on the shores of the Nile has been gathered to his fathers. I am aware of the fate I have to expect, Cambyses. I will not plead for a life whose end has been attained. Crœsus, I understand your reproachful looks. You grieve for the murdered children. But life is such a web of wretchedness and disappointment, that I agree with your philosopher Solon in thinking those fortunate to whom, as in former days to Kleobis and Biton,[152] the gods decree an early death. If I have ever been dear to you, Cambyses—if my counsels have been of any use, permit me as a last favor to say a few more words. Psamtik knows the causes that rendered us foes to each other. Ye all, whose esteem is worth so much to me, shall

---

152. Crœsus, after having shown Solon his treasures, asked him whom he held to be the most fortunate of men, hoping to hear his own name. The sage first named Tellus, a famous citizen of Athens, and then the brothers Kleobis and Biton. These were two handsome youths, who had gained the prize for wrestling, and one day, when the draught-animals had not returned from the field, dragged their mother themselves to the distant temple, in presence of the people. The men of Argos praised the strength of the sons,—the women praised the mother who possessed these sons. She, transported with delight at her sons' deed and the people's praise, went to the statue of the goddess and besought her to give them the best that could fall to the lot of men. When her prayer was over and the sacrifice offered, the youths fell asleep, and never woke again. They were dead. Herod. I. 31. Cicero, Tuscul. I. 47.

know them too. This man's father placed me in his son's stead at the head of the troops which had been sent to Cyprus. Where Psamtik had earned humiliation, I won success and glory. I also became unintentionally acquainted with a secret, which seriously endangered his chances of obtaining the crown; and lastly, I prevented his carrying off a virtuous maiden from the house of her grandmother, an aged woman, beloved and respected by all the Greeks. These are the sins which he has never been able to forgive; these are the grounds which led him to carry on war to the death with me directly I had quitted his father's service. The struggle is decided now. My innocent children have been murdered at thy command, and I have been pursued like a wild beast. That has been thy revenge. But mine!—I have deprived thee of thy throne and reduced thy people to bondage. Thy daughter I have called my slave, thy son's death-warrant was pronounced by my lips, and my eyes have seen the maiden whom thou persecutedst become the happy wife of a brave man. Undone, sinking ever lower and lower, thou hast watched me rise to be the richest and most powerful of my nation. In the lowest depth of thine own misery— and this has been the most delicious morsel of my vengeance—thou wast forced to see me—me, Phanes!— shedding tears that could not be kept back, at the sight of thy misery. The man, who is allowed to draw even one breath of life, after beholding his enemy so low, I hold to be happy as the gods themselves. I have spoken."

He ceased, and pressed his hand on his wound. Cambyses gazed at him in astonishment, stepped forward, and was just going to touch his girdle—an action which would have been equivalent to the signing of a death-warrant—[153] when his eye caught sight of the chain, which he himself had hung round the Athenian's neck as a reward for the clever way in which he had proved the innocence of Nitetis. The sudden recollection of the woman he loved, and of the countless services rendered him by Phanes, calmed his wrath—his hand dropped. One minute the severe ruler stood gazing lingeringly at his disobedient friend; the next, moved by a sudden impulse, he raised his right hand again, and pointed imperiously to the gate leading from the court.

Phanes bowed in silence, kissed the king's robe, and descended slowly into the court. Psamtik watched him, quivering with excitement, sprang towards the veranda, but before his lips could utter the curse which his heart had prepared, he sank powerless on to the ground.

Cambyses beckoned to his followers to make immediate preparations for a lion-hunt in the Libyan mountains.

CHAPTER XIII.

The waters of the Nile had begun to rise again. Two months had passed away since Phanes' disappearance, and much had happened.

153. The same sign was used by the last Darius to denote that his able Greek general Memnon, who had offended him by his plainness of speech, was doomed to death. As he was being led away, Memnon exclaimed, in allusion to Alexander, who was then fast drawing near: " Thy remorse will soon prove my worth; my avenger is not far off." Droysen, *Alex. d. Grosse*, I. p. 240. Diod. XVII. 30. Curtius III. 2.

The very day on which he left Egypt, Sappho had given birth to a girl, and had so far regained strength since then under the care of her grandmother, as to be able to join in an excursion up the Nile, which Crœsus had suggested should take place on the festival of the goddess Neith. Since the departure of Phanes, Cambyses' behavior had become so intolerable, that Bartja, with the permission of his brother, had taken Sappho to live in the royal palace at Memphis, in order to escape any painful collision. Rhodopis, at whose house Crœsus and his son, Bartja, Darius and Zopyrus were constant guests, had agreed to join the party.

On the morning of the festival-day they started in a gorgeously decorated boat, from a point between thirty and forty miles below Memphis, favored by a good north-wind and urged rapidly forward by a large number of rowers.

A wooden roof or canopy, gilded and brightly painted, sheltered them from the sun. Crœsus sat by Rhodopis; Theopompus the Milesian lay at her feet. Sappho was leaning against Bartja. Syloson, the brother of Polykrates, had made himself a comfortable resting-place next to Darius, who was looking thoughtfully into the water. Gyges and Zopyrus busied themselves in making wreaths for the women, from the flowers handed them by an Egyptian slave.

"It seems hardly possible," said Bartja, "that we can be rowing against the stream. The boat flies like a swallow."

"This fresh north-wind brings us forward," answered Theopompus. "And then the Egyptian boatmen understand their work splendidly."

"And row all the better just because we are sailing

against the stream," added Crœsus. "Resistance always brings out a man's best powers."

"Yes," said Rhodopis, "sometimes we even make difficulties, if the river of life seems too smooth."

"True," answered Darius. "A noble mind can never swim with the stream. In quiet inactivity all men are equal. We must be seen fighting, to be rightly estimated."

"Such noble-minded champions must be very cautious, though," said Rhodopis, "lest they become contentious and quarrelsome. Do you see those melons lying on the black soil yonder, like golden balls? Not one would have come to perfection if the sower had been too lavish with his seed. The fruit would have been choked by too luxuriant tendrils and leaves. Man is born to struggle and to work, but in this, as in everything else, he must know how to be moderate if his efforts are to succeed. The art of true wisdom is to keep within limits."

"Oh, if Cambyses could only hear you!" exclaimed Crœsus. "Instead of being contented with his immense conquests, and now thinking for the welfare of his subjects, he has all sorts of distant plans in his head. He wishes to conquer the entire world, and yet, since Phanes left, scarcely a day has passed in which he has not been conquered himself by the Div of drunkenness."

"Has his mother no influence over him?" asked Rhodopis. "She is a noble woman."

"She could not even move his resolution to marry Atossa, and was forced to be present at the marriage-feast."

"Poor Atossa!" murmured Sappho.

"She does not pass a very happy life as Queen of Persia," answered Crœsus; "and her own naturally impetuous disposition makes it all the more difficult for her to live contentedly with this husband and brother; I am sorry to hear it said that Cambyses neglects her sadly, and treats her like a child. But the marriage does not seem to have astonished the Egyptians, as brothers and sisters often marry here."[154]

"In Persia too," said Darius, putting on an appearance of the most perfect composure, "marriages with very near relations are thought to be the best."*

"But to return to the king," said Crœsus, turning the conversation for Darius' sake. "I can assure you, Rhodopis, that he may really be called a noble man. His violent and hasty deeds are repented of almost as soon as committed, and the resolution to be a just and merciful ruler has never forsaken him. At supper, for instance, lately, before his mind was clouded by the influence of wine, he asked us what the Persians thought of him in comparison with his father.".

"And what was the answer?" said Rhodopis.

"Intaphernes got us out of the trap cleverly enough," answered Zopyrus, laughing. "He exclaimed: 'We are of opinion that you deserve the preference, inasmuch as you have not only preserved intact the inheritance bequeathed you by Cyrus, but have extended his dominion beyond the seas by your conquest of Egypt.' This answer did not seem to please the

---

[154]. Marriages with a sister or a deceased wife's brother were not uncommon among the Egyptians. This is confirmed by numerous testimonies. Diod. I. 27. *Cod. Justin.* V. *Tit.* V. Leg. VIII. Also by Greek writers. Cor. Nep. I. v. *Cim.* I. The history of the Ptolemies, and especially of Philadelphus, is full of examples of such marriages.

* See note 130.

king, however, and poor Intaphernes was not a little horrified to hear him strike his fist on the table and cry, 'Flatterer, miserable flatterer!' He then turned to Crœsus and asked his opinion. Our wise friend answered at once: 'My opinion is that you have not attained to the greatness of your father; for,' added he in a pacifying tone, 'one thing is wanting to you— a son such as Cyrus bequeathed us in yourself.'" [155]

"First-rate, first-rate," cried Rhodopis clapping her hands and laughing. "An answer that would have done honor to the ready-witted Odysseus himself. And how did the king take your honeyed pill?"

"He was very much pleased, thanked Crœsus, and called him his friend."

"And I," said Crœsus taking up the conversation, "used the favorable opportunity to dissuade him from the campaigns he has been planning against the long-lived Ethiopians, the Ammonians and the Carthaginians. Of the first of these three nations we know scarcely anything but through fabulous tales; by attacking them we should lose much and gain little. The oasis of Ammon is scarcely accessible to a large army, on account of the desert by which it is surrounded; besides which, it seems to me sacrilegious to make war upon a god in the hope of obtaining possession of his treasures, whether we be his worshippers or not. As to the Carthaginians, facts have already justified my predictions. Our fleet is manned principally by Syrians and Phœnicians, and they have, as might be expected, refused to go to war against their brethren. Cambyses laughed at my reasons, and ended by swearing, when he was already somewhat intoxicated, that he could carry out

---

155. Herod. III. 34.

difficult undertakings and subdue powerful nations, even without the help of Bartja and Phanes."

"What could that allusion to you mean, my son?" asked Rhodopis.

"He won the battle of Pelusiam," cried Zopyrus, before his friend could answer. "He and no one else!"

"Yes," added Crœsus, "and you might have been more prudent, and have remembered that it is a dangerous thing to excite the jealousy of a man like Cambyses. You all of you forget that his heart is sore, and that the slightest vexation pains him. He has lost the woman he really loved; his dearest friend is gone; and now you want to disparage the last thing in this world that he still cares for,—his military glory."

"Don't blame him," said Bartja, grasping the old man's hand. "My brother has never been unjust, and is far from envying me what I must call my good fortune, for that my attack arrived just at the right time can hardly be reckoned as a merit on my part. You know he gave me this splendid sabre, a hundred thorough-bred horses, and a golden hand-mill* as rewards of my bravery."

Crœsus' words had caused Sappho a little anxiety at first; but this vanished on hearing her husband speak so confidently, and by the time Zopyrus had finished his wreath and placed it on Rhodopis' head, all her fears were forgotten.

Gyges had prepared his for the young mother. It was made of snow-white water-lilies, and, when she placed it among her brown curls, she looked so won-

* See note 219.

derfully lovely in the simple ornament, that Bartja could not help kissing her on the forehead, though so many witnesses were present. This little episode gave a merry turn to the conversation; every one did his best to enliven the others, refreshments of all kinds were handed round, and even Darius lost his gravity for a time and joined in the jests that were passing among his friends.

When the sun had set, the slaves set elegantly-carved chairs, footstools, and little tables on the open part of the deck. Our cheerful party now repaired thither and beheld a sight so marvellously beautiful as to be quite beyond their expectations.

The feast of Neith, called in Egyptian "the lamp-burning," was celebrated by a universal illumination, which began at the rising of the moon.[156] The shores of the Nile looked like two long lines of fire. Every temple, house and hut was ornamented with lamps according to the means of its possessors. The porches of the country-houses and the little towers on the larger buildings were all lighted up by brilliant flames, burning in pans of pitch and sending up clouds of smoke, in which the flags and pennons waved gently backwards and forwards. The palm-trees and sycamores were silvered by the moonlight and threw strange fantastic reflections on the red waters of the Nile—red from the fiery glow of the houses on their shores. But strong and glowing as was the light of the illumination, its rays had not power to reach the middle of the giant

---

156. Herodotus (II. 62.) speaks of this "burning of lamps" (λυχνοκαία) in honor of the goddess Neith (Pallas Athene). In Homer, Pallas Athene appears with an oil-lamp in her hand. *Odyss.* XIX. 34. Strabo (396) speaks of an eternal lamp, which was kept burning in honor of Athene Polias in her ancient temple on the Acropolis.

river, where the boat was making its course, and the pleasure-party felt as if they were sailing in dark night between two brilliant days. Now and then a brightly-lighted boat would come swiftly across the river and seem, as it neared the shore, to be cutting its way through a glowing stream of molten iron.

Lotus-blossoms, white as snow, lay on the surface of the river, rising and falling with the waves, and looking like eyes in the water. Not a sound could be heard from either shore. The echoes were carried away by the north-wind, and the measured stroke of the oars and monotonous song of the rowers were the only sounds that broke the stillness of this strange night—a night robbed of its darkness.

For a long time the friends gazed without speaking at the wonderful sight, which seemed to glide past them. Zopyrus was the first to break the silence by saying, as he drew a long breath: "I really envy you, Bartja. If things were as they should be, every one of us would have his dearest wife at his side on such a night as this."

"And who forbade you to bring one of your wives?" answered the happy husband.

"The other five," said the youth with a sigh. "If I had allowed Oroetes' little daughter Parysatis, my youngest favorite, to come out alone with me to-night, this wonderful sight would have been my last; to-morrow there would have been one pair of eyes less in the world."

Bartja took Sappho's hand and held it fast, saying, "I fancy *one* wife will content me as long as I live."

The young mother pressed his hand warmly again, and said, turning to Zopyrus: "I don't quite trust you, my friend. It seems to me that it is not the anger of your wives you fear, so much as the commission of an offence against the customs of your country. I have been told that my poor Bartja gets terribly scolded in the women's apartments for not setting eunuchs to watch over me, and for letting me share his pleasures."

"He does spoil you terribly," answered Zopyrus, "and our wives are beginning to quote him as an example of kindness and indulgence, whenever we try to hold the reins a little tight. Indeed there will soon be a regular women's mutiny at the king's gate, and the Achæmenidæ who escaped the swords and arrows of the Egyptians, will fall victims to sharp tongues and floods of salt tears."

"Oh! you most impolite Persian!" said Syloson laughing. "We must make you more respectful to these images of Aphrodite."

"You Greeks! that's a good idea," answered the youth. "By Mithras, our wives are quite as well off as yours. It's only the Egyptian women, that are so wonderfully free."

"Yes, you are quite right," said Rhodopis. "The inhabitants of this strange land have for thousands of years granted our weaker sex the same rights, that they demand for themselves. Indeed, in many respects, they have given us the preference. For instance, by the Egyptian law it is the daughters, not the sons, who are commanded to foster and provide for their aged parents, showing how well the fathers of this now humbled people understood women's nature, and how rightly they acknowledged that she far surpasses man in thoughtful solicitude and self-forgetful love. Do not laugh at these worshippers of animals. I confess that I cannot understand them, but I feel true admiration for a people in the teaching of whose priests, even Pythagoras, that great master in the art of knowledge, assured me lies a wisdom as mighty as the Pyramids."

"And your great master was right," exclaimed Darius. "You know that I obtained Neithotep's freedom, and, for some weeks past, have seen him and Onuphis very constantly, indeed they have been teaching me. And oh, how much I have learnt already from those two old men, of which I had no idea before! How much that is sad I can forget, when I am listening to them! They are acquainted with the entire history of the heavens and the earth. They know the name of every king, and the circumstances of every important event that has occurred during the last four thousand years, the courses of the stars, the works of their own artists and sayings of their sages, during the same immense period of time. All this knowledge is recorded in huge books, which have been preserved in a palace at Thebes,* called the "place of healing for the soul." Their laws are a fountain of pure wisdom, and a comprehensive intellect has been shown in the adaptation of all their state institutions to the needs of the country. I wish we could boast of the same regularity and order at home. The idea that lies at the root of all their knowledge is the use of numbers, the only means by which it is possible to calculate the course of the stars, to ascertain and determine the limits of all that exists, and, by the application of which in the shortening and lengthening of the strings of musical instruments, tones can be regulated.[157] Numbers are

---

157. Zeller, *Geschichte d. Philosophie der Griechen*, I. 292. We agree with Iamblichus in supposing, that these Pythagorean views were derived from the Egyptian mysteries.

* See note 51.

the only certain things; they can neither be controlled nor perverted. Every nation has its own ideas of right and wrong; every law can be rendered invalid by circumstances; but the results obtained from numbers can never be overthrown. Who can dispute, for instance, that twice two make four? Numbers determine the contents of every existing thing; whatever is, is equal to its contents, numbers therefore are the true being, the essence of all that is."

"In the name of Mithras, Darius, do leave off talking in that style, unless you want to turn my brain," interrupted Zopyrus. "Why, to hear you, one would fancy you'd been spending your life among these old Egyptian speculators and had never had a sword in your hand. What on earth have we to do with numbers?"

"More than you fancy," answered Rhodopis. "This theory of numbers belongs to the mysteries of the Egyptian priests, and Pythagoras learnt it from the very Onuphis who is now teaching you, Darius. If you will come to see me soon, I will show you how wonderfully that great Samian brought the laws of numbers and of the harmonies into agreement."[158]—But look, there are the Pyramids!"

The whole party rose at these words, and stood speechless, gazing at the grand sight which opened before them.

The Pyramids lay on the left bank of the Nile, in the silver moonshine, massive and awful, as if bruising the earth beneath them with their weight; the giant graves of mighty rulers. They seemed examples of man's creative power, and at the same time warnings

---

158. Aristotle, *Metaphys.* I. 5.

of the vanity and mutability of earthly greatness. For where was Chufu now,—the king who had cemented that mountain of stone with the sweat of his subjects? Where was the long-lived Chafra who had despised the gods, and, defiant in the consciousness of his own strength, was said to have closed the gates of the temples in order to make himself and his name immortal by building a tomb of superhuman dimensions?[159] Their empty sarcophagi are perhaps tokens, that the judges of the dead found them unworthy of rest in the grave, unworthy of the resurrection, whereas the builder of the third and most beautiful pyramid, Menkera, who contented himself with a smaller monument, and re-opened the gates of the temples, was allowed to rest in peace in his coffin of blue basalt.[160]

There they lay in the quiet night, these mighty pyramids, shone on by the bright stars, guarded by the watchman of the desert—the gigantic sphinx,—and

[159]. Herodotus repeats, in good faith, that the builders of the great Pyramids were despisers of the gods. The tombs of their faithful subjects at the foot of these huge structures prove, however, (especially in E. de Rougé's *Recherches sur les monuments qu'on peut attribuer aux VI. premières dynasties, &c.*), that they owe their bad repute to the hatred of the people, who could not forget the era of their hardest bondage, and branded the memories of their oppressors wherever an opportunity could be found. We might use the word "tradition" instead of "the people," for this it is which puts the feeling and tone of mind of the multitude into the form of history.

[160]. Bunsen, *Aegyptens Stelle in der Weltgeschichte* II. 169 and following, Pl. XVII. and in Vyse, *Pyramids of Ghizeh* II. Unfortunately the sarcophagus went down on the coast of Spain, in the ship which was conveying it to Europe. The Arabian geographer, Idrisi, states that shortly before the date at which he was then writing (1240) the pyramid had been opened, and that a mummy had been found in the sarcophagus with a gold plate by its side covered with unknown characters. Birch's translation of the inscription restored by Lepsius is probably the first. It is given in *Vyse's Pyramids* II. p. 94. The inscription restored by Lepsius and artistic representations of every portion of the city of the dead in Memphis, may be found in Ebers, *Aegypten in Bild und Wort* I. p. 33 and following.

overlooking the barren rocks of the Libyan stony mountains. At their feet, in beautifully-ornamented tombs, slept the mummies of their faithful subjects, and opposite the monument of the pious Menkera stood a temple, where prayers were said by the priests for the souls of the many dead buried in the great Memphian city of the dead. In the west, where the sun went down behind the Libyan mountains,—where the fruitful land ended and the desert began—there the people of Memphis had buried their dead; and as our gay party looked towards the west they felt awed into a solemn silence.

But their boat sped on before the north-wind; they left the city of the dead behind them and passed the enormous dikes* built to protect the city of Menes from the violence of the floods; the city of the Pharaohs came in sight, dazzlingly bright with the myriads of flames which had been kindled in honor of the goddess Neith, and when at last the gigantic temple of Ptah** appeared, the most ancient building of the most ancient land, the spell broke, their tongues were loosed, and they burst out into loud exclamations of delight.

It was illuminated by thousands of lamps; a hundred fires burnt on its Pylons, its battlemented walls and roofs. Burning torches flared between the rows of sphinxes which connected the various gates with the main building, and the now empty house of the god Apis[161] was so surrounded by colored fires that it

---

[161]. More has been said on the characteristic marks of the sacred bull Apis farther on in the text, and on the festival held at his discovery. Great lamentation was made at his death, and he was buried with incredible pomp. In the reign of Ptolemy Lagi the Apis having died of old age, his keeper not only expended on his funeral all the ready money then in store, but borrowed 50 silver talents from the king for

* See vol. I. note 141.   ** See vol. I. note 56.

gleamed like a white limestone rock in a tropical sunset. Pennons, flags and garlands waved above the brilliant picture; music and loud songs could be heard from below.

"Glorious," cried Rhodopis in enthusiasm, "glorious! Look how the painted walls and columns gleam in the light, and what marvellous figures the shadows of the obelisks and sphinxes throw on the smooth yellow pavement!"

"And how mysterious the sacred grove looks yonder!" added Crœsus. "I never saw anything so wonderful before."

"I have seen something more wonderful still," said Darius. "You will hardly believe me when I tell you that I have witnessed a celebration of the mysteries of Neith."

"Tell us what you saw, tell us!" was the universal outcry.

"At first Neithotep refused me admission, but when I promised to remain hidden, and besides, to obtain the

the same purpose (£6,750). Some of the priests who presided over the Apis-temple are said to have expended 100 talents (£22,500) on the animal's burial. Diod. I. 84. The Egyptians ascribed the gift of prophecy to Apis, (Plin. VIII. 71.), and seem to have considered him as symbolizing a period of 25 years. This supposition has been confirmed by the results of Mariette's excavations in the Serapeum and in the Apis-tombs, and by the deciphering of inscriptions on the so-called Apis-stelae. Mariette found a stone statue of the bull, covered with beautiful inscriptions, and a number of colossal Apis-sarcophagi. The statue was sent to Paris. A. Mariette, *Le Sérapéum de Memphis*. The dates on these Apis-stelae are of the greatest importance for the chronology of later Egyptian history, especially that of the 26th dynasty, which can be accurately determined by their means. We recommend as interesting Mariette's *La mère d'Apis*. He was said by many of the ancient writers to have been generated by a moonbeam, and dedicated to the moon as the Mnevis-bull of Heliopolis to the sun. Pomp. Mela. I. 9. 7. We cannot here discuss the place he held in the Egyptian religion. Much on this subject is to be found in Reinisch, *Die Aegyptischen Denkmäler in Miramar* p. 178. Also in Mariette's writings.

freedom of his child, he led me up to his observatory, from which there is a very extensive view, and told me that I should see a representation of the fates of Osiris and his wife Isis.[162]

"He had scarcely left, when the sacred grove became so brightly illuminated by colored lights that I was able to see into its innermost depths.

"A lake,* smooth as glass, lay before me, surrounded by beautiful trees and flower-beds. Golden boats were sailing on this lake and in them sat lovely boys and girls dressed in snow-white garments, and singing sweet songs as they passed over the water. There were no rowers to direct these boats, and yet they moved over the ripples of the lake in a graceful order, as if guided by some magic unseen hand. A large ship sailed in the midst of this little fleet. Its deck glittered with precious stones. It seemed to be steered by one beautiful boy only, and, strange to say, the rudder he guided consisted of one white lotus-flower, the delicate leaves of which seemed scarcely to touch the water. A very lovely woman, dressed like a queen, lay on silken cushions in the middle of the vessel; by her side sat a man of larger stature than that of ordinary mortals. He wore a crown of ivy on his flowing curls, a panther-skin hung over his shoulders and he held a crooked staff in the right hand. In the back part of the ship was a roof made of ivy, lotus-blossoms and roses; beneath it stood a milk-white

162. These performances in the sacred grove of Neith seemed to have belonged to the external apparatus of the mysteries. The stage on which they took place was the lake of *Sa-el-Hagar*. It exists to this day, and Herodotus (II. 170.) implies that near it was a tomb of Osiris. He says (171) "These plays represented the fates of the above-mentioned, and were called Mysteries." See note 164.

* See vol. I. note 150.

cow[163] with golden horns, covered with a cloth of purple. The man was Osiris, the woman Isis, the boy at the helm their son Horus, and the cow was the animal sacred to the immortal Isis. The little boats all skimmed over the water, singing glad songs of joy as they passed by the ship, and receiving in return showers of flowers and fruits, thrown down upon the lovely singers by the god and goddess within. Suddenly I heard the roll of thunder. It came crashing on, louder, and louder, and in the midst of this awful sound a man in the skin of a wild boar, with hideous features and bristling red hair, came out of the gloomiest part of the sacred grove, plunged into the lake, followed by seventy creatures like himself, and swam up to the ship of Osiris.[164]

"The little boats fled with the swiftness of the wind, and the trembling boy helmsman dropped his lotus-blossom.

"The dreadful monster then rushed on Osiris, and, with the help of his comrades, killed him, threw the body into a coffin and the coffin into the lake,[165] the waters of which seemed to carry it away as if by magic. Isis meanwhile had escaped to land in one of the small boats, and was now running hither and

163. The ivy was the plant of Osiris, the cow, the animal sacred to Isis. Diod. I. 17. Plut. *Isis and Orisis* 37. Herod. II 41. Isis is almost always represented with the head of a cow, and is again and again called "*ehe*" (the cow). There must certainly be a connection between this word and the name Io.

164. We have taken our description of this spectacle entirely from the Osiris-myth, as we find it in Plutarch, *Isis and Orisis* 13-19. Diod. I. 22. and a thousand times repeated on the monuments. Horus is called "the avenger of his father," &c. We copy the battle with all its phases from an inscription at Edfu, interpreted by Naville.

165. Here we have departed in some measure from Plutarch's version, in which Typhon artfully induces Osiris to lie down in the coffin.

thither on the shores of the lake, with streaming hair, lamenting her dead husband and followed by the virgins who had escaped with her. Their songs and dances, while seeking the body of Osiris, were strangely plaintive and touching, and the girls accompanied the dance by waving black Byssus scarfs in wonderfully graceful curves. Neither were the youths idle; they busied themselves in making a costly coffin for the vanished corpse of the god, accompanying their work with dances and the sound of castanets. When this was finished they joined the maidens in the train of the lamenting Isis and wandered on the shore with them, singing and searching.

"Suddenly a low song rose from some invisible lips. It swelled louder and louder and announced, that the body of the god had been transported by the currents of the Mediterranean to Gebal* in distant Phœnicia. This singing voice thrilled to my very heart; Neithotep's son, who was my companion, called it "the wind of rumor."

"When Isis heard the glad news, she threw off her mourning garments and sang a song of triumphant rejoicing, accompanied by the voices of her beautiful followers. Rumor had not lied; the goddess really found the sarcophagus and the dead body of her husband on the northern shore of the lake.[166] They

---

[166]. It is natural, that Isis should find the body of her husband in the north. The connection between Phœnicia and Egypt in this myth, as it has been handed down to us by Plutarch, is very remarkable. We consider the explanation of the close affinity between the Isis-and-Osiris and the Adonis myths to lie in the fact, that Egyptians and Phœnicians lived together on the shores of the Delta where the latter had planted their colonies. Plutarch's story of the finding of Osiris' dead body is very charming. *Isis and Osiris. Ed. Parth.* 15. The

*Better known by its Greek name of Byblos.

brought both to land with dances; Isis threw herself on the beloved corpse, called on the name of Osiris and covered the mummy with kisses, while the youths wove a wonderful tomb of lotus-flowers and ivy.

"When the coffin had been laid under this beautiful vault, Isis left the sad place of mourning and went to look for her son. She found him at the east end of the lake, where for a long time I had seen a beautiful youth practising arms with a number of companions.

"While she was rejoicing over her newly-found child, a fresh peal of thunder told that Typhon had returned. This time the monster rushed upon the beautiful flowering grave, tore the body out of its coffin, hewed it into fourteen pieces[167] and strewed them over the shores of the lake.

"When Isis came back to the grave, she found nothing but faded flowers and an empty coffin; but at fourteen different places on the shore fourteen beautiful colored flames were burning. She and her virgins ran

coffin had been overgrown and enclosed by an Erica, which supported the roof of the king of Byblus. This was wafted to Isis' ears by a marvellous breath of rumor (πνεύματι δαιμονίῳ φήμης). She went to Byblus and seated herself by a spring, weeping and in poor raiment. She spoke with no one save with the maidens of the queen, whose hair she braided and breathed into them a wonderful perfume, which she alone possessed. When the queen saw her maidens, she felt a desire towards this marvellous stranger, whose hair and skin breathed ambrosial odors, and sent for her. Isis soon became her friend and was appointed nurse to the queen's little child . . . Isis nourished it, by putting her finger into its mouth instead of the breast . . . she herself took the form of a swallow, and flew round the supporting pillar uttering plaintive cries . . . Finally she reveals herself as the goddess and asks for the pillar, draws it lightly away from under the roof, peels the Erica covering from the coffin of Osiris, and anoints him with bitter tears.

167. In 26 pieces, according to Diodorus, (I. 21.) which Typhon distributes among the same number of his companions. Plut. *(Is. and Os.* 18.) agrees with the monuments in stating the number as fourteen. These are separately specified on the latter.

to these flames, while Horus led the youths to battle against Typhon on the opposite shore.

"My eyes and ears hardly sufficed for all I had to see and hear. On the one shore a fearful and interesting struggle, peals of thunder and the braying of trumpets; on the other the sweet voices of the women, singing the most captivating songs to the most enchanting dances, for Isis had found a portion of her husband's body at every fire and was rejoicing.

"That was something for you, Zopyrus! I know of no words to describe the grace of those girls' movements, or how beautiful it was to see them first mingling in intricate confusion, then suddenly standing in faultless, unbroken lines, falling again into the same lovely tumult and passing once more into order, and all this with the greatest swiftness. Bright rays of light flashed from their whirling ranks all the time, for each dancer had a mirror[168] fastened between her shoulders, which flashed while she was in motion, and reflected the scene when she was still.

"Just as Isis had found the last limb but one[169] of the murdered Osiris, loud songs of triumph and the flourish of trumpets resounded from the opposite shore.

"Horus had conquered Typhon, and was forcing his way into the nether regions to free his father. The gate to this lower world opened on the west side of the

---

168. Dupuis, *Origine des Cultes*. This mirror-dance is most charmingly described by Th. Moore in his *Epicurean*. Nothing determinate can be said about it.

169. Isis sought the last limb in vain. Typhon (Set) had thrown it into the Nile. The goddess made an artificial limb, and from thence arose a worship, which seems to us to have been imported into Egypt from Phœnicia. Diod. I. 22. Plutarch, *Isis and Osiris* 18.

lake and was guarded by a fierce female hippopotamus.[170]

"And now a lovely music of flutes and harps came nearer and nearer, heavenly perfumes rose into the air, a rosy light spread over the sacred grove, growing brighter every minute, and Osiris came up from the lower world, led by his victorious son. Isis hastened to embrace her risen and delivered husband, gave the beautiful Horus his lotus-flower again instead of the sword, and scattered fruits and flowers over the earth, while Osiris seated himself under a canopy wreathed with ivy, and received the homage of all the spirits of the earth and of the Amenti."*

Darius was silent. Rhodopis began:

"We thank you for your charming account; but this strange spectacle must have a higher meaning, and we should thank you doubly if you would explain that to us."

"Your idea is quite right," answered Darius, "but what I know I dare not tell. I was obliged to promise Neithotep with an oath, not to tell tales out of school."[171]

"Shall I tell you," asked Rhodopis, "what conclu-

---

170. Lepsius considers the animal that kept guard over the lower world, and was generally represented sitting in front of Osiris, to have been a female hippopotamus. Sometimes, however, it is represented as a female dog, and generally of a mongrel form bearing some resemblance to a hippopotamus. Whatever it be, Cerberus certainly owes his origin to this "voracious beast of the Amenthes."

171. Herodotus, in speaking of the Osiris of the mysteries, says (II. 170.) "This sanctuary is holy to him, whose name I hold it sin to mention here;" and (171.) "Though I know much about the mysteries, I am silent in deep reverence."

* The lower world, in Egyptian *Amenti*, properly speaking, the West or kingdom of death, to which the soul returns at the death of the body, as the sun at his setting. In a hieroglyphic inscription of the time of the Ptolemies the Amenti is called Hades.

sions various hints from Pythagoras and Onuphis have led me to draw, as to the meaning of this drama? Isis seems to me to represent the bountiful earth; Osiris, humidity or the Nile, which makes the earth fruitful; Horus, the young spring; Typhon, the scorching drought. The bounteous earth, robbed of her productive power, seeks this beloved husband with lamentations in the cooler regions of the north, where the Nile discharges his waters. At last Horus, the young springing power of nature, is grown up and conquers Typhon, or the scorching drought. Osiris, as is the case with the fruitful principle of nature, was only apparently dead, rises from the nether regions and once more rules the blessed valley of the Nile, in concert with his wife, the bounteous earth."

"And as the murdered god behaved properly in the lower regions," said Zopyrus, laughing, "he is allowed, at the end of this odd story, to receive homage from the inhabitants of Hamestegan, Duzakh and Gorothman,[172] or whatever they call these abodes for the Egyptian spirit-host."

"They are called Amenti," said Darius, falling into his friend's merry mood; but you must know that the history of this divine pair represents not only the life of nature, but also that of the human soul, which, like the murdered Osiris, lives an eternal life, even when the body is dead."

"Thank you," said the other; "I'll try to remember

---

172. *Haméstegán*—the abode of those whose good and bad deeds were equal; *Duzakh*—Hell; Gorothman—the Paradise of the Persians. Spiegel, *Avesta* I. p. 23. *Ulmai Islam*. Vullers, *Fragments*. The "contemplation from the seven heavens," seems to have belonged to a later period. (*The Ardai-Viraf nameh, &c.* Translated from the Persian by J. A. Pope.) Spiegel, *Avesta*, Farg. XIX. note to §. 121.

that if I should chance to die in Egypt. But really, cost what it may, I must see this wonderful sight soon."

"Just my own wish," said Rhodopis. "Age is inquisitive."

"You will never be old," interrupted Darius. "Your conversation and your features have remained alike beautiful, and your mind is as clear and bright as your eyes."

"Forgive me for interrupting you," said Rhodopis, as if she had not heard his flattering words, "but the word 'eyes' reminds me of the oculist Nebenchari, and my memory fails me so often, that I must ask you what has become of him, before I forget. I hear nothing now of this skilful operator to whom the noble Kassandane owes her sight."

"He is much to be pitied," replied Darius. "Even before we reached Pelusium he had begun to avoid society, and scorned even to speak with his countryman Onuphis. His gaunt old servant was the only being allowed to wait on or be with him. But after the battle his whole behavior changed. He went to the king with a radiant countenance, and asked permission to accompany him to Sais, and to choose two citizens of that town to be his slaves. Cambyses thought he could not refuse anything to the man, who had been such a benefactor to his mother, and granted him full power to do what he wished. On arriving at Amasis' capital, he went at once to the temple of Neith, caused the high-priest (who had moreover placed himself at the head of the citizens hostile to Persia), to be arrested, and with him a certain oculist named Petammon. He then informed them that, as punishment for the burning of certain papers, they would be condemned to serve a Persian to whom he should sell them, for the term of their natural lives, and to perform the most menial services of slaves in a foreign country. I was present at this scene, and I assure you I trembled before the Egyptian as he said these words to his enemies. Neithotep, however, listened quietly, and when Nebenchari had finished, answered him thus: 'If thou, foolish son, hast betrayed thy country for the sake of thy burnt manuscripts, the deed has been neither just nor wise. I preserved thy valuable works with the greatest care, laid them up in our temple, and sent a complete copy to the library at Thebes.* Nothing was burnt but the letters from Amasis to thy father, and a worthless old chest. Psamtik and Petammon were present, and it was then and there resolved that a new family tomb in the city of the dead should be built for thee as a compensation for the loss of papers, which, in order to save Egypt, we were unfortunately forced to destroy. On its walls thou canst behold pleasing paintings of the gods to whom thou hast devoted thy life, the most sacred chapters from the book of the dead, and many other beautiful pictures touching thine own life and character.'"[173]

[173]. Descriptions and drawings of such ancient Egyptian tombs are to be found in all the modern works on the land of the Pharaohs. Among them Ebers, *Aegypten in Bild und Wort*. Where there were mountains, the tombs were hewn in the rock; on the level Delta sepulchres were erected. Both were well supplied with inscriptions. For the uninitiated in such matters, the minute particulars given by Brugsch in his description of the tomb of Ti will be instructive. The following inscription on a tomb-stela in the Egyptian Museum at Boolak (Cairo) is particularly interesting. (Mariette's Catalogue p. 76. N. 51.) "O ye great ones, ye prophets, priests, orators and all ye that shall come after me in the millions of years; if any one shall set my name at the end, and set his own name in its place (on the Stele), God

* See note 51.

"The physician turned very pale—asked first to see his books, and then his new and beautifully-fitted-up tomb. He then gave his slaves their freedom, (notwithstanding which they were still taken to Memphis as prisoners of war), and went home, often passing his hand across his forehead on the way, and with the uncertain step of one intoxicated. On reaching his house he made a will, bequeathing all he possessed to the grandson of his old servant Hib, and, alleging that he was ill, went to bed. The next morning he was found dead. He had poisoned himself with the fearful strychnos-juice."*

"Miserable man" said Crœsus. "The gods had blinded him, and he reaped despair instead of revenge, as a reward for his treachery."

"I pity him," murmured Rhodopis. "But look, the rowers are taking in their oars. We are at the end of our journey; there are your litters and carriages waiting for you. It was a beautiful trip. Farewell, my dear ones; come to Naukratis soon. I shall return at once with Theopompus and Syloson. Give little Parmys a thousand kisses from me, and tell Melitta never to take her out at noon. It is dangerous for the eyes.** Good-night, Crœsus; good-night, friends, farewell my dear son."

---

will requite him with the destruction of his likeness upon earth; if he erase my name upon this, so will God do also unto him." At the time in which Nebenchari lived, (during the 26th dynasty), it was customary to have chapters from the Ritual of the Dead painted on the inner walls of the tombs. Lepsius, *Aelteste Texte des Todtenbuchs* p. 14. A. 1. One of the largest and most richly-ornamented tombs in the Theban Necropolis belongs to a noble of Psamtik's reign. Many chapters from the Ritual of the Dead are found on the walls of the chamber containing the sarcophagus of Amen em ha of the 18th dynasty at Abd el Qurnah, in the western part of Thebes.

* See note 7. ** See vol. I. note 290.

The Persians left the vessel with many a nod and farewell word, and Bartja, looking round once more, missed his footing and fell on the landing-pier.

He sprang up in a moment without Zopyrus' help, who came running back, calling out, "Take care, Bartja! It's unlucky to fall in stepping ashore. I did the very same thing, when we left the ship that time at Naukratis."

CHAPTER XIV.

WHILE our friends were enjoying their row on the Nile, Cambyses' envoy, Prexaspes, had returned from a mission to the long-lived Ethiopians.[174] He praised their strength and stature, described the way to their country as almost inaccessible to a large army, and had plenty of marvellous tales to tell. How, for instance, they always chose the strongest and handsomest man in their nation for their king, and obeyed him unconditionally: how many of them reached the age of 120 years, and some even passed it: how they ate nothing but boiled flesh, drank new milk and washed in a spring the waters of which had the scent of violets, gave a remarkable lustre to their skins, and were so light that wood could not swim in them: how their captives wore golden fetters, because other metals were rare and dear in their country; and lastly, how they covered the bodies of the dead with plaster or stucco, over which a coating of some glass-like material was poured, and kept the pillars thus formed one year in

[174]. Herod. II. 20-25.

their houses, during which time sacrifices were offered to them, and at the year's end they were placed in rows around the town.

The king of this strange people had accepted Cambyses' presents, saying, in a scornful tone, that he knew well his friendship was of no importance to the Persians, and Prexaspes had only been sent to spy out the land. If the prince of Asia were a just man, he would be contented with his own immense empire and not try to subjugate a people who had done him no wrong. "Take your king this bow," he said, "and advise him not to begin the war with us, until the Persians are able to bend such weapons as easily as we do. Cambyses may thank the gods, that the Ethiopians have never taken it into their heads to conquer countries which do not belong to them."

He then unbent his mighty bow of ebony, and gave it to Prexaspes to take to his lord.

Cambyses laughed at the bragging African, invited his nobles to a trial of the bow the next morning, and rewarded Prexaspes for the clever way in which he had overcome the difficulties of his journey and acquitted himself of his mission. He then went to rest, as usual intoxicated, and fell into a disturbed sleep, in which he dreamed that Bartja was seated on the throne of Persia, and that the crown of his head touched the heavens.[175]

This was a dream, which he could interpret without the aid of soothsayer or Chaldean. It roused his anger first, and then made him thoughtful.

He could not sleep, and such questions as the following came into his mind: "Haven't you given

175. Herod. III. 30.

your brother reason to feel revengeful? Do you think he can forget that you imprisoned and condemned him to death, when he was innocent? And if he should raise his hand against you, would not all the Achæmenidæ take his part? Have I ever done, or have I any intention of ever doing anything to win the love of these venal courtiers? Since Nitetis died and that strange Greek fled, has there been a single human being, in whom I have the least confidence or on whose affection I can rely?"

These thoughts and questionings excited him so fearfully, that he sprang from his bed, crying: "Love and I have nothing to do with one another. Other men may be kind and good if they like; I must be stern, or I shall fall into the hands of those who hate me—hate me because I have been just, and have visited heavy sins with heavy chastisements. They whisper flattering words in my ear; they curse me when my back is turned. The gods themselves must be my enemies, or why do they rob me of everything I love, deny me posterity and even that military glory which is my just due? Is Bartja so much better than I, that everything which I am forced to give up should be his in hundred-fold measure? Love, friendship, fame, children,—everything flows to him as the rivers to the sea, while my heart is parched like the desert. But I am king still. I can show him which is the stronger of us two, and I will, though his forehead may touch the heavens. In Persia there can be only one great man. He or I,—I or he. In a few days I'll send him back to Asia and make him satrap of Bactria. There he can nurse his child and listen to his wife's songs, while I am winning glory in Ethiopia, which it shall not be in his power to lessen. Ho, there, dressers! bring my robes and a good morning-draught of wine. I'll show the Persians that I'm fit to be King of Ethiopia, and can beat them all at bending a bow. Here, give me another cup of wine. I'd bend that bow, if it were a young cedar and its string a cable!" So saying he drained an immense bowl of wine and went into the palace-garden, conscious of his enormous strength and therefore sure of success.

All his nobles were assembled waiting for him there, welcomed him with loud acclamations, and fell on their faces to the ground before their king.

Pillars, connected by scarlet cords, had been quickly set up between the closely-cut hedges and straight avenues.* From these cords, suspended by gold and silver rings, yellow and dark blue hangings[176] fluttered in the breeze. Gilded wooden benches had been placed round in a large circle, and nimble cup-bearers handed wine in costly vessels to the company assembled for the shooting-match.

At a sign from the king the Achæmenidæ rose from the earth.

Cambyses glanced over their ranks, and his face brightened on seeing that Bartja was not there. Prexaspes handed him the Ethiopian bow, and pointed out a target at some distance. Cambyses laughed at the large size of the target, weighted the bow with his right hand, challenged his subjects to try their fortune

---

176. Book of Esther I. 6. There the hangings are white, green and blue or violet. (English version.) In the text we have given red, yellow and dark blue, because these were the Persian colors. See p. 266 and note 141.

* See vol. I. note 7.

first, and handed the bow to the aged Hystaspes, as the highest in rank among the Achæmenidæ.

While Hystaspes first, and then all the heads of the six other highest families in Persia, were using their utmost efforts to bend this monster weapon in vain, the king emptied goblet after goblet of wine, his spirits rising as he watched their vain endeavors to solve the Ethiopian's problem. At last Darius, who was famous for his skill in archery, took the bow. Nearly the same result. The wood was inflexible as iron and all his efforts only availed to move it one finger's breadth. The king gave him a friendly nod in reward for his success, and then, looking round on his friends and relations in a manner that betokened the most perfect assurance, he said: "Give me the bow now, Darius. I will show you, that there is only one man in Persia who deserves the name of king;—only one who can venture to take the field against the Ethiopians;—only one who can bend this bow."

He grasped it tightly with his left hand, taking the string, which was as thick as a man's finger and made from the intestines of a lion, in his right, fetched a deep breath, bent his mighty back and pulled and pulled; collected all his strength for greater and greater efforts, strained his sinews till they threatened to break, and the veins in his forehead were swollen to bursting, did not even disdain to use his feet and legs, but all in vain. After a quarter of an hour of almost superhuman exertion, his strength gave way, the ebony, which he had succeeded in bending even farther than Darius, flew back and set all his further endeavors at nought. At last, feeling himself thoroughly exhausted, he dashed the bow on to the ground in a passion, crying: "The

Ethiopian is a liar! no mortal man has ever bent that bow. What is impossible for my arm is possible for no other. In three days we will start for Ethiopia. I will challenge the impostor to a single combat, and ye shall see which is the stronger. Take up the bow, Prexaspes, and keep it carefully. The black liar shall be strangled with his own bow-string. This wood is really harder than iron, and I confess that the man who could bend it, would really be my master. I should not be ashamed to call him so, for he must be of better stuff than I."

As he finished speaking, Bartja appeared in the circle of assembled Persians. His glorious figure was set off to advantage by his rich dress, his features were bright with happiness and a feeling of conscious strength. He passed through the ranks of the Achæmenidæ with many a friendly nod, which was warmly returned, and going straight to his brother, kissed his robe, looked up frankly and cheerfully into his gloomy eyes, and said: " I am a little late, and ask your forgiveness, my lord and brother. Or have I really come in time? Yes, yes, I see there's no arrow in the target yet, so I am sure you, the best archer in the world, cannot have tried your strength yet. But you look so enquiringly at me. Then I will confess that our child kept me. The little creature laughed to-day for the first time, and was so charming with its mother, that I forgot how time was passing while I watched them. You have all full leave to laugh at my folly; I really don't know how to excuse myself. See, the little one has pulled my star from the chain. But I think, my brother, you will give me a new one to-day if I should hit the bull's eye. Shall I shoot first, or will you begin, my Sovereign?"

"Give him the bow, Prexaspes," said Cambyses, not even deigning to look at his brother.

Bartja took it and was proceeding to examine the wood and the string, when Cambyses suddenly called out, with a mocking laugh: "By Mithras, I believe you want to try your sweet looks on the bow, and win its favor in that fashion, as you do the hearts of men. Give it back to Prexaspes. It's easier to play with beautiful women and laughing children, than with a weapon like this, which mocks the strength even of real men."

Bartja blushed with anger and annoyance at this speech, which was uttered in the bitterest tone, picked up the giant arrow that lay before him, placed himself opposite the target, summoned all his strength, bent the bow, by an almost superhuman effort, and sent the arrow into the very centre of the target, where its iron point remained, while the wooden shaft split into a hundred shivers.[177]

Most of the Achæmenidæ burst into loud shouts of delight at this marvellous proof of strength; but Bartja's nearest friends turned pale and were silent; they were watching the king, who literally quivered with rage, and Bartja, who was radiant with pride and joy.

Cambyses was a fearful sight at that moment. It seemed to him as if that arrow, in piercing the target, had pierced his own heart, his strength, dignity and honor. Sparks floated before his eyes, in his ears was

[177]. Herodotus tells this story (III. 30.), and we are indebted to him also for our information of the events which follow. The following inscription, said to have been placed over the grave of Darius, and communicated by Onesikritus, (Strabo 730.) proves that the Persians were very proud of being reputed good archers: "I was a friend to my friends, the best rider and archer, a first-rate hunter; I could do everything."

a sound like the breaking of a stormy sea on the shore; his cheeks glowed and he grasped the arm of Prexaspes who was at his side. Prexaspes only too well understood what that pressure meant, when given by a royal hand, and murmured: "Poor Bartja!"

At last the king succeeded in recovering his presence of mind. Without saying a word, he threw a gold chain to his brother, ordered his nobles to follow him, and left the garden, but only to wander restlessly up and down his apartments, and try to drown his rage in wine. Suddenly he seemed to have formed a resolution and ordered all the courtiers, except Prexaspes, to leave the hall. When they were alone, he called out in a hoarse voice and with a look that proved the extent of his intoxication: "This life is not to be borne! Rid me of my enemy, and I will call you my friend and benefactor."

Prexaspes trembled, threw himself at the king's feet and raised his hands imploringly; but Cambyses was too intoxicated, and too much blinded by his hatred to understand the action. He fancied the prostration was meant as a sign of devotion to his will, signed to him to rise, and whispered, as if afraid of hearing his own words: "Act quickly and secretly; and, as you value your life, let no one know of the upstart's death. Depart, and when your work is finished, take as much as you like out of the treasury. But keep your wits about you. The boy has a strong arm and a winning tongue. Think of your own wife and children, if he tries to win you over with his smooth words."

As he spoke he emptied a fresh goblet of pure wine, staggered through the door of the room, calling out as he turned his back on Prexaspes: "Woe be to you if that upstart, that woman's hero, that fellow who has robbed me of my honor, is left alive."

Long after he had left the hall, Prexaspes stood fixed on the spot where he had heard these words. The man was ambitious, but neither mean nor bad, and he felt crushed by the awful task allotted to him. He knew that his refusal to execute it would bring death or disgrace on himself and on his family; but he loved Bartja, and besides, his whole nature revolted at the thought of becoming a common, hired murderer. A fearful struggle began in his mind, and raged long after he left the palace. On the way home he met Crœsus and Darius. He fancied they would see from his looks that he was already on the way to a great crime, and hid himself behind the projecting gate of a large Egyptian house. As they passed, he heard Crœsus say: "I reproached him bitterly, little as he deserves reproach in general, for having given such an inopportune proof of his great strength. We may really thank the gods, that Cambyses did not lay violent hands on him in a fit of passion. He has followed my advice now and gone with his wife to Sais. For the next few days Bartja must not come near the king; the mere sight of him might rouse his anger again, and a monarch can always find unprincipled servants . . ."

The rest of the sentence died away in the distance, but the words he had heard were enough to make Prexaspes start, as if Crœsus had accused him of the shameful deed. He resolved in that moment that, come what would, his hands should not be stained with the blood of a friend. This resolution restored him his old erect bearing and firm gait for the time, but when he reached the dwelling which had been assigned as his abode in Sais his two boys ran to the door to meet him. They had stolen away from the play-ground of the sons of the Achæmenidæ, (who, as was always the case, had accompanied the king and the army), to see their father for a moment. He felt a strange tenderness, which he could not explain to himself, on taking them in his arms, and kissed the beautiful boys once more on their telling him that they must go back to their play-ground again, or they should be punished. Within, he found his favorite wife playing with their youngest child, a sweet little girl. Again the same strange, inexplicable feeling of tenderness. He overcame it this time for fear of betraying his secret to his young wife, and retired to his own apartment early.

Night had come on.

The sorely-tried man could not sleep; he turned restlessly from side to side. The fearful thought, that his refusal to do the king's will would be the ruin of his wife and children, stood before his wakeful eyes in the most vivid colors. The strength to keep his good resolution forsook him, and even Crœsus' words, which, when he first heard them had given his nobler feelings the victory, now came in as a power on the other side. "A monarch can always find unprincipled servants." Yes, the words were an affront, but at the same time a reminder, that though he might defy the king's command a hundred others would be ready to obey it. No sooner had this thought become clear to him, than he started up, examined a number of daggers which hung, carefully arranged, above his bed, and laid the sharpest on the little table before him.

He then began to pace the room in deep thought, often going to the opening which served as a window, to cool his burning forehead and see if dawn were near.

When at last daylight appeared, he heard the sounding brass* calling the boys to early prayer. That reminded him of his sons and he examined the dagger a second time. A troop of gaily-dressed courtiers rode by on their way to the king. He put the dagger in his girdle; and at last, on hearing the merry laughter of his youngest child sound from the women's apartments, he set the tiara hastily on his head, left the house without taking leave of his wife, and, accompanied by a number of slaves, went down to the Nile. There he threw himself into a boat and ordered the rowers to take him to Sais.

A few hours after the fatal shooting-match, Bartja had followed Crœsus' advice and had gone off to Sais with his young wife. They found Rhodopis there. She had yielded to an irresistible impulse and, instead of returning to Naukratis, had stopped at Sais. Bartja's fall on stepping ashore had disturbed her, and she had with her own eyes seen an owl fly from the left side close by his head. These evil omens, to a heart which had by no means outgrown the superstitions of the age, added to a confused succession of distressing dreams which had disturbed her slumbers, and her usual wish to be always near Bartja and Sappho, led her to decide quickly on waiting for her granddaughter at Sais.

Bartja and Sappho were delighted to find such a

* See vol. I. p. 239.

welcome guest, and after she had dandled and played with her great grandchild, the little Parmys,[178] to her heart's content, they led her to the rooms which had been prepared for her. They were the same in which the unhappy Tachot had spent the last months of her fading existence. Rhodopis could not see all the little trifles which showed, not only the age and sex of the former occupant, but her tastes and disposition, without feeling very sad. On the dressing-table were a number of little ointment-boxes and small bottles for perfumes, cosmetics, washes and oils.[179] Two larger boxes, one in the form of a Nile-goose,[180] and another on the side of which a woman playing on a lute had been painted, had once contained the princess's costly golden ornaments, and the metal mirror with a handle in the form of a sleeping maiden,[181] had once reflected her beautiful face with its pale pink flush. Everything in the room, from the elegant little couch resting on lions' claws, to the delicately-carved ivory combs[182] on the toilet-table, proved that the outward adornments of life had possessed much charm for the former owner of these rooms. The golden *sistrum* and the delicately-wrought

178. Herodotus states, that beside Atossa, &c., Darius took a daughter of the deceased Bartja, named Parmys, to be his wife. Herod. III. 88. She is also mentioned VII. 78.

179. Wilkinson III. 381. 383. We learn from the monuments, that the Egyptians were accustomed to anoint themselves in divers ways from a very early period. We read of a paint for the eyes called *Mestem* as early as the 12th dynasty. The staining of the finger-nails so customary still in Egypt, though forbidden, was practised in the time of the Pharaohs, (this can be proved by the mummies), and perfumed locks were indispensable to a beauty of those days. *Papyr. d'Orb.* 9. 3. Plut. *Isis and Osiris* 15.

180. From Wilkinson II. 360. Leyden Museum.

181. From the handle of a saucer or vase used for ornaments, in Wilkinson II. 359. See also Wilkinson III. 386. 1. 2.

182. Combs found at Thebes. Wilkinson III. 381.

nabla, the strings of which had long ago been broken, testified to her taste for music, while the broken spindle* in the corner, and some unfinished nets of glass beads [183] shewed that she had been fond of woman's usual work.

It was a sad pleasure to Rhodopis to examine all these things, and the picture which she drew in her own mind of Tachot after the inspection, differed very little from the reality. At last interest and curiosity led her to a large painted chest. She lifted the light cover and found, first, a few dried flowers; then a ball, round which some skilful hand had wreathed roses and leaves, once fresh and bright, now, alas, long ago dead and withered. Beside these were a number of amulets in different forms, one representing the goddess of truth, another containing spells written on a strip of papyrus and concealed in a little golden case. Then her eyes fell on some letters written in the Greek character. She read them by the light of the lamp. They were from Nitetis in Persia to her supposed sister, and were written in ignorance of the latter's illness. When Rhodopis laid them down her eyes were full of tears. The dead girl's secret lay open before her. She knew now that Tachot had loved Bartja, that he had given her the faded flowers, and that she had wreathed the ball with roses because he had thrown it to her. The amulets must have been intended either to heal her sick heart, or to awaken love in his.

As she was putting the letters back in their old

---

183. Bead-work has been found on very many of the mummies in almost all the larger museums. In Wilkinson III. 90. 101. is a drawing of the celebrated large glass bead, in which a hieroglyphic inscription had been cut.

* See note 104.

place, she touched some cloths which seemed put in to fill up the bottom of the chest, and felt a hard round substance underneath. She raised them, and discovered a bust made of colored wax, such a wonderfully-exact portrait of Nitetis, that an involuntary exclamation of surprise broke from her, and it was long before she could turn her eyes away from Theodorus' marvellous work.

She went to rest and fell asleep, thinking of the sad fate of Nitetis, the Egyptian Princess.

The next morning Rhodopis went into the garden —the same into which we led our readers during the lifetime of Amasis—and found Bartja and Sappho in an arbor overgrown with vines.

Sappho was seated in a light wicker-work chair. Her child lay on her lap, stretching out its little hands and feet, sometimes to its father, who was kneeling on the ground before them, and then to its mother whose laughing face was bent down over her little one.

Bartja was very happy with his child. When the little creature buried its tiny fingers in his curls and beard, he would draw his head back to feel the strength of the little hand, would kiss its rosy feet, its little round white shoulders and dimpled arms. Sappho enjoyed the fun, always trying to draw the little one's attention to its father.

Sometimes, when she stooped down to kiss the rosy baby lips, her forehead would touch his curls and he would steal the kiss meant for the little Parmys.

Rhodopis watched them a long time unperceived, and, with tears of joy in her eyes, prayed the gods that they might long be as happy as they now were. At last she came into the arbor to wish them good-morning, and bestowed much praise on old Melitta for appearing at the right moment, parasol in hand, to take her charge out of the sunshine before it became too bright and hot, and put her to sleep.

The old slave had been appointed head-nurse to the high-born child, and acquitted herself in her new office with an amount of importance which was very comical. Hiding her old limbs under rich Persian robes, she moved about exulting in the new and delightful right to command, and kept her inferiors in perpetual motion.

Sappho followed Melitta into the palace, first whispering in her husband's ear with her arm round his neck: "Tell my grandmother everything and ask whether you are right."

Before he could answer, she had stopped his mouth with a kiss, and then hurried after the old woman who was departing with dignified steps.

The prince smiled as he watched her graceful walk and beautiful figure, and said, turning to Rhodopis: "Does not it strike you, that she has grown taller lately."

"It seems so," answered Rhodopis. "A woman's girlhood has its own peculiar charm, but her true dignity comes with motherhood. It is the feeling of having fulfilled her destiny, which raises her head and makes us fancy she has grown taller."

"Yes," said Bartja, "I think she is happy. Yesterday our opinions differed for the first time, and as she was leaving us just now, she begged me, privately, to lay the question before you, which I am very glad to do, for I honor your experience and wisdom just as much, as I love her childlike inexperience."

Bartja then told the story of the unfortunate shooting-match, finishing with these words: "Crœsus blames my imprudence, but I know my brother; I know that when he is angry he is capable of any act of violence, and it is not impossible that at the moment when he felt himself defeated he could have killed me; but I know too, that when his fierce passion has cooled, he will forget my boastful deed, and only try to excel me by others of the same kind. A year ago he was by far the best marksman in Persia, and would be so still, if drink and epilepsy had not undermined his strength. I must confess I feel as if I were becoming stronger every day."

"Yes," interrupted Rhodopis, "pure happiness strengthens a man's arm, just as it adds to the beauty of a woman, while intemperance and mental distress ruin both body and mind far more surely even than old age. My son, beware of your brother; his strong arm has become paralyzed, and his generosity can be forfeited too. Trust my experience, that the man who is the slave of one evil passsion, is very seldom master of the rest; besides which, no one feels humiliation so bitterly as he who is sinking—who knows that his powers are forsaking him. I say again, beware of your brother, and trust the voice of experience more than that of your own heart, which, because it is generous itself, believes every one else to be so."

"I see," said Bartja, "that you will take Sappho's side. Difficult as it will be for her to part from you, she has still begged me to return with her to Persia. She thinks that Cambyses may forget his anger, when I am out of sight. I thought she was over-anxious, and besides, it would disappoint me not to take part in the expedition against the Ethiopians."

"But I entreat you," interrupted Rhodopis, "to follow her advice. The gods only know what pain it will give me to lose you both, and yet I repeat a thousand times: Go back to Persia, and remember that none but fools stake life and happiness to no purpose. As to the war with Ethiopia, it is mere madness; instead of subduing those black inhabitants of the south, you yourselves will be conquered by heat, thirst and all the horrors of the desert. In saying this I refer to the campaigns in general; as to your own share in them, I can only say that if no fame is to be won there, you will be putting your own life and the happiness of your family in jeopardy literally for nothing, and that if, on the other hand, you should distinguish yourself again, it would only be giving fresh cause of jealousy and anger to your brother. No, go to Persia, as soon as you can."

Bartja was just beginning to make various objections to these arguments, when he caught sight of Prexaspes coming up to them, looking very pale.

After the usual greeting, the envoy whispered to Bartja, that he should like to speak with him alone. Rhodopis left them at once, and he began, playing with the rings on his right hand as he spoke, in a constrained, embarrassed way. "I come from the king. Your display of strength irritated him yesterday, and he does not wish to see you again for some time. His orders are, that you set out for Arabia to buy up all the camels [184] that are to be had. As these animals can

---

184. Camels are never represented on the Egyptian monuments, whereas they were in great use among the Arabians and Persians, and are now a necessity on the Nile. They must have existed in Egypt, however. Hekekyan-Bey discovered the bones of a dromedary in a deep bore. Representations of these creatures were probably forbid-

bear thirst very long, they are to be used in conveying food and water for our army on the Ethiopian campaign. There must be no delay. Take leave of your wife, and (I speak by the king's command) be ready to start before dark. You will be absent at least a month. I am to accompany you as far as Pelusium. Kassandane wishes to have your wife and child near her during your absence. Send them to Memphis as soon as possible; under the protection of the queen-mother, they will be in safety."

Prexaspes' short, constrained way of speaking did not strike Bartja. He rejoiced at what seemed to him great moderation on the part of his brother, and at receiving a commission which relieved him of all doubt on the question of leaving Egypt, gave his friend, (as he supposed him to be), his hand to kiss and an invitation to follow him into the palace.

In the cool of the evening, he took a short but very affectionate farewell of Sappho and his child, who was asleep in Melitta's arms, told his wife to set out as soon as possible on her journey to Kassandane, called out jestingly to his mother-in-law, that at least this time she had been mistaken in her judgment of a man's character, (meaning his brother's), and sprang on to his horse.

As Prexaspes was mounting, Sappho whispered to him, "Take care of that reckless fellow, and remind him of me and his child, when you see him running into unnecessary danger."

"I shall have to leave him at Pelusium," answered

den. We know this was the case with the cock, of which bird there were large numbers in Egypt. It is remarkable, that camels were not introduced into Barbary until after the birth of Christ. H. Barth, *Wanderungen am Gestade des Mittelmeers p.* 3 and following.

the envoy, busying himself with the bridle of his horse in order to avoid meeting her eyes.

"Then may the gods take him into their keeping!" exclaimed Sappho. clasping her husband's hand, and bursting into tears, which she could not keep back. Bartja looked down and saw his usually trustful wife in tears. He felt sadder than he had ever felt before. Stooping down lovingly from his saddle, he put his strong arm round her waist, lifted her up to him, and as she stood supporting herself on his foot in the stirrup, pressed her to his heart, as if for a long last farewell. He then let her safely and gently to the ground, took his child up to him on the saddle, kissed and fondled the little creature, and told her laughingly to make her mother very happy while he was away, exchanged some warm words of farewell with Rhodopis, and then, spurring his horse till the creature reared, dashed through the gateway of the Pharaohs' palace, with Prexaspes at his side.

When the sound of the horses' hoofs had died away in the distance, Sappho laid her head on her grandmother's shoulder and wept uncontrollably. Rhodopis remonstrated and blamed, but all in vain, she could not stop her tears.

CHAPTER XV.

On the morning after the trial of the bow, Cambyses was seized by such a violent attack of his old illness, that he was forced to keep his room for two days and nights, ill in mind and body; at times raging like a madman, at others weak and powerless as a little child.

On the third day he recovered consciousness and remembered the awful charge he had laid on Prexaspes, and that it was only too possible he might have executed it already. At this thought he trembled, as he had never trembled in his life before. He sent at once for the envoy's eldest son, who was one of the royal cup-bearers. The boy said his father had left Memphis, without taking leave of his family. He then sent for Darius, Zopyrus and Gyges, knowing how tenderly they loved Bartja, and enquired after their friend. On hearing from them that he was at Sais, he sent the three youths thither at once, charging them, if they met Prexaspes on the way, to send him back to Memphis without delay. This haste and the king's strange behavior were quite incomprehensible to the young Achæmenidæ; nevertheless they set out on their journey with all speed, fearing that something must be wrong.

Cambyses, meanwhile, was miserably restless, inwardly cursed his habit of drinking and tasted no wine the whole of that day. Seeing his mother in the palace-gardens, he avoided her; he durst not meet her eye.

The next eight days passed without any sign of Prexaspes' return; they seemed to the king like a year. A hundred times he sent for the young cup-bearer and asked if his father had returned; a hundred times he received the same disappointing answer.

At sunset on the thirteenth day, Kassandane sent to beg a visit from him. The king went at once, for now he longed to look on the face of his mother; he fancied it might give him back his lost sleep.

After he had greeted her with a tenderness so rare from him, that it astonished her, he asked for what reason she had desired his presence. She answered, that Bartja's wife had arrived at Memphis under singular circumstances and had said she wished to present a gift to Cambyses. He gave Sappho an audience at once, and heard from her that Prexaspes had brought her husband an order to start for Arabia, and herself a summons to Memphis from the queen-mother. At these words the king turned very pale, and his features were agitated with pain as he looked at his brother's lovely young wife. She felt that something unusual was passing in his mind, and such dreadful forebodings arose in her own, that she could only offer him the gift in silence and with trembling hands.

"My husband sends you this," she said, pointing to the ingeniously-wrought box, which contained the wax likeness of Nitetis. Rhodopis had advised her to take this to the king in Bartja's name, as a propitiatory offering.

Cambyses showed no curiosity as to the contents of the box, gave it in charge to a eunuch, said a few words which seemed meant as thanks to his sister-in-law, and left the women's apartments without even so much as enquiring after Atossa, whose existence he seemed to have forgotten.

He had come to his mother, believing that the visit would comfort and calm his troubled mind, but Sappho's words had destroyed his last hope, and with that his last possibility of rest or peace. By this time either Prexaspes would already have committed the murder, or perhaps at that very moment might be raising his dagger to plunge it into Bartja's heart.

How could he ever meet his mother again after Bartja's death? how could he answer her questions or those of that lovely Sappho, whose large, anxious, appealing eyes had touched him so strangely?

A voice within told him, that his brother's murder would be branded as a cowardly, unnatural, and unjust deed, and he shuddered at the thought. It seemed fearful, unbearable, to be called an assassin. He had already caused the death of many a man without the least compunction, but that had been done either in fair fight, or openly before the world. He was king, and what the king did was right. Had he killed Bartja with his own hand, his conscience would not have reproached him; but to have had him privately put out of the way, after he had given so many proofs of possessing first-rate manly qualities, which deserved the highest praise—this tortured him with a feeling of rage at his own want of principle,—a feeling of shame and remorse which he had never known before. He began to despise himself. The consciousness of having acted, and wished to act justly, forsook him, and he began to fancy, that every one who had been executed by his orders, had been, like Bartja, an innocent victim of his fierce anger. These thoughts became so intolerable, that he began to drink once more in the hope of drowning them. But now the wine had precisely the opposite effect, and brought such tormenting thoughts, that, worn out as he was already by epileptic fits and his habit of drinking, both body and mind threatened to give way to the agitation caused by the events of the last months. Burning and shivering by turns, he was at last forced to lie down. While the attendants were disrobing him, he remembered his brother's present, had the box fetched and opened, and then desired to be left alone. The Egyptian paintings on the outside of the box reminded him of Nitetis, and then he asked himself what she would have said to his deed. Fever had already begun, and his mind was wandering as he took the beautiful wax bust out of the box. He stared in horror at the dull, immovable eyes. The likeness was so perfect, and his judgment so weakened by wine and fever, that he fancied himself the victim of some spell, and yet could not turn his eyes from those dear features. Suddenly the eyes seemed to move. He was seized with terror, and, in a kind of convulsion, hurled what he thought had become a living head against the wall. The hollow, brittle wax broke into a thousand fragments, and Cambyses sank back on to his bed with a groan.

From that moment the fever increased. In his delirium the banished Phanes appeared, singing a scornful Greek song and deriding him in such infamous words, that his fists clenched with rage. Then he saw his friend and adviser, Crœsus, threatening him in the very same words of warning, which he had used when Bartja had been sentenced to death by his command on account of Nitetis: "Beware of shedding a brother's blood; the smoke thereof will rise to heaven and become a cloud, that must darken the days of the murderer, and at last cast down the lightnings of heaven upon his head."

And in his delirious fancy this figure of speech became a reality. A rain of blood streamed down upon him from dark clouds; his clothes and hands were wet with the loathsome moisture. He went down to the Nile to cleanse himself, and suddenly saw Nitetis coming towards him. She had the same sweet smile with which Theodorus had modelled her. Enchanted with this lovely vision, he fell down before her and took her hand, but he had scarcely touched it, when drops of blood appeared at the tips of her delicate fingers, and she turned away from him with every sign of horror. He humbly implored her to forgive him and come back; she remained inexorable. He grew angry, and threatened her, first with his wrath, and then with awful punishments. At last, as she only answered his threats by a low scornful laugh, he ventured to throw his dagger at her. She crumbled at once into a thousand pieces, like the wax statue. But the derisive laughter echoed on, and became louder. Many voices joined in it, each trying to outbid the other. And the voices of Bartja and Nitetis were the loudest,—their tone the most bitter. At last he could bear these fearful sounds no longer and stopped his ears; this was of no use, and he buried his head, first in the glowing desert-sand and then in the icy cold Nile-water, until his senses forsook him. On awaking, the actual state of things seemed incomprehensible to him. He had gone to bed in the evening, and yet he now saw, by the direction of the sun's rays which fell on his bed, that, instead of dawning as he had expected, the day was growing dark. There could be no mistake; he heard the chorus of priests singing farewell to the setting Mithras.

Then he heard a number of people moving behind a curtain, which had been hung up at the head of his bed. He tried to turn in his bed, but could not; he was too weak. At last, finding it impossible to discover whether he was in real life or still in a dream, he called for his dressers and the courtiers, who were accustomed to be present when he rose. They appeared in a moment, and with them his mother, Prexaspes, a number of the learned among the Magi, and some Egyptians who were unknown to him. They told him, that he had been lying in a violent fever for weeks, and had only escaped death by the special mercy of the gods, the skill of the physicians, and the unwearied nursing of his mother. He looked enquiringly first at Kassandane, then at Prexaspes, lost consciousness again, and fell into a deep sleep, from which he awoke the next morning with renewed strength.

In four days he was strong enough to sit up and able to question Prexaspes on the only subject, which occupied his thoughts.

In consideration of his master's weakness the envoy was beginning an evasive reply, when a threatening movement of the king's gaunt, worn hand, and a look which had by no means lost its old power of awing into submission, brought him to the point at once, and in the hope of giving the king a great pleasure and putting his mind completely at rest, he began: "Rejoice, O King! the youth, who dared to desire the disparagement of thy glory, is no more. This hand slew him and buried his body at Baal-Zephon. The sand of the desert and the unfruitful waves of the Red Sea were the only witnesses of the deed;[185] and no creature knows thereof beside thyself, O King, thy servant Prexaspes, and the gulls and cormorants, that hover over his grave."

The king uttered a piercing shriek of rage, was seized

---

185. Herodotus says (III. 30.): "Some say that after Prexaspes had led Bartja to the Red Sea (ἐς τὴν Ἐρυθρήν θάλασσαν . . ποσβιγαγόντα) he murdered him there." It is possible, but by no means certain, that in this place Herodotus is speaking of the Persian Gulf.

by a fresh shivering-fit, and sank back once more in raving delirium.

Long weeks passed, every day of which threatened his death. At last, however, his strong constitution gained the day, but his mind had given way, and remained disordered and weak up to his last hour.

When he was strong enough to leave the sick-room and to ride and shoot once more, he abandoned himself more than ever to the pleasure of drinking, and lost every remnant of self-control.

The delusion had fixed itself in his disordered mind, that Bartja was not dead, but transformed into the bow of the King of Ethiopia, and that the Feruer* of his father Cyrus had commanded him to restore Bartja to his original form, by subjugating the black nation.

This idea, which he confided to every one about him as a great secret, pursued him day and night and gave him no rest, until he had started for Ethiopia with an immense host. He was forced, however, to return without having accomplished his object, after having miserably lost the greater part of his army by heat and the scarcity of provisions. An historian, who may almost be spoken of as contemporary,[186] tells us that the wretched soldiers, after having subsisted on herbs as long as they could, came to deserts where there was no sign of vegetation, and in their despair resorted to an expedient almost too fearful to describe. Lots were drawn by every ten men, and he on whom the lot fell was killed and eaten by the other nine.

At last things went so far, that his subjects compelled

---

186. Herodotus visited Egypt some 60 years after the death of Cambyses, 454 B. C. He describes the Ethiopian campaign, III. 25.

* The spiritual part of man—his soul and reason. See vol. 1. note 271.

this madman to return, but only, with their slavish Asiatic feelings, to obey him all the more blindly, when they found themselves once more in inhabited regions.

On reaching Memphis with the wreck of his army, he found the Egyptians in glorious apparel celebrating a festival. They had found a new Apis* and were rejoicing over the reappearance of their god, incarnate in the sacred bull.

As Cambyses had heard at Thebes, that the army he had sent against the oasis of Ammon [187] in the Libyan desert, had perished miserably in a Khamsin, or Simoom,[188] and that his fleet, which was to conquer Carthage, had refused to fight with a people of their own race,[189] he fancied that the Memphians must be celebrating a festival of joy at the news of his misfortunes, sent for their principal men, and after reproaching them with their conduct, asked why they had been gloomy and morose after his victories, but joyous at hearing of his misfortunes. The Memphians answered by explaining the real ground for their merry-making, and told him, that

---

187. The oracle of Jupiter Ammon, which afterwards became so celebrated through having pronounced Alexander to be a son of the god, was in this oasis. Curtius IV. 7. Crœsus had already bestowed attention upon this oracle. Herod. I. 46. On its mode of utterance. Iamblichus. *De Myst.* 3. Tacit. *Hist.* IV, 83. On this marvellous oasis, which is now called Siwah, see Minutoli, *Reise zum Tempel des Jupiter Ammon, &c.* and especially Parthey's *zur Erdkunde des alten Aegyptens.* Berlin 1859. Also Brugsch, *Geographische Inschriften.* Popularly described by G. Rasch, and recently by G. Rohlfs. The oasis is called Wach or el Wach, *Abulfedæ Descrip. Aegypt.* 1746.

188. A fearful south-west wind, which blows in Egypt and the Libyan desert. The best information on this is to be found in Gregoire's *Du Khamsine et de ses efforts.* A similar wind, known as the "Samum," is called by the Turks "Schamyele." Possibly the dreadful fiend Samiel, so fatal to the caravans, derived his name from this wind.

189. Herod. III. 26. 17. 19.

* See note 161.

the appearance of the sacred bull was always celebrated in Egypt with the greatest rejoicings. Cambyses called them liars, and, as such, sentenced them to death.[190] He then sent for the priests; received, however, exactly the same answer from them.

With the bitterest irony he asked to be allowed to make the acquaintance of this new god, and commanded them to bring him. The bull Apis was brought and the king told that he was the progeny of a virgin cow and a moonbeam, that he must be black, with a white triangular spot on the forehead, the likeness of an eagle on his back, and on his side the crescent moon. There must be two kinds of hair on his tail, and on his tongue an excrescence in the form of the sacred beetle Scarabæus.[191]

190. So says Herod. III. 27. Plutarch, *Is. and Os.* 12. In several places we have laid stress upon the Persians' esteem for truth. Things are, alas, very different now. Brugsch, in his *Perser und Germanen*, assures us, that he had nowhere met with such hardened liars as in Persia. In the book of *Kawus*, the wise Shah *Kjekjawus*, as early as the 11th century A. D., advises his son and successor rather to tell a lie, which sounds like truth, than the truth when it seems improbable. *B. d. Kawus*, translated by Diez. p. 376. Herodotus, on the other hand, writing (I. 138.) of the same nation in the 5th century B. C. says: "They hold lying and debt to be the greatest disgrace," and in the Vendidad lying is constantly spoken of as one of the most grievous sins. Brugsch may be right in saying, that such a deceitful people needed repeated commands on the subject of truth. See Vol. I. note 142.

191. On the characteristic signs of Apis, see Herod. III. 28. Whether the white spot on his forehead was to be a triangle or a square, depends on the different readings of Herodotus; the testimony of the monuments is for the triangle. According to Ammian Marcellinus, he was to have a half-moon on the right side; Strabo (807) speaks of him as black with a white forehead, and white on some other portions of his body. Aelian says the sacred bull had twenty-nine marks. Ovid calls him: *variis coloribus Apis.* The monuments explain these differences, by proving that the sacred bulls were not always alike. Sometimes Apis is represented entirely black, at others with characteristic white spots. Champollion, *Pantheon Eg.* Pl. 37. On the Apis-statue, discovered by Mariette and now in Paris, many of these marks have been traced. They are painted on the body of the animal in black. The coloring of the head, unfortunately, has been rubbed off. There are several bronze figures of the god with the sun-disc and the Uræus

When Cambyses saw this deified creature he could discover nothing remarkable in him, and was so enraged that he plunged his sword into its side.[192] As the blood streamed from the wound and the animal fell, he broke out into a piercing laugh, and cried: "Ye fools! so your gods are flesh and blood; they can be wounded. Such folly is worthy of you. But ye shall find, that it is not so easy to make a fool of me. Ho, guards! flog these priests soundly, and kill every one whom you find taking part in this mad celebration." The command was obeyed and fearfully exasperated the Egyptians.

Apis died of his wound; the Memphians buried him secretly in the vaults belonging to the sacred bulls,* near the Serapeum, and, led by Psamtik, attempted an insurrection against the Persians. This was very quickly put down, however, and cost Psamtik his life,[193]—a life the stains and severities of which deserve to be forgiven, in consideration of his unwearied, ceaseless efforts to deliver his people from a foreign yoke, and his death in the cause of freedom.

Cambyses' madness had meanwhile taken fresh forms. After the failure of his attempt to restore Bartja, (transformed as he fancied into a bow) to his original

between his horns, a broad collar round his neck, and on his back two vultures, whose extended wings reach to the fore and hind legs; between these birds a small but costly covering is spread over his back. On the forehead is a spot in the form of the triangle, which had a symbolic meaning. "All the good skin-marks" of the Apis are frequently mentioned on the monuments.

192. According to Herod. III. 29. Cambyses' sword slipped and ran into the leg of the sacred bull. As the king died also of a wound in the thigh, this just suits Herodotus, who always tries to put the retribution that comes after presumptuous crime in the strongest light; but it is very unlikely that the bull should have died of a mere thigh-wound.

193. Herod. III. 15.

* See note 161.

shape, his irritability increased so frightfully that a single word, or even a look, was sufficient to make him furious.

Still his true friend and counsellor, Crœsus, never left him, though the king had more than once given him over to the guards for execution. But the guards knew their master; they took good care not to lay hands on the old man, and felt sure of impunity, as the king would either have forgotten his command, or repented of it by the next day. Once, however, the miserable whip-bearers paid a fearful penalty for their lenity. Cambyses, while rejoicing that Crœsus was saved, ordered his deliverers to be executed for disobedience without mercy.[194]

It would be repugnant to us to repeat all the tales of barbarous cruelties, which are told of Cambyses at this insane period of his life; but we cannot resist mentioning a few which seem to us especially characteristic.

While sitting at table one day, already somewhat intoxicated, he asked Prexaspes what the Persians thought of him. The envoy, who in hopes of deadening his tormenting conscience by the performance of noble and dangerous acts, let no opportunity pass of trying to exercise a good influence over his sovereign, answered that they extolled him on every point, but thought he was too much addicted to wine.

These words, though spoken half in jest, put the king into a violent passion, and he almost shrieked: "So the Persians say, that the wine has taken away my senses, do they? on the contrary, I'll show them that they've lost their own." And as he spoke he bent his bow, took aim for a moment at Prexaspes' eldest son, who, as cup-bearer, was standing at the back

[194]. Herod. III. 36.

of the hall waiting for and watching every look of his sovereign, and shot him in the breast. He then gave orders that the boy's body should be opened and examined. The arrow had pierced the centre of his heart. This delighted the senseless tyrant, and he called out with a laugh: "Now you see, Prexaspes, it's the Persians who have lost their judgment, not I. Could any one have hit the mark better?"

Prexaspes stood there, pale and motionless, compelled to watch the horrid scene, like Niobe when chained to Sipylus. His servile spirit bowed before the ruler's power, instead of arming his right hand with the dagger of revenge, and when the frantic king asked him the same question a second time, he actually answered, pressing his hand on his heart: "A god could not have hit the mark more exactly." [195]

A few weeks after this, the king went to Sais, and there was shown the rooms formerly occupied by his bride. This brought back all the old painful recollections in full force, and at the same time his clouded memory reminded him, though without any clearness of detail, that Amasis had deceived both Nitetis and himself. He cursed the dead king and furiously demanded to be taken to the temple of Neith, where his mummy was laid. There he tore the embalmed body out of its sarcophagus, caused it to be scourged, to be stabbed with pins, had the hair torn off and maltreated it in every possible way. In conclusion, and contrary to the ancient Persian religious law, which held the pollution of pure fire by corpses to be a deadly sin,

---

[195]. Herod. III. 35. certainly means by τὸν ϑεὸν Apollo who hits his mark from afar. Seneca *(De Ira* III. 14.), in telling the story, says plainly "Apollo."

he caused Amasis' dead body to be burnt, and condemned the mummy of his first wife, which lay in a sarcophagus at Thebes, her native place, to the same fate.[196]

On his return to Memphis, Cambyses did not shrink from personally ill-treating his wife and sister, Atossa.

He had ordered a combat of wild beasts to take place, during which, amongst other entertainments of the same kind, a dog was to fight with a young lion. The lion had conquered his antagonist, when another dog, the brother of the conquered one, broke away from his chain, attacked the lion, and with the help of the wounded dog, vanquished him.

This scene delighted Cambyses, but Kassandane and Atossa, who had been forced by the king's command to be present, began to weep aloud.

The tyrant was astonished, and on asking the reason for their tears, received as answer from the impetuous Atossa, that the brave creature who had risked its own life to save its brother, reminded her of Bartja. She would not say by whom he had been murdered, but his murder had never been avenged.

These words so roused the king's anger, and so goaded his conscience, that in a fit of insane fury he struck the daring woman, and might possibly have killed her, if his mother had not thrown herself into his arms and exposed her own body to his mad blows.[197]

Her voice and action checked his rage, for he had

196. Herod. III. 16. The officers of the French frigate Luxor, which was sent to fetch the obelisk of Thebes, found a sarcophagus at el Qurnah containing a half-burnt mummy, probably that of the wife of Amasis.

197. Herod. III. 32.

not lost reverence for his mother; but her look of intense anger and contempt, which he clearly saw and could not forget, begot a fresh delusion in his mind. He believed from that moment, that the eyes of women had power to poison him; he started and hid himself behind his companions whenever he saw a woman, and at last commanded that all the female inhabitants of the palace at Memphis, his mother not excepted, should be sent back to Ecbatana. Araspes and Gyges were appointed to be their escort thither.

The caravan of queens and princesses had arrived at Sais; they alighted at the royal palace. Croesus had accompanied them thus far on their way from Egypt.

Kassandane had altered very much during the last few years. Grief and suffering had worn deep lines in her once beautiful face, though they had had no power to bow her stately figure.

Atossa, on the contrary, was more beautiful than ever, notwithstanding all she had suffered. The refractory and impetuous child, the daring spirited girl, had developed into a dignified, animated and determined woman. The serious side of life, and three sad years passed with her ungovernable husband and brother, had been first-rate masters in the school of patience, but they had not been able to alienate her heart from her first love. Sappho's friendship had made up to her in some measure for the loss of Darius.

The young Greek had become another creature, since the mysterious departure of her husband. Her rosy color and her lovely smile were both gone. But she was wonderfully beautiful, in spite of her paleness, her downcast eyelashes and languid attitude. She looked like Ariadne waiting for Theseus. Longing and expectation lay in every look, in the low tone of her voice, in her measured walk. At the sound of approaching steps, the opening of a door or the unexpected tones of a man's voice, she would start, get up and listen, and then sink back into the old waiting, longing attitude, disappointed but not hopeless. She began to dream again, as she had been so fond of doing in her girlish days.

She was her old self only when playing with her child. Then the color came back to her cheeks, her eyes sparkled, she seemed once more to live in the present, and not only in the past or future.

Her child was everything to her. In that little one Bartja seemed to be still alive, and she could love the child with all her heart and strength, without taking one iota from her love to him. With this little creature the gods had mercifully given her an aim in life and a link with the lower world, the really precious part of which had seemed to vanish with her vanished husband. Sometimes, as she looked into her baby's blue eyes, so wonderfully like Bartja's, she thought: Why was not she born a boy? He would have grown more like his father from day to day, and at last, if such a thing indeed could ever be, a second Bartja would have stood before me.

But such thoughts generally ended soon in her pressing the little one closer than ever to her heart, and blaming herself for ingratitude and folly.

One day Atossa put the same idea in words, exclaiming: "If Parmys were only a boy! He would have grown up exactly like his father, and have been a second Cyrus for Persia." Sappho smiled sadly at her friend, and covered the little one with kisses, but Kassandane said: "Be thankful to the gods, my child, for having given you a daughter. If Parmys were a boy, he would be taken from you as soon as he had reached his sixth year, to be brought up with the sons of the other Achæmenidæ, but your daughter will remain your own for many years."

Sappho trembled at the mere thought of parting from her child; she pressed its little fair curly head close to her breast, and never found fault with her treasure again for being a girl.

Atossa's friendship was a great comfort to her poor wounded heart. With her she could speak of Bartja as much and as often as she would, and was always certain of a kind and sympathizing listener. Atossa had loved her vanished brother very dearly. And even a stranger would have enjoyed hearing Sappho tell of her past happiness. Her words rose into real eloquence in speaking of those bright days; she seemed like an inspired poetess. Then she would take her lyre, and with her clear, sweet, plaintive voice sing the love-songs of the elder Sappho, in which all her own deepest feelings were so truly expressed, and fancy herself once more with her lover sitting under the sweet-scented acanthus in the quiet night, and forget the sad reality of her present life. And when, with a deep sigh, she laid aside the lyre and came back out of this dream-kingdom, the tears were always to be seen in Kassandane's eyes, though she did not understand the language in which Sappho had been singing, and Atossa would bend down and kiss her forehead.

Thus three long years had passed, during which Sappho had seldom seen her grandmother, for, as the mother of Parmys, she was by the king's command, forbidden to leave the harem, unless permitted and accompanied either by Kassandane or the eunuchs.

On the present occasion Crœsus, who had always loved, and loved her still, like a daughter, had sent for Rhodopis to Sais. He, as well as Kassandane, understood her wish to take leave of this, her dearest and most faithful friend, before setting out for Persia; besides which Kassandane had a great wish to see one in whose praise she had heard so much. When Sappho's tender and sad farewell was over therefore, Rhodopis was summoned to the queen-mother.

A stranger, who saw these two women together, would have thought both were queens; it was impossible to decide which of the two had most right to the title.

Crœsus, standing as he did in as close a relation to the one as to the other, undertook the office of interpreter, and the ready intellect of Rhodopis helped him to carry on an uninterrupted flow of conversation.

Rhodopis, by her own peculiar attractions, soon won the heart of Kassandane, and the queen knew no better way of proving this than by offering, in Persian fashion, to grant her some wish.

Rhodopis hesitated a moment; then raising her hands as if in prayer, she cried: "Leave me my Sappho, the consolation and beauty of my old age."

Kassandane smiled sadly. "It is not in my power to grant that wish," she answered. "The laws of Persia command, that the children of the Achæmenidæ shall be brought up at the king's gate. I dare not allow the little Parmys, Cyrus' only grandchild, to leave me, and, much as Sappho loves you, you know she would not part from her child. Indeed, she has become so dear to me now, and to my daughter, that though I well understand your wish to have her, I could never allow Sappho to leave us."

Seeing that Rhodopis' eyes were filling with tears, Kassandane went on: "There is, however, a good way out of our perplexity. Leave Naukratis, and come with us to Persia. There you can spend your last years with us and with your granddaughter, and shall be provided with a royal maintenance."

Rhodopis shook her head, hoary but still so beautiful, and answered in a suppressed voice: "I thank you, noble queen, for this gracious invitation, but I feel unable to accept it. Every fibre of my heart is rooted in Greece, and I should be tearing my life out by leaving it forever. I am so accustomed to constant activity, perfect freedom, and a stirring exchange of thought, that I should languish and die in the confinement of a harem. Crœsus had already prepared me for the gracious proposal you have just made, and I have had a long and difficult battle to fight, before I could decide on resigning my dearest blessing for my highest good. It is not easy, but it is glorious,—it is more worthy of the Greek name—to live a good and beautiful life, than a happy one—to follow duty rather than pleasure. My heart will follow Sappho, but my intellect and experience belong to the Greeks; and if you should ever hear that the people of Hellas are ruled by themselves alone, by their own gods, their own laws, the beautiful and the good, then you will know that the work on which Rhodopis, in league with the noblest and best of her countrymen, has staked her life, is accomplished. Be not angry with the Greek woman, who confesses that she would rather die free as a beggar than live in bondage as a queen, though envied by the whole world."

Kassandane listened in amazement. She only understood part of what Rhodopis had said, but felt that she had spoken well and nobly, and at the conclusion gave her her hand to kiss. After a short pause, Kassandane said: "Do what you think right, and remember, that as long as I and my daughter live, your granddaughter will never want for true and faithful love."

"Your noble countenance and the fame of your great virtue are warrant enough for that," answered Rhodopis.

"And also," added the queen, "the duty which lies upon me to make good the wrong, that has been done your Sappho."

She sighed painfully and went on: "The little Parmys shall be carefully educated. She seems to have much natural talent, and can sing the songs of her native country already after her mother. I shall do nothing to check her love of music, though, in Persia the religious services are the only occasions in which that art is studied by any but the lower classes."[198]

At these words Rhodopis' face glowed. "Will you permit me to speak openly, O Queen?" she said.

"Speak without fear," was Kassandane's answer.

"When you sighed so painfully just now in speaking of your dear lost son, I thought: Perhaps that

---

198. *Book of Kawus* p. 732. Brugsch, *Reise nach Persien* p. 389. On the musical instruments used in Persia, see Chardin V. p. 69–71.

brave young hero might have been still living, if the Persians had understood better how to educate their sons. Bartja told me in what that education consisted. To shoot, throw the spear, ride, hunt, speak the truth, and perhaps also to distinguish between the healing and noxious properties of certain plants: that is deemed a sufficient educational provision for a man's life. The Greek boys are just as carefully kept to the practice of exercises for hardening and bracing the body; for these exercises are the founders and preservers of health, the physician is only its repairer and restorer. If, however, by constant practice a Greek youth were to attain to the ·strength of a bull, the truth of the Deity, and the wisdom of the most learned Egyptian priest, we should still look down upon him were he wanting in two things which only early example and music, combined with these bodily exercises, can give: grace and symmetry. You smile because you do not understand me, but I can prove to you that music, which, from what Sappho tells me, is not without its moving power for your heart, is as important an element in education as gymnastics, and, strange as it may sound, has an equal share in effecting the perfection of both body and mind. The man who devotes his attention exclusively to music will, if he be of a violent disposition, lose his savage sternness at first; he will become gentle and pliable as metal in the fire. But at last his courage will disappear too; his passionate temper will have changed into irritability, and he will be of little worth as a warrior, the calling and character most desired in your country. If, on the other hand, he confines himself to gymnastics only, he will, like Cambyses, excel in manliness and strength; but his mind—here my comparison ceases—will remain obtuse and blind, his perceptions will be confused, He will not listen to reason, but will endeavor to carry everything by force, and, lacking grace and proportion, his life will probably become a succession of rude and violent deeds. On this account we conclude that music is necessary not only for the mind, and gymnastics not only for the body, but that both, working together, elevate and soften the mind and strengthen the body—give manly grace, and graceful manliness."[199]

After a moment's pause Rhodopis went on: "The youth who has not received such an education, whose roughness has never been checked even in childhood, who has been allowed to vent his temper on every one, receiving flattery in return and never hearing reproof; who has been allowed to command before he has learnt to obey, and who has been brought up in the belief that splendor, power and riches are the highest good, can never possibly attain to the perfect manhood, which we beseech the gods to grant our boys. And if this unfortunate being happens to have been born with an impetuous disposition, ungovernable and eager passions, these will be only nourished and increased by bodily exercise unaccompanied by the softening influence of music, so that at last a child, who possibly came into the world with good qualities, will, merely through the defects in his education, degenerate into a destructive animal, a sensual self-destroyer, and a mad and furious tyrant."

Rhodopis had become animated with her subject. She ceased, saw tears in the eyes of the queen, and

[199]. The fundamental ideas of this speech are drawn from Plato's ideal "State."

felt that she had gone too far and had wounded a mother's heart,—a heart full of noble feeling. She touched her robe, kissed its border, and said softly: "Forgive me."

Kassandane looked her forgiveness, courteously saluted Rhodopis and prepared to leave the room. On the threshold, however, she stopped and said: "I am not angry. Your reproaches are just; but you too must endeavor to forgive, for I can assure you that he who has murdered the happiness of your child and of mine, though the most powerful, is of all mortals the most to be pitied. Farewell! Should you ever stand in need of ought, remember Cyrus' widow, and how she wished to teach you, that the virtues the Persians desire most in their children are magnanimity and liberality."

After saying this she left the apartment.

On the same day Rhodopis heard that Phanes was dead. He had retired to Crotona in the neighborhood of Pythagoras and there passed his time in reflection, dying with the tranquillity of a philosopher.

She was deeply affected at this news and said to Crœsus: "Greece has lost one of her ablest men, but there are many, who will grow up to be his equals. The increasing power of Persia causes me no fear; indeed, I believe that when the barbarous lust of conquest stretches out its hand towards us, our manyheaded Greece will rise as a giant with one head of divine power, before which mere barbaric strength must bow as surely as body before spirit."

Three days after this, Sappho said farewell for the

last time to her grandmother, and followed the queens to Persia. Notwithstanding the events which afterwards took place, she continued to believe that Bartja would return, and full of love, fidelity and tender remembrance, devoted herself entirely to the education of her child and the care of her aged mother-in-law, Kassandane.

Little Parmys became very beautiful, and learnt to love the memory of her vanished father next to the gods of her native land, for her mother's tales had brought him as vividly before her as if he had been still alive and present with them.

Atossa's subsequent good fortune and happiness did not cool her friendship. She always called Sappho her sister. The hanging-gardens were the latter's residence in summer, and in her conversations there with Kassandane and Atossa one name was often mentioned—the name of her, who had been the innocent cause of events which had decided the destinies of great kingdoms and noble lives—the Egyptian Princess.

CHAPTER XVI.

HERE we might end this tale, but that we feel bound to give our readers some account of the last days of Cambyses. We have already described the ruin of his mind, but his physical end remains still to be told, and also the subsequent fate of some of the other characters in our history.

A short time after the departure of the queens, news

reached Naukratis that Oroetes, the satrap of Lydia, had, by a stratagem, allured his old enemy, Polykrates, to Sardis and crucified him there,* thus fulfilling what Amasis had prophecied of the tyrant's mournful end. This act the satrap had committed on his own responsibility, events having taken place in the Median kingdom which threatened the fall of the Achæmenidæan dynasty.[200]

The king's long absence in a foreign country had either weakened or entirely dissipated, the fear which the mere mention of his name had formerly inspired in those who felt inclined to rebel. The awe that his subjects had formerly felt for him, vanished at the tidings of his madness, and the news that he had wantonly exposed the lives of thousands of their countrymen to certain death in the deserts of Libya and Ethiopia, inspired the enraged Asiatics with a hatred which, when skilfully fed by the powerful Magi, soon roused, first the Medes and Assyrians, and then the Persians, to defection and open insurrection. Motives of self-interest led the ambitious high-priest, Oropastes, whom Cambyses had appointed regent in his absence, to place himself at the head of this movement. He flattered the people by remitting their taxes, by large gifts and larger promises, and finding his clemency gratefully recognized, determined on an imposture, by which he hoped to win the crown of Persia for his own family.

He had not forgotten the marvellous likeness between

---

200. Herodotus has been our main guide in this part of our tale also (Herod. III. 61–68.); and the inscription of Bisitun or Behistân. Ktesias lived at the Persian court, it is true, but his information, though in this place it somewhat tallies with that of Herodotus, is far more improbable.

* See note 75.

his brother Gaumata (who had been condemned to lose his ears) and Bartja, the son of Cyrus, and on hearing that the latter, the universal favorite, as he well knew, of the Persian nation, had disappeared, resolved to turn this to account by passing off his brother as the vanished prince, and setting him on the throne in place of Cambyses. The hatred felt throughout the entire kingdom towards their insane king, and the love and attachment of the nation to Bartja, made this stratagem so easy of accomplishment, that when at last messengers from Oropastes arrived in all the provinces of the empire declaring to the discontented citizens that, notwithstanding the rumor they had heard, the younger son of Cyrus was still alive, had revolted from his brother, ascended his father's throne and granted to all his subjects freedom from tribute and from military service during a period of three years, the new ruler was acknowledged throughout the kingdom with rejoicings.

The pretended Bartja, who was fully aware of his brother's mental superiority, had obeyed his directions in every particular, had taken up his residence in the palace of Nisaea,[201] in the plains of Media, placed the crown on his head, declared the royal harem his own, and had shown himself once from a distance to the people, who were to recognize in him the murdered Bartja. After that time, however, for fear of being at last unmasked, he concealed himself in his palace, giving

201. Spiegel, *Inscription of Behistán:* "There is a fortress, Cikathauvatis by name, a district, Niçáya by name, in Media, there he killed him." What town is meant here cannot be determined, but the district of Nisaja was celebrated principally for its good pasture for horses. Eustath. in *Dionys. Perieg.* p. 178. According to Diod. XVII. 10. and Arrian, *Anab.* VII. 13. there were more than 150,000 horses in this district, distinguished by their large size. According to Herodotus, the whole of this part of our story took place in Susa.

himself up, after the manner of Asiatic monarchs, to every kind of indulgence, while his brother held the sceptre with a firm hand, and conferred all the important offices of state on his friends and family.

No sooner did Oropastes feel firm ground under his feet, than he despatched the eunuch Ixabates to Egypt, to inform the army of the change of rulers that had taken place and persuade them to revolt in favor of Bartja, who he knew had been idolized by the soldiers.

The messenger had been well chosen, fulfilled his mission with much skill, and had already won over a considerable part of the army for the new king, when he was taken prisoner by some Syrians, who brought him to Memphis in hopes of reward.

On arriving in the city of the Pyramids he was brought before the king, and promised impunity on condition of revealing the entire truth.

The messenger then confirmed the rumor, which had reached Egypt, that Bartja had ascended the throne of Cyrus and had been recognized by the greater part of the empire.

Cambyses started with terror at these tidings, as one who saw a dead man rise from his grave. He was by this time fully aware that Bartja had been murdered by Prexaspes at his own command, but in this moment he began to suspect that the envoy had deceived him and spared his brother's life. The thought had no sooner entered his mind than he uttered it, reproaching Prexaspes so bitterly with treachery, as to elicit from him a tremendous oath, that he had murdered and buried the unfortunate Bartja with his own hand.

Oropastes' messenger was next asked whether he

had seen the new king himself. He answered that he had not, adding that the supposed brother of Cambyses had only once appeared in public, and had then shown himself to the people from a distance. On hearing this, Prexaspes saw through the whole web of trickery at once, reminded the king of the unhappy misunderstandings to which the marvellous likeness between Bartja and Gaumata had formerly given rise, and concluded by offering to stake his own life on the correctness of his supposition. The explanation pleased the king, and from that moment his diseased mind was possessed by one new idea to the exclusion of all others—the seizure and slaughter of the Magi.

The host was ordered to prepare for marching. Aryandes,[202] one of the Achæmenidæ, was appointed satrap of Egypt, and the army started homeward without delay. Driven by this new delusion, the king took no rest by day or night, till at last his over-ridden and ill-used horse fell with him, and he was severely wounded in the fall by his own dagger.[203]

After lying insensible for some days, he opened his eyes and asked first to see Araspes, then his mother, and lastly Atossa, although these three had set out on

202. Herod. IV. 166.

203. Herod. III. 64. In Spiegel's translation of the inscription of Behistân we read: "Thereupon Kambujiya died, having killed himself." Oppert gives the same translation of *Uvâmarsiyus*. Bensey thus: "Thereupon Kambuija died of exceeding anger." Ktesias, *Pers.* 12. says that Cambyses wounded himself with a knife in the thigh, accidentally, and died of the wound. This, as well as the account given by Herodotus, agrees with the inscription: "He ended, '*uvâmarsiyus*,' dying from himself," for even the Greeks allow that Cambyses died by his own weapon, though not by his own will. We reject the idea of wilful suicide all the more gladly, as just on this point Herodotus and Ktesias agree, and the dying speech which Herodotus puts into the mouth of Cambyses bears a decidedly Perso-Iranian character. M. Duncker, *Geschichte d. Alterth.* II. p. 544. Herodot. III. 65.

their journey home months before. From all he said it appeared that during the last four years, from the attack of fever until the present accident, he had been living in a kind of sleep. He seemed astonished and pained at hearing what had happened during these years. But of his brother's death he was fully aware. He knew that Prexaspes had killed him by his—the king's—orders and had told him that Bartja lay buried on the shores of the Red Sea.—During the night which followed this return to his senses it became clear to himself also, that his mind had been wandering for a long time. Towards morning he fell into a deep sleep, and this so restored his strength, that on waking he called for Crœsus and required an exact relation of the events that had passed during the last few years.

His old friend and adviser obeyed; he felt that Cambyses was still entrusted to his care, and in the hope, faint as it was, of bringing him back to the right way, he did not suppress one of the king's acts of violence in his relation.

His joy was therefore great at perceiving, that his words made a deep impression on the newly-awakened mind of the king. With tears in his eyes, and with the ashamed look of a child, he grieved over his wrong deeds and his madness, begged Crœsus to forgive him, thanked him for having borne so long and faithfully with him, and commissioned him to ask Kassandane and Sappho especially for forgiveness, but also, Atossa and all whom he had unjustly offended.

The old man wept too, but his tears were tears of joy and he repeatedly assured Cambyses that he would recover and have ample opportunity of making amends for the past. But to all this Cambyses shook his head resolutely, and, pale and wan as he looked, begged Crœsus to have his couch carried on to a rising ground in the open air, and then to summon the Achæmenidæ. When these orders, in spite of the physicians, had been obeyed, Cambyses was raised into an upright sitting position, and began, in a voice which could be heard at a considerable distance:

"The time to reveal my great secret has arrived, O ye Persians. Deceived by a vision, provoked and annoyed by my brother, I caused him to be murdered in my wrath. Prexaspes wrought the evil deed by my command, but instead of bringing me the peace I yearned for, that deed has tortured me into madness and death. By this my confession ye will be convinced, that my brother Bartja is really dead. The Magi have usurped the throne of the Achæmenidæ. Oropastes, whom I left in Persia as my vicegerent and his brother Gaumata, who resembles Bartja so nearly that even Crœsus, Intaphernes and my uncle, the noble Hystaspes, were once deceived by the likeness, have placed themselves at their head. Woe is me, that I have murdered him who, as my nearest kinsman, should have avenged on the Magi this affront to my honor. But I cannot recall him from the dead, and I therefore appoint you the executors of my last will. By the Feruer* of my dead father, and in the name of all good and pure spirits, I conjure you not to suffer the government to fall into the hands of the unfaithful Magi. If they have obtained possession thereof by artifice, wrest it from their hands in like manner; if by force, use force to win it back. Obey this my last will, and the earth will yield you its fruits abundantly; your wives, your

* See vol. I. note 271.

flocks and herds shall be blessed and freedom shall be your portion. Refuse to obey it, and ye shall suffer the corresponding evils; yea, your end, and that of every Persian shall be even as mine."

After these words the king wept and sank back fainting, on seeing which, the Achæmenidæ rent their clothes and burst into loud lamentations. A few hours later Cambyses died in Crœsus' arms. Nitetis was his last thought; he died with her name on his lips and tears of penitence in his eyes.[204] When the Persians had left the unclean corpse, Crœsus knelt down beside it and cried, raising his hand to heaven: " Great Cyrus, I have kept my oath. I have remained this miserable man's faithful adviser even unto his end."

The next morning the old man betook himself, accompanied by his son Gyges, to the town of Barene, which belonged to him,[205] and lived there many years as a father to his subjects, revered by Darius and praised by all his contemporaries.

After Cambyses' death the heads of the seven Persian tribes[206] held a council, and resolved, as a first measure, on obtaining certain information as to the person of the usurper. With this view, Otanes sent a confidential eunuch to his daughter Phædime, who, as

204. Herod. III. 65. 66. mentions expressly the sentimental-sounding penitence of Cambyses.

205. Ktesias, *Pers.* 4.

206. The names of the seven conspiring chiefs, given by Herodotus agree for the most part with those in the cuneiform inscriptions. Spiegel, *Keilinschriften* p. 37. In Herod. III. 70. the names are: Otanes, Intaphernes, Gobryas, Megabyzus, Aspatines, Hydarnes and Darius Hystaspis. In the inscription *Utána: Vindafraná, Gaubaruva, Ardumanis, Vidarna, Bagabukhsa? and Darayavus*.

they knew, had come into the possession of the new
king with the rest of Cambyses' harem. Before the
messenger returned, the greater part of the army had
dispersed, the soldiers seizing this favorable opportunity to return to their homes and families, after so
many years of absence. At last, however, the long-
expected messenger came back and brought for answer, that the new king had only visited Phædime once,
but that during that visit she had, at great personal
risk, discovered that he had lost both ears. Without
this discovery, however, she could assert positively that
though there were a thousand points of similarity between the usurper and the murdered Bartja, the former
was in reality none other than Gaumata, the brother of
Oropastes. Her old friend Boges had resumed his
office of chief of the eunuchs, and had revealed to her
the secrets of the Magi. The high-priest had met the
former keeper of the women begging in the streets of
Susa, and had restored him to his old office with the
words: "You have forfeited your life, but I want men
of your stamp." In conclusion, Phædime entreated
her father to use every means in his power for the overthrow of the Magi, as they treated her with the greatest
contempt and she was the most miserable of women.

Though none of the Achæmenidæ had really for a
moment believed, that Bartja was alive and had seized
on the throne, so clear an account of the real person of
the usurper was very welcome to them, and they
resolved at once to march on Nisæa with the remnant
of the army and overthrow the Magi either by craft or
force.

They entered the new capital unassailed, and finding that the majority of the people seemed content

with the new government, they also pretended to acknowledge the king as the son of Cyrus, to whom they were prepared to do homage. The Magi, however, were not deceived; they shut themselves up in their palace, assembled an army in the Nisæan plain,* promised the soldiers high pay, and used every effort to strengthen the belief of the people in Gaumata's disguise. On this point no one could do them more injury, or, if he chose, be more useful to them, than Prexaspes. He was much looked up to by the Persians, and his assurance, that he had not murdered Bartja, would have been sufficient to lame the fast-spreading report of the real way in which the youth had met his death. Oropastes, therefore, sent for Prexaspes, who, since the king's dying words, had been avoided by all the men of his own rank and had led the life of an outlaw, and promised him an immense sum of money, if he would ascend a high tower and declare to the people, assembled in the court beneath, that evil-disposed men had called him Bartja's murderer, whereas he had seen the new king with his own eyes and had recognized in him the younger son of his benefactor. Prexaspes made no objection to this proposal, took a tender leave of his family while the people were being assembled, uttered a short prayer before the sacred fire-altar and walked proudly to the palace. On his way thither he met the chiefs of the seven tribes and seeing that they avoided him, called out to them: "I am worthy of your contempt, but I will try to deserve your forgiveness."

Seeing Darius look back, he hastened towards him, grasped his hand and said: "I have loved you like a

* See note 201.

son; take care of my children when I am no more, and use your pinions, winged Darius." Then, with the same proud demeanor he ascended the tower.

Many thousands of the citizens of Nisæa were within reach of his voice, as he cried aloud: "Ye all know that the kings who have, up to the present time, loaded you with honor and glory, belonged to the house of the Achæmenidæ. Cyrus governed you like a real father, Cambyses was a stern master, and Bartja would have guided you like a bridegroom, if I, with this right hand which I now show you, had not slain him on the shores of the Red Sea. By Mithras, it was with a bleeding heart that I committed this wicked deed, but I did it as a faithful servant in obedience to the king's command. Nevertheless, it has haunted me by day and night; for four long years I have been pursued and tormented by the spirits of darkness, who scare sleep from the murderer's couch. I have now resolved to end this painful, despairing existence by a worthy deed, and though even this may procure me no mercy at the bridge of Chinvat,* in the mouths of men, at least, I shall have redeemed my honorable name from the stain with which I defiled it. Know then, that the man who gives himself out for the son of Cyrus, sent me hither; he promised me rich rewards if I would deceive you by declaring him to be Bartja, the son of the Achæmenidæ. But I scorn his promises and swear by Mithras and the Feruers of the kings, the most solemn oaths I am acquainted with, that the man who is now ruling you is none other than the Magian Gaumata, he who was deprived of his ears, the brother of the king's vicegerent and high-priest, Oropastes, whom ye all know. If it be your will to

* See note 15.

forget all the glory ye owe to the Achæmenidæ, if to this ingratitude ye choose to add your own degradation, then acknowledge these creatures and call them your kings; but if ye despise a lie and are ashamed to obey worthless impostors, drive the Magi from the throne before Mithras has left the heavens, and proclaim the noblest of the Achæmenidæ, Darius, the exalted son of Hystaspes, who promises to become a second Cyrus, as your king. And now, in order that ye may believe my words and not suspect that Darius sent me hither to win you over to his side, I will commit a deed, which must destroy every doubt and prove that the truth and glory of the Achæmenidæ are dearer to me, than life itself. Blessed be ye if ye follow my counsels, but curses rest upon you, if ye neglect to reconquer the throne from the Magi and revenge yourselves upon them.—Behold, I die a true and honorable man!"

With these words he ascended the highest pinnacle of the tower and cast himself down head foremost, thus expiating the one crime of his life by an honorable death.[207]

The dead silence with which the people in the court below had listened to him, was now broken by shrieks of rage and cries for vengeance. They burst open the gates of the palace and were pressing in with cries of "Death to the Magi," when the seven princes of the Persians appeared in front of the raging crowd to resist their entrance.

At sight of the Achæmenidæ the citizens broke into shouts of joy, and cried more impetuously than ever, "Down with the Magi! Victory to King Darius!"

The son of Hystaspes was then carried by the crowd

207. Herod. III. 75.

to a rising ground, from which he told the people that the Magi had been slain by the Achæmenidæ, as liars and usurpers. Fresh cries of joy arose in answer to these words, and when at last the bleeding heads of Oropastes and Gaumata were shown to the crowd, they rushed with horrid yells through the streets of the city, murdering every Magian they could lay hold of. The darkness of night alone was able to stop this awful massacre.[208]

Four days later, Darius, the son of Hystaspes, was chosen as king by the heads of the Achæmenidæ, in consideration of his high birth and noble character, and received by the Persian nation with enthusiasm. Darius had killed Gaumata with his own hand, and the high-priest had received his death-thrust from the hand of Megabyzus, the father of Zopyrus. While Prexaspes was haranguing the people, the seven conspiring Persian princes, Otanes, Intaphernes, Gobryas, Megabyzus, Aspatines, Hydarnes and Darius, (as representative of his aged father Hystaspes), had entered the palace by a carelessly-guarded gate, sought out the part of the building occupied by the Magi, and then, assisted by their own knowledge of the palace, and the fact that most of the guards had been sent to keep watch over the crowd assembled to hear Prexaspes easily penetrated to the apartments in which at that moment they were

---

208. Herod. III. 79. In this place Herodotus also says that the Persians kept this day as a great festival, and called it "the murder of the Magi." Wlastoff, in his *Nouvelles annales des voyages*. Vol. 177. gives us some new thoughts on this period of Persian history, with which, however, we are as little inclined to agree as with Malcolm, Anquetil and others, in their conjecture that the Darius of the inscriptions is the Gustasps of Firdusi. It is unquestionably far more probable, that the inscription of Behistân was intended to hand down the deeds of Darius to posterity, than to commemorate religious occurrences.

to be found. Here they were resisted by a few eunuchs, headed by Boges, but these were overpowered and killed to a man. Darius became furious on seeing Boges, and killed him at once. Hearing the dying cries of these eunuchs, the Magi rushed to the spot and prepared to defend themselves. Oropastes snatched a lance from the fallen Boges, thrust out one of Intaphernes' eyes and wounded Aspatines in the thigh, but was stabbed by Megabyzus. Gaumata fled into another apartment and tried to bar the door, but was followed too soon by Darius and Gobryas; the latter seized, threw him, and kept him down by the weight of his own body, crying to Darius, who was afraid of making a false stroke in the half-light, and so wounding his companion instead of Gaumata, "Strike boldly, even if you should stab us both." Darius obeyed, and fortunately only hit the Magian.[209]

Thus died Oropastes, the high-priest, and his brother Gaumata, better known under the name of the "pseudo" or "pretended Smerdis."

A few weeks after Darius' election to the throne, which the people said had been marvellously influenced by divine miracles and the clever cunning of a groom,[210] he celebrated his coronation brilliantly at Pasargadæ, and with still more splendor, his marriage

---

209. Herod. III. 73.

210. Herod. (III. 85.) relates, that the seven conspirators agreed to take a ride out of the city, and that he whose horse was the first to neigh at the rising sun should be king. He then tells the well-known tale of the trick said to have been played by Darius' groom, and adds that at the same time, though the sky was clear, it had thundered and lightened. The former part of this history is probable, as horses were sacred to the sun, and the neighing of Darius' horse as Mithras rose, would therefore be regarded as a sign from heaven. But the claims of Darius to the throne were too well-founded, to need the support of a groom's cunning.

with his beloved Atossa.[211] The trials of her life had ripened her character, and she proved a faithful, beloved and respected companion to her husband through the whole of that active and glorious life, which, as Prexaspes had foretold, made him worthy of the names by which he was afterwards known—Darius the Great, and a second Cyrus.[212]

As a general he was circumspect and brave, and at the same time understood so thoroughly how to divide his enormous realm, and to administer its affairs, that he must be classed with the greatest organizers of all times and countries. That his feeble successors were able to keep this Asiatic Colossus of different countries together for two hundred years after his death, was entirely owing to Darius. He was liberal of his own, but sparing of his subjects' treasures, and made truly royal gifts without demanding more than was his due. He introduced a regular system of taxation, in place of the arbitrary exactions practised under Cyrus and Cambyses, and never allowed himself to be led astray in the carrying out of what seemed to him right, either by difficulties or by the ridicule of the Achæmenidæ, who nicknamed him the "shopkeeper," on account of what seemed, to their exclusively military tastes, his petty financial measures. It is by no means one of his smallest merits, that he introduced

---

211. Atossa is constantly mentioned as the favorite wife of Darius, and he appointed her son Xerxes to be his successor, though he had three elder sons by the daughter of Gobryas. Herodotus (VII. 3.) speaks with emphasis of the respect and consideration in which Atossa was held, and Aeschylus, in his *Persians*, mentions her in her old age, as the much-revered and noble matron.

212. For instance in the *Frogs* of Aristophanes (V. 1035.) Darius is called "the great."

one system of coinage through his entire empire, and consequently through half the then known world.[213]

Darius respected the religions and customs of other nations. When the writing of Cyrus, of the existence of which Cambyses had known nothing, was found in the archives of Ecbatana, he allowed the Jews to carry on the building of their temple to Jehovah;[214] he also left the Ionian cities free to govern their own communities independently. Indeed, he would hardly have sent his army against Greece, if the Athenians had not insulted him.

In Egypt he had learnt much; among other things, the art of managing the exchequer of his kingdom wisely; for this reason he held the Egyptians in high esteem, and granted them many privileges, amongst others a canal to connect the Nile with the Red Sea, which was greatly to the advantage of their commerce.[215]

[213]. Herod. III. 89. Böckh, *Metrologie* p. 45 and 129. In Rawlinson's *Herodotus*, Vol. II. p. 460. Essay III.

[214]. Ezra VI. 2-12. Zechariah 1-8. On the various stages of the work, see Bunsen, *Bibelwerk*. *Biblische Jahrbücher* CCCXXIII-XXV.

[215]. Traces of this canal can be found as early as the days of Setos I.; his son Rameses II. caused the works to be continued. Under Necho they were recommenced, and possibly finished by Darius. In the time of the Ptolemies, at all events, the canal was already completed. Herod. II. 158. Diod. I. 33. The French, in undertaking to reconstruct the Suez canal, have had much to encounter from the unfriendly commercial policy of the English and their influence over, the internal affairs of Egypt, but the unwearied energy and great talent of Monsr. de Lesseps and the patriotism of the French nation have at last succeeded in bringing their great work to a successful close. Whether it will pay is another question. See G. Ebers, *Der Kanal von Suez*. *Nordische Revue*, October 1864. The maritime canal connecting the Mediterranean with the Red Sea has also been completed since 1869. We were among those, who attended the brilliant inauguration ceremonies, and now willingly recall many of the doubts expressed in our work *Durch Gosen zum Sinai*. The number of ships passing through the canal is constantly increasing. Direct lines to Bombay leave London, Liverpool, Marseilles, Genoa, Trieste, Brin-

During the whole of his reign, Darius endeavored to make amends for the severity with which Cambyses had treated the Egyptians; even in the later years of his life he delighted to study the treasures of their wisdom, and no one was allowed to attack either their religion or customs, as long as he lived. The old high-priest Neithotep enjoyed the king's favor to the last, and Darius often made use of his wise old master's astrological knowledge.

The goodness and clemency of their new ruler was fully acknowledged by the Egyptians; they called him a deity,[216] as they had called their own kings, and yet, in the last years of his reign, their desire for independence led them to forget gratitude and to try to shake off his gentle yoke, which was only oppressive because it had originally been forced on them.

Their generous ruler and protector did not live to see the end of this struggle.[217]

disi and Odessa. Many ships of lighter draught are built specially for this voyage, and it appears that cotton can be transported from India to Mediterranean and English ports more cheaply in steamers through the canal, than in sailing vessels around the Cape. We refer the reader also to Stephan's essay on the Suez Canal in his admirable work *Das heutige Aegypten* p. 425 and following.

216. The name of Darius occurs very often on the monuments as Ntariusch. It is most frequently found in the inscriptions on the temple in the Oasis el-Khargah, recently photographed by G. Rohlfs. The Egypto-Persian memorial fragments, bearing inscriptions in the hieroglyphic and cuneiform characters are very interesting. *Description de l'Eg. ant.* V. Pl. 29. Lepsius, *Monatsbericht der Berliner Akademie der Wissenschaft.* May 17, 1866. p. 285, &c. Darius's name in Egyptian was generally "Ra, the beloved of Ammon." On a porcelain vessel in Florence, and in some papyri in Paris and Florence he is called by the divine titles of honor given to the Pharaohs.

217. The first rebellion in Egypt, which broke out under Aryandes, the satrap appointed by Cambyses, was put down by Darius in person. He visited Egypt, and promised 100 talents (£22,500) to any one who would find a new Apis. Polyaen. VII. 11. 7. No second outbreak took place until 486 B. C. about 4 years before the death of Darius. Herod. VII. 1. Xerxes conquered the rebels two years after his accession, and appointed his brother Achæmenes satrap of Egypt.

It was reserved for Xerxes, the successor and son of Darius and Atossa,* to bring back the inhabitants of the Nile valley to a forced and therefore insecure obedience.

Darius left a worthy monument of his greatness in the glorious palace which he built on Mount Rachmed, the ruins of which are the wonder and admiration of travellers to this day. Six thousand Egyptian workmen, who had been sent to Asia by Cambyses, took part in the work and also assisted in building a tomb for Darius and his successors, the rocky and almost inaccessible chambers of which have defied the ravages of time, and are now the resort of innumerable wild pigeons.

He caused the history of his deeds to be cut, (in the cuneiform character and in the Persian, Median and Assyrian languages), on the polished side of the rock of Bisitun or Behistân, not far from the spot where he saved Atossa's life. The Persian part of this inscription ** can still be deciphered with certainty, and contains an account of the events related in the last few chapters, very nearly agreeing with our own and that of Herodotus. The following sentences occur amongst others: "Thus saith Darius the King: That which I have done, was done by the grace of Auramazda in every way. I fought nineteen battles after the rebellion of the kings. By the mercy of Auramazda I conquered them. I took nine kings captive. One was a Median, Gaumata by name. He lied and said: 'I am Bardiya (Bartja), the son of Cyrus.' He caused Persia to rebel."

* See note 211.
** The cuneiform character called Persian-Achæmedian.

Some distance lower down, he names the chiefs who helped him to dethrone the Magi, and in another place the inscription has these words: "Thus saith the King Darius: That which I have done was done in every way by the grace of Auramazda. Auramazda helped me, and such other gods as there be. Auramazda and the other gods gave me help, because I was not swift to anger, nor a liar, nor a violent ruler, neither I nor my kinsmen. I have shown favor unto him who helped my brethren, and I have punished severely him who was my enemy. Thou who shalt be king after me, be not merciful unto him who is a liar or a rebel, but punish him with a severe punishment. Thus saith Darius the King: Thou who shalt hereafter behold this tablet which I have written, or these pictures, destroy them not, but so long as thou shalt live preserve them, &c."

It now only remains to be told that Zopyrus, the son of Megabyzus, continued to the last the king's most faithful friend.

A courtier once showed the king a pomegranate, and asked him of what one gift of fortune he would like so many repetitions, as there were seeds in that fruit. Without a moment's hesitation Darius answered, " Of my Zopyrus."[218]

The following story will prove that Zopyrus, on his part, well understood how to return his royal friend's kindness. After the death of Cambyses, Babylon revolted from the Persian empire. Darius besieged the city nine months in vain, and was about to raise the

---

218. Plutarch tells this story (in his *Apophthegmata* p. 173.) of Zopyrus, and Herodotus of Megabyzus, the conqueror of Thrace. Herod, IV. 193.

siege, when one day Zopyrus appeared before him bleeding, and deprived of his ears and nose, and explained that he had mutilated himself thus in order to cheat the Babylonians, who knew him well, as he had formerly been on intimate terms with their daughters. He said he wished to tell the haughty citizens, that Darius had thus disfigured him, and that he had come to them for help in revenging himself. He thought they would then place troops at his disposal, with which he intended to impose upon them by making a few successful sallies at first. His ultimate intention was to get possession of the keys, and open the Semiramis gate to his friends.

These words, which were spoken in a joking tone, contrasted so sadly with the mutilated features of his once handsome friend, that Darius wept, and when at last the almost impregnable fortress was really won by Zopyrus' stratagem, he excaimed: "I would give a hundred Babylons, if my Zopyrus had not thus mutilated himself."

He then appointed his friend lord of the giant city, gave him its entire revenues, and honored him every year with the rarest presents. In later days he used to say that, with the exception of Cyrus, who had no equal, no man had ever performed so generous a deed as Zopyrus.[219]

Few rulers possessed so many self-sacrificing friends as Darius, because few understood so well how to be grateful.

When Syloson, the brother of the murdered Poly-

---

219. Herod. III. 160. Among other presents Zopyrus received a gold hand-mill weighing six talents, the most honorable and distinguished gift a Persian monarch could bestow upon a subject. According to Ktesias, Megabyzus received this gift from Xerxes.

krates, came to Susa and reminded the king of his former services, Darius received him as a friend, placed ships and troops at his service, and helped him to recover Samos.

The Samians made a desperate resistance, and said, when at last they were obliged to yield: "Through Syloson we have much room in our land."*

Rhodopis lived to hear of the murder of Hipparchus, the tyrant of Athens, by Harmodius and Aristogiton, and died at last in the arms of her best friends, Theopompus the Milesian and Kallias the Athenian, firm in her belief of the high calling of her countrymen.

All Naukratis mourned for her, and Kallias sent a messenger to Susa, to inform the king and Sappho of her death.

A few months later the satrap of Egypt received the following letter from the hand of the king:

"Inasmuch as we ourselves knew and honored Rhodopis, the Greek, who has lately died in Naukratis, —inasmuch as her granddaughter, as widow of the lawful heir to the Persian throne, enjoys to this day the rank and honors of a queen,—and lastly, inasmuch as I have lately taken the great-grandchild of the same Rhodopis, Parmys,** the daughter of Bartja and Sappho, to be my third lawful wife, it seems to me just to grant royal honors to the ancestress of two queens. I therefore command thee to cause the ashes of Rhodopis, whom we have always esteemed as the greatest and rarest among women, to be buried in the greatest and rarest of all monuments, namely, in one of the

* See note 96.   ** See note 197.

Pyramids. The costly urn, which thou wilt receive herewith, is sent by Sappho to preserve the ashes of the deceased."

Given in the new imperial palace at Persepolis.

DARIUS, son of Hystaspes.

King.

THE END.

www.ingramcontent.com/pod-product-compliance
Lightning Source LLC
Chambersburg PA
CBHW031421230426
43668CB00007B/391